MW00980018

THE
BOOK OF
TAROT

THE
BOOK OF
TAROT

A SPIRITUAL KEY TO
UNDERSTANDING THE CARDS

SAHAR
HUNEIDI-PALMER

ARCTURUS

To Merryn Jose, daughter of Maureen Treanor,
my former mentor, and friend,
The Hermit who lit my path and still guides me along.
To Maureen, The High Priestess, who peered into my tea cup and said:

"Sahar, just sit and write for ten minutes each day."

And, I did!
With gratitude and love.

Rider-Waite-Smith Tarot cards copyright Arcturus Publishing Ltd.
All other images courtesy of Shutterstock.

ARCTURUS

This edition published in 2022 by Arcturus Publishing Limited
26/27 Bickels Yard, 151–153 Bermondsey Street,
London SE1 3HA

Copyright © Arcturus Holdings Limited

All rights reserved. No part of this publication may be reproduced, stored in a
retrieval system, or transmitted, in any form or by any means, electronic, mechanical,
photocopying, recording or otherwise, without prior written permission in
accordance with the provisions of the Copyright Act 1956 (as amended). Any
person or persons who do any unauthorised act in relation to this publication may be
liable to criminal prosecution and civil claims for damages.

ISBN: 978-1-3988-1297-0
AD010236UK

Printed in China

Contents

CHAPTER ONE

TAROT OVERVIEW

There are numerous books on the Tarot, so what distinguishes this book from others? *The Book of Tarot* gives you an overview of how the Tarot evolved into what it is today. It also teaches you everything you need to know to begin using the Tarot as a tool for self-development guidance and inspiration, providing clear definitions, methodology and interpretations for each card, based on The Rider-Waite-Smith deck. Published in 1909, it was the first deck in English by Arthur Edward Waite, an American-born British poet, intellectual and mystic. Pamela Colman Smith illustrated all the cards, including the 'pip' or Minor Arcana ones. Originally known as The Rider-Waite Tarot, it was later renamed The Rider-Waite-Smith Deck to honour the work of the artist who illustrated it and commemorate her contribution.

Pamela Colman Smith was a British occultist, artist, illustrator, writer and publisher. Her creative and innovative illustrations, particularly of the Minor cards, were quite an accomplishment at the time. Prior to this deck, Minor cards were not illustrated. The Rider-Waite-Smith marked a significant departure from preceding Tarot cards, which were mostly based on the 16th-century *Tarot of Marseilles* (the latter was used to play card games), which was the standard Tarot deck at the time. The *Marseilles* was based on previous Italian card games decks developed in the 15th century. In this book, however, the Major arcana sequence follows the *Tarot of Marseilles*'s order, which is more relevant to the numerological interpretations, as you shall discover later. The Rider-Waite-Smith Tarot swiftly rose to prominence as one of the most popular Tarot cards, setting the bar for all succeeding modern decks.

The Book of Tarot aims to demonstrate how the Tarot can assist your own self-development and transform your life experiences into wisdom. The self-development process is depicted by the journey of The Fool, the first card of the Tarot, who undergoes a transformative journey to awaken his consciousness. Viewing the Tarot as a journey helps you remember the cards' sequence and the significance of their numbers, meanings and interpretations. These meanings and interpretations are also updated in *The Book of Tarot* to provide you with contemporary understanding and practical interpretations based on the author's practical experience as a Tarot reader for more than three decades.

What is the Tarot?

The Tarot we know today is one of the most popular and sophisticated divination systems.

Divination is defined by *Encyclopaedia Britannica* as "the process of finding the hidden meaning or origin of events and occasionally foretelling the future". In ancient Rome, however, divination was concerned with discovering the 'will of the gods'. Even though scholars now do not confine the word to its original meaning, it nevertheless conveys seeking guidance from higher realms (in other words, out of the box). *The Book of Tarot* places guidance in your hands, strengthens your intuition, and helps you develop a deeper connection with yourself for your highest good.

The Tarot is a comprehensive guidance system because of the deck's evolution into a complex composition over a millennium. It evokes interpretations on several levels, from the mundane to the spiritual. Consulting the Tarot offers perspective, guidance and an overview, as well as a context for detailed insights into real-life situations. Using the Tarot in this way assists your decision-making towards a more fulfilling life journey. Moreover, context for guidance

is determined by the way the cards are laid. There are numerous ways to lay out the cards, known as a 'spread', in which the placement of any card has a meaning. Each spread provides unique insights that help you construct a complete picture of your situation.

Whenever the cards are arranged in a spread, they tell a tale or provide a snapshot of your current situation. Each spread weaves the tapestry of your life. It can also reflect issues you need to confront and work on, as well as what's in your subconscious. You are encouraged to innovate and create your own spreads. With practice, you will get to know the cards well and your Tarot deck will become like a close, trusted friend with whom you can consult and seek counsel at any time, to clear your mind.

The Tarot process of guidance is referred to as a 'reading'. Tarot readers typically provide readings for clients to answer a question or provide advice or guidance. A reading begins with shuffling a deck of Tarot cards and then dealing them out according to the sequence of a spread. A Tarot reader's task is to interpret the symbolic images of the cards in the context of a spread, considering the meaning of the adjacent cards. One of the more complex Tarot spreads, such as the 12-house astrological spread, can provide more detailed information. Here you will see the Tarot in action!

When the cards are laid out over the 12 houses, the Tarot provides a rich matrix of information through 12 Major arcana cards and 12 Minor arcana cards laid over two rows. Each card is interpreted in context according to the astrological house it falls into, its relationship to adjacent cards, as well as cards directly underneath it (or over it) in the row below (or above). More about this spread later. However, the Tarot is more than just a divination tool. It is also useful for meditation, reflection, creative brainstorming, and triggering your intuition to realign and direct your energies to creating an enjoyable life.

THE TAROT STORY

Since its conception in 9th-century China, as a deck to entertain Royalty and play money-taking card games, the Tarot metamorphosed and evolved to become a tool for deeper spiritual self-understanding that awakens innate intuitive abilities. The Tarot tells the story of its main character, The Fool (card zero), who starts out as a zero and transforms into a hero. By going through life's struggles and difficulties, The Fool gains self-knowledge and mastery of the duality of being part human and part spirit. He matures and awakens as he passes

from one experience to the next. These experiences are necessary training, however – 'lessons' if you like – for his growth and development. As soon as he learns one lesson, he encounters the next, until we finally see him fully transformed at the end of his journey as a figure floating gracefully and in balance as the final card of the Tarot: The World (number 21).

The Enlightenment Thinkers

The Tarot cards, however, have been on a journey of development ever since they were created. By the 18th century, esotericists reflected deeply on the nature and mechanics of the world through the Tarot, and it fired their imagination. You will find a wealth of symbolism steeped in millennia of wisdom from Classical Greek philosophers and mystics who wondered whether there was more to life. Their understanding influenced the teachings of 14th-century clergy who sought spiritual enlightenment outside of the restrictive state church's principles. They challenged the dogma and authority of the Catholic Church, and were increasingly interested in science: finding order, or other principles, that governed their lives outside of religion. The Church, however, waged war on it at the time, describing it as "the devil's instrument" – the earliest reference to the much-feared and misunderstood card, The Devil. The clergy who defected became known as The Enlightenment Thinkers. They wanted the educational system to be modernized and play a more central role in transmitting their new ideas and principles.

Their schools of thought influenced Western scholars in late-17th and 18th-century Europe and England, who claimed that Tarot cards held hidden knowledge encoded in them, which led to the birth of spiritual enlightenment. Distinct schools of thought emerged separately, and each interpreted the Tarot in their own way, adding 'hidden' symbols to the cards to support their beliefs. Moreover, 'spiritual' knowledge and beliefs, outside the teachings of the state church, were coded and eventually reflected in the illustrations of the Tarot cards – as in the case of the Rider-Waite-Smith Tarot deck. Several claimed that the Tarot secrets were rooted in ancient civilizations and cultures such as ancient Egypt or The Holy Kabbalah. Each scholar 'projected' their own beliefs on the Tarot, however, enriching it further. In return, the Tarot gave them the guidance they sought. Although modern Tarot scholars have found no evidence to support such claims

to date, the magic of the Tarot endures. Now this magic is between your hands.

You will discover that the 'hidden knowledge' in the Tarot is about balancing both aspects of the self: intellect and emotions, reason and intuition, passive and active, feminine and masculine, conscious and unconscious, action and lack of, etc. We hope that you will realize that the magic of the Tarot lies in its symbols. Michael Dummett, an English academic who has been considered one of the most prominent British philosophers of the last century, and a scholar in the field of card-game history, wrote: *Without the Tarot, the Magic of the Ancients is a closed book.* This 'magic' is now at your disposal. Allow the cards to speak to you, and you shall discover what they represent to you as your imagination and intuition are invigorated.

THE TAROT MATRIX

A traditional Tarot deck consists of 78 trump cards, as they were referred to in the past. The 78 cards are divided into two distinct types: 22 Major Arcana (Greater Secrets) cards and 56 Minor Arcana (Lesser Secrets), which resemble modern playing cards. **The Major Arcana** (Major cards) have names or titles on the cards, as well as numbers from zero to 21. They contain elements or symbolism from a wide range of different themes, including religion, mythology, historical persons and events, astrology, alchemy and numerology, to mention a few. The title of some cards directly indicates their meaning, such as Strength, Temperance and Justice. Other Major card titles describe a quality for a person in their attitude to life, such as The Magician, or The Hermit. Also, there are cards with astronomical names, such as The Moon, The Sun and The Star, symbolizing the effect of heavenly bodies on life's journey.

The first card is The Fool, which carries the number zero. Major cards tell the story of The Fool's journey into self-awareness and enlightenment. They are referred to as face cards because they contain a picture of the main figures whom The Fool meets along his journey. Major cards represent Major turning points and lessons The Fool must learn to mature and become wiser. The cards end with The World, number 21, in which The Fool is self-transformed into an asexual being, a balanced fusion between female and male, earthly and spiritual aspects, having attained mystical knowledge.

STARTING A TAROT JOURNAL

The Tarot is a tool for improving your intuition and self-awareness. Tarot and intuition are inextricably linked. As you gaze upon, analyze and become familiar with each card, the rich imagery on the Tarot cards helps spark or engage your intuition and imagination. To begin with, the Rider-Waite-Smith deck is wonderful, nearly self-explanatory thanks to its vivid pictures. In a Tarot reading, you would tie each card's significance to its context, based on its location in the spread.

As a result, it's critical to start your own Tarot journal straight away, as you'll be introduced to each of the 78 cards separately in Chapter Three. Each card is followed by a meditation or exercise to help you connect with the card and link it to your life. Record your unfolding adventure as you link it to The Fool's in your Tarot journal. After each exercise, start writing down your thoughts, observations and insights. This will allow you to form your own tool for self-discovery. The symbolism and illustrations on each card will help your mind unravel, think beyond the box, and receive guidance as you interact with the Tarot cards. The cards appear to tell a story when laid out in a spread. This story will evoke deeper insights and provide you with a new perspective on a situation. Learning the Tarot allows you to take a step back and analyze the story of the cards in front of you.

As you learn about The Fool's own path to enlightenment, this creative visual process of reflection is not only enjoyable, but also serves to strengthen your capacity to delve deeply into understanding what your own life patterns are, and how you may change or improve them. You will have a meta-resource of information that will tickle your mind's imagination by uncovering the symbology, mythology, numerology and meaning of each card as well as its interpretation in combination with other cards. It's an invitation to connect with yourself, your strengths and weaknesses, and discover how and why you generate your life's experiences.

Furthermore, Tarot cards are numbered, which is significant because numbers represent a process. Understanding the vibrational quality of numbers allows you to gain insight into your own subtle process of dealing with relationships, work and money. Numbers can also shed light on the meaning of each card. Keep a Tarot diary, because you will undoubtedly have your own insights, and by the time you finish Chapter Five, you will have learned how all components of the Tarot are interconnected. Furthermore, the abundance of knowledge and insights will prepare you to face and overcome the various challenges you may have in your life. You become buoyant along the way, bounce back swiftly from adversity, and continue to pursue your life's purpose

with the same zeal as The Fool!

So here's a suggestion: choose a diary and pen that appeal to you so that you enjoy writing in it and using your pen. If you dangle a carrot in front of you, you'll keep writing. When it comes to mastering the Tarot, your Tarot journal will be your most valuable asset. Happy self-discovery!

The Tarot

MAJOR ARCANA

Generally, the 22 Major cards reflect the human psyche as well as the many stages of an individual's personal development path. They represent major changes and turning points, while the Minor cards depict daily activities and situations. Major cards are titled as well as numbered; the title is a description of the figure on the card, such as The Magician, The Hanged Man or Strength. The Major cards serve as the foundation for interpreting the Tarot cards, symbolizing the path of personal development, enlightenment and self-awakening. Major cards also represent an important person to the reader or the querent (the person asking for the reading) at the time of the reading and indicate the beginning of new cycles and significant transitions in the person's life, as follows:

The Fool (0), The Magician (1), The High Priestess (2), The Empress (3), The Emperor (4), The Hierophant (5), The Lovers (6), The Chariot (7), Justice (8), The Hermit (9), Wheel of Fortune (10), Strength (11), The Hanged Man (12), Death (13), Temperance (14), The Devil (15), The Tower (16), The Star (17), The Moon (18), The Sun (19), Judgement (20) and The World (21).

If you are new to the Tarot, it is a good idea to get to know the Major cards first, before you start adding the Minor cards in Tarot spreads. This method will provide a structure to your readings by presenting the general picture first, followed by details or solutions presented in the Minor cards. If, for example, The Tower card comes up in a spread, it will indicate sudden upheaval in your life. You will know that a cycle of stability might suddenly change. When following it with the Minor cards, the Five of Cups, for example, might be associated with The Tower. You might discover that the reason for (and solution to) this upheaval is your emotional attitude. The Five of Cups indicates that it is time to 'stop crying over spilt milk', and move forward, towards better opportunities of which you are not even aware (see the sections Tarot Spreads and Sample Readings for more details).

The Drama of the Tarot

When you lay out the cards in a spread, the Major cards have a way of drawing your attention to what you need to give importance to. A card or two will always pop out at you to communicate a message. The most feared cards are possibly The Devil, Death, and Judgement. However, their images are dramatic to convey a crucial transformative message that should not be overlooked: "You are stuck in a situation that you have outgrown; your emotions are getting the worst of you;" or that "this phase must end to bring about the next step in your personal evolution," respectively.

Foretold events or cycle outcomes are not always as dramatic as they may seem. You must, however, pay close attention to such cards that leap out at you, because they signify a critical turning point in your life. When shuffling at the start of a reading, one technique to highlight those crucial turning points is to reverse two Major and five Minor cards before you lay out the cards. If they show up in a reading, pay attention to them.

Reversed Meanings

Moreover, when ominous cards appear reversed (upside down) in a reading, they have a more positive meaning – for instance, The Hanged Man and The Devil. The first reversed denotes the end of a

CARD	NUMBER	INTERPRETATION	REVERSED MEANING
THE FOOL	0	Taking a risk, start of a new endeavour, new cycle	Foolishness, bad risk
THE MAGICIAN	1	The initiator, creative and logical	Confusion, disorganized mind
THE HIGH PRIESTESS	2	Intuition, the unknown	Self-delusion
THE EMPRESS	3	Abundance, potential fulfilled	Limited abundance
THE EMPEROR	4	Structure and authority	Disorganised, stern, inflexible
THE HIEROPHANT	5	Higher mind, innate spiritual understanding	Materialistic
THE LOVERS	6	Partnerships (romantic or business), decision	Dysfunctional partnership, indecisiveness
THE CHARIOT	7	Efforts rewarded, victory	Lack of control
JUSTICE	8	Prudence, legal matters	Dissolution of agreements
THE HERMIT	9	Inner wisdom, the teacher	Introversion
WHEEL OF FORTUNE	10	Unexpected change	Negative cycle
STRENGTH	11	Mastering spirit-matter, self-healer	Inability to control passion
THE HANGED MAN	12	Surrender, sacrifice the 'old'	Useless sacrifice, waiting over
DEATH	13	Death of the old, birth of the new, end/loss	Fear of change
TEMPERANCE	14	Harmony, resolution of conflict	Imbalance
THE DEVIL	15	Enslaved to obsession, lust, restrictions	End of restraints, beginning of flow
THE TOWER	16	Sudden upheaval, destruction of the old	Disruptive behaviour
THE STAR	17	Hope, bliss, optimism	Let go of doubt
THE MOON	18	Illusion, the unconscious, the unknown	Self-deception
THE SUN	19	Joy, success	Success awaits
JUDGEMENT	20	Total transformation	Forced changes
THE WORLD	21	Fulfilment	Recognition awaits

Figure 1 Major Arcana key interpretations and numerology

waiting period. The Devil reversed signifies that you are about to be released from your 'bondage'; Death reversed suggests your unwillingness to embrace the changes you are undergoing; and Judgement reversed denotes that you are undergoing a crucial metamorphosis and there is nothing you can do about it!

By the time you have learned the individual meaning of each Tarot card in the deck in Chapter Three, you will be prepared to start reading the cards as you learn about Tarot spreads in Chapter Five. To arrive at the meaning of any reversed card, consider its upright qualities and attributes, and what happens to them when the card is literally turned upside down. What objects would fall off when the figures are reversed? This might help trigger your own interpretations of the card in a spread. Below is a quick key interpretation of each card in upright and reversed position:

THE MINOR ARCANA SUITS

The Minor Arcana are 56 cards which are divided into four suits (Wands, Cups, Swords and Pentacles) and show people in everyday situations. The person in the image is usually holding a tool in his hands, such as a Pentacle (money), Wand (drive), Cup (emotions) or Sword (swift, decisive action). This tool represents one of the elements of nature and denotes the suit to which the card belongs. Each suit has 10 numbered 'pips' cards, the first of which is known as the 'Ace'; the remainder are numbered from 2 to 10. The Page (or Princess), Knight (or Prince), Queen and King are the next four Royal Court Cards in each suit. Each suit has a ruling element that corresponds to the four elements of nature and carries specific attributes:

Wands symbolize the element of fire and represent drive (self-motivation). They relate to personal initiative and growth energy. They signify innovative thinking, innate creativity and the ability to start new undertakings. They represent the yang aspect, or the masculine aspect of energy. They are associated with springtime because they symbolize growth. In a modern playing-card deck, the suit of clubs is their counterpart.

Cups symbolize the element of water and represent emotions. Cups represent love, happiness and feelings. As such, they are associated with fertility, children, beauty, relationships and emotions towards, or inflected by, other people. The subconscious and intuition are also represented by cups since they reflect fluctuating emotions and innate senses rather than intellect or reason. As such, they represent the yin aspect, or the feminine. Cups represent summer. The suit of hearts is the modern-day equivalent.

Swords symbolize the element of air and depict intellect, mental state and decisions. Conflict, aggression, force, ambition, strife, deception, treachery and hatred are all represented by swords. They show 'quick' actions as well as thoughts (which led to the action) that can be positive or bad, deliberate or rash. Both sides are portrayed in the cards of this Minor arcana suit. Swords represent autumn. Spades is their equivalent in playing cards.

Pentacles symbolize the earth element and represent money, financial matters and material gain. The first symbol featured in the Tarot is coins, which are represented by pentacles. They are linked to financial and property interests. They were previously represented as discs or coins in Tarot decks. In everyday life, the coins signify the 'fruits of labour', that is, every activity has a return or result. Pentacles are related to physical health (without which you cannot earn money). In a modern playing-card deck, the suit of pentacle corresponds to diamonds. Pentacles represent winter.

THE FOUR ELEMENTS

The Tarot and conventional playing cards have a few similarities that come from their shared roots. One of these parallels is the deck's division into four suits. Spades, diamonds, hearts and clubs are the suits found in standard playing-card decks. While the names of the Tarot suits vary from deck to deck, the most common names for them, as we have seen, are Swords (Blades, sometimes Crystals), Wands (Staves, Rods), Cups and Pentacles (Coins or Disks). These suits are essentially like standard decks of playing cards. Enigmatically, however, the order of the cards, as well as the four suits they consisted of, have remained unchanged since about the 14th century.

Around the 14th century, in China, illustrated pip cards began to appear with four suits or coins to play money-taking games. The first illustrations that appeared were of coins and strings of coins. The string of coins symbol appeared to resemble a stick (the word for string in Chinese is the same as the word for stick). As the Tarot cards moved to other civilisations, they evolved with each culture. Strings were misinterpreted as sticks, and the suit of batons, or sticks, was born in the Mamluks of Egypt cards (as well as cups, swords and coins). Moreover, a historical reference points to specifically Moorish designs in Barcelona dated to 1414. "These cards are possibly the earliest set of European playing cards that came to us," according to Simon Wintle, a playing-cards historian.

In Europe, card games were referred

to as *naipero*, *naips* or *nayps*. Mark R. Johnson, author of *The Casino, Card and Betting Game Reader: Communities, Cultures, and Play*, mentions in his book historical references to card playing in Barcelona dating to 1380: "There is also a record of Rodrigo Borges, who set up a shop as a painter and card maker (*pintor y naipero*)." European cards evolved from the suit system and composition of these cards, explains Wintle, "which corresponds with the Italian 'naipi' and Spanish 'naipes', and possibly the English 'knave'."

These early cards were termed 'naib', derived from the Early Mamluks' deck of the 13th century (1250-1517) named *mulûk wa-nuwwâb* (Kings and Deputies, singular is *malek wa naib*, king and deputy). The cards had four suits: *darâhim* (coins) *suyûf* (scimitars), *jawkân* (polo sticks) and *tûmân* (multitudes). And the Court Cards were named as follows: *malik* (king), *nâib* (deputy), and *thanî nâib* (second deputy); the pip cards were numbered 0-10. In 14th- and 15th-century Europe, card playing became popular, and several upmarket gilded versions were created for the elite. However, the Mamluk patterns of the four suits can still be traced in all European decks.

Wands represent Fire: The masculine principle of 'taking initiative' or drive.

Wands reflect: vitality, common strength, willpower, violence, passion, optimism, drive, confidence, carriage, aggression, dominance and leadership. Fire, or drive, is the catalyst for growth and is associated with the season spring. The wand can be compared to a branch of a tree that is just beginning to grow. You will notice the colour of the wand suit – mostly auburn, the shade of branches. All 'spring' cards include budding leaves on wands, indicating the first stage of growth throughout this season.

Cups represent Water: The feminine principle of feeling, nurturing and intuition. They depict emotional support needed to manifest what we want, psychic ability, receptivity, reflection, passivity, emotion, love, sensitivity, nourishment, sexuality, fertility, children, family life, desire and psychic ability. The water element is mostly confined within the cup. Occasionally the water flows, or is spilled on the ground, and sometimes leads into a lake or river. The fluid state of water indicates that emotions ebb and flow. Water is a mutable element. Water is a reminder of summer, when seedlings planted in the spring are watered.

Swords represent Air: The masculine principle of thinking and acting. It is ideas

SUIT	ELEMENT	SEASON/ TIMING	KEYWORD	INTERPRETATION/ QUALITIES	CORRESPONDING PLAYING CARD SUIT	RIDER-WAITE-SMITH SUITS
Wands	Fire	Spring	Ideas	Male aspect, inspiration, initiation, renewal, manifestation of ideas, growth. Communication and self-expression.	♣	 ACE OF WANDS
Cups	Water	Summer	Emotions	Female aspect. Emotions, creativity, happiness, love, intuition, acceptance, flow, the need for emotional support.	♥	 ACE OF CUPS
Swords	Air	Autumn	Thoughts	Sharp mind, mental activity, intellect, logical thinking, decisions that shape ideas.	♠	 ACE OF SWORDS
Pentacles	Earth	Winter	Finance	Material manifestation of creation. Money, material wealth, success, business, physical body, foundation, property.	♦	 ACE OF PENTACLES

Figure 2 The four suits and corresponding elements

in motion, if you like, intellect, reason, swiftness of action, logic, methodology, discrimination, and discernment. The figure here is taking an action. The motion and number of swords depicted on a card indicate the type of action it represents (they depict a sword in action). Any activity involving a sword is quick. A swooshing sword is represented in the various images, and you can nearly hear the sound as the blade slices into the air! Swords depict conflict, the greyness of autumn that contrasts with the bright, warm summer season. Any action is preceded by a thought. Thoughts are influenced by preceding emotions. Any action that is too rash, without reason, can lead to disastrous consequences. A message of warning in the changeable autumn season!

Pentacles represent Earth: The feminine aspect of life-giving force. In general, they depict manifestation into physical reality, stability of material gain (money flowing in), physical health, work, materialistic gain, home life, the material world. They are attributed to the winter season. The figures are either clad in black or riding on a black steed (the Knight). They are associated with winter, which is the final cycle of seeding, watering and harvesting. Here we see the

tangible (manifested) result of the growth process depicted as pentacles.

THE COURT CARDS

Each Minor card suit is numbered 1 to 10, and there are four Royal Cards, or Court Cards: a Page, Knight, Queen and King. Court Card pictures depict a single person, their age, status, abilities, qualities and mental condition. Different facets of their personalities are mirrored in each suit in relation to the element it corresponds to (see table below). Each deck, therefore, has 16 Court Cards.

When a Court Card occurs in a spread, it may represent a person in the reader's life or the person for whom the reading is given (commonly referred to as the querent) who possesses the card's specific characteristics. It could also represent the person's qualities that have not been expressed or developed yet.

Pages represent children or young people of either gender and depict innocence. They represent youthful promise, dreams and other traits based on the suit, or element, they belong to.

Knights represent older youth, men and women, mature male-essence

Figure 3 The Court Cards

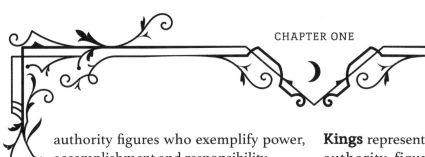

authority figures who exemplify power, accomplishment and responsibility.

Queens represent mature maternal figures, usually women who, like kings, wield power. They represent the feminine aspect of wisdom, assurance, fertility and life-giving abilities.

Kings represent the male aspect, mature authority figures, usually men, who exemplify power, accomplishment and responsibility.

Key attributes and meanings are summarized in the table below:

CARD	KEYWORDS	WANDS	CUPS	SWORDS	PENTACLES
KING	Masculine aspect, older man, authority figure, personality, vision, experience	Important, successful, kind, business-minded	Mature, caring, balanced, kind in high position	Powerful, professional, good mind, tough	Financial wizard, wealthy
QUEEN	Feminine aspect, older woman, authority figure, personality, profession, ability	Capable and kind, practical woman. Brunette	Loving, helpful, intuitive	Lonely, mentally able woman, has overcome problems	Abundant, helpful businesswoman. Dark skin/hair
KNIGHT	Young men, movement, action	Business-related travel	Loving sensitive person	Assertive man, moves quickly	Money-minded, methodical
PAGE	Children, genre, timing	Energetic	Poetic, soft emotional	Bright, difficult	Investment
COMPLEXION	Physical appearance	Strawberry blonde, freckled, brown hair	Fair, light hair/ skin	Salt & pepper hair	Dark skin/hair

Figure 4 Court Cards: keywords and meanings

Tarot Symbology

The Tarot reflects a progression of generations of users, as well as other people's thoughts, ideologies and interpretations that built on the wisdom of past generations; those created their own system of interpretation and imposed it on the Tarot. However, one thing connects all Tarot readers across generations: a desire for a deeper connection with themselves, and more meaningful life experiences through seeking guidance.

The Tarot today is therefore a compounded symbolic language represented by images, numbers and a hierarchical structure. When you look at the cards in a spread, all these combinations evoke feelings or senses, allowing you to connect to timeless legends to discover a meaning that is relevant to you today. Each card on its own has an enigmatic meaning and is open to interpretation. It may evoke a different meaning for each Tarot reader – that is what the Tarot does. More themes are presented in Chapter Four.

Let's begin by taking a deeper look into the Tarot. You will notice that the Tarot has a rhythm to it. This rhythm is represented by the numbering of the cards, the naming of the Major card drawings, the identification of the four elements as the four seasons signifying cycles and timing, and other subtle meanings hidden in each picture (such as astrological symbols, Hebrew letters and more, which will be explored later). Each season, or cycle, contains cycles within it; that is, there is a process within a process. This makes the Tarot's structure more akin to a matrix of hierarchy, triggering intuition on multiple levels. In many ways, it is comparable to a piece of music or an opera. All its components come together to tell a story that evokes different sensations that vary from one time to the next, and each person to the other. The hierarchy's rhythm is expressed in the classifications of the Tarot cards as follows:

1. **Major Cards** depict main events or turning points in one's life.

2. **Court Cards** are given higher importance and are represented by Kings, Queens, Knights and Pages. Their illustrations and suit depict a single figure in a similar manner to the figures of the Major cards, as well as the characteristics of each figure. They stand a level above the numbered pip cards, although they are not numbered.

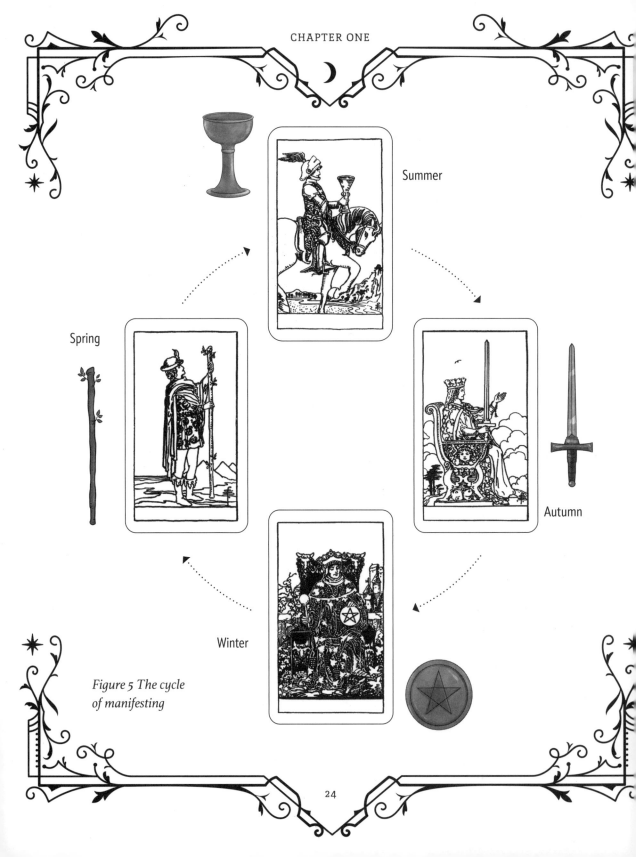

Summer

Spring

Autumn

Winter

*Figure 5 The cycle
of manifesting*

3. Minor Cards reflect the cycles and processes of everyday situations.

4. Assigned Ascending Numbers: The ascending numbers on the cards imply a process from beginning to end. Each stage has a meaning or a vibration.

5. The Four Elements Associated with the Four Suits reflect a cycle of seasons, and fluctuating cycles within each season (cards are numbered from 1 to 10).

TAROT CYCLES

The hierarchy of structure in the Tarot cards is what holds the key to their secrets. It conveys cycles within cycles. The Major cards tell the story of Major cycles of growth and development. Some are upward cycles; others represent inevitable down cycles which are necessary for self-growth. Minor cycles of the Minor cards, their ascending numbers, and the figures of the Court Cards reflect other 'lesser' cycles of growth and of fluctuating emotional (cups) and mental (swords) states, as well as attitudes toward achieving goals (wands) and making money (pentacles) in the material world, respectively.

Cause and Effect Cycle

Cycles of life are presented as seasons of the Minor cards' symbols. Each season represents one of the four elements: **Wands** represent the beginning of growth in spring. **Cups** represent summer, and the element of water needed to nurture the seeds planted in the spring. **Swords** represent the autumn or fall season, where action taken is the harvesting of the fruits. And finally, **Pentacles**, which represent the element of earth, and the winter season, represent material gain secured from selling the harvest.

Seasons are also related to timing. The pip cards' illustrations depict images of real-life situations in each season. When you arrange the pip cards in four rows, one for each season (or element), you will notice that they symbolize actions we all engage in, such as starting creative endeavours, nurturing them, and protecting what we create. They can be hostile at times, but always yield a tangible outcome – whether positive or negative. First one must initiate action and plant seeds (Wands/spring), then nurture it (Cups/summer) by watering it (supportive emotions), then harvest it (Swords/autumn, shaping the crop), and finally reap the fruits of one's labour (Pentacles/winter, physical reality). A full cycle of cause and effect that requires self-awareness: initiative (wands), feelings (cups), thoughts/actions (swords) and results (pentacles), respectively.

2. Nurture

1. Take Intiative

3. Harvest

Figure 6 The steps of manifesting

4. Tangible Result (of drive, emotions, actions)

Cycles highlight a process, and the cycle of the Court Cards represents personal development in terms of characteristics, abilities and skills, which leads to the responsibility that comes as one matures. Pages grow into Knights by developing their skills and inner abilities. They become wiser authority figures: Queens (feminine/creative aspect) and Kings (masculine/doer aspect). The sovereignty here refers to mastering the self. Through never-ending cycles of growth, fulfilment of purpose is attained by mastering the balance between the conflicting aspects and qualities of being human – a spirit, a life force, in a physical body (The World).

TAROT NUMEROLOGY

The ascending numbers indicate an order to the path of self-awareness, or a process. Surprisingly, the Tarot's numbers have remained consistent since at least the 13th century, though, at the time, the Tarot was just used for amusement and games.

Numerology of the Tarot is a good example of how the Tarot evolved as it passed through different civilisations. Numerology is a branch of mathematics defined as the study of the numerical value of letters in words, names and concepts. Although the term 'numerology' was first used in the English language in 1907,

philosophers of the ancient Classical Greek world, such as Pythagoras, Aristotle, and Plato, studied numerology as early as 500 BCE. They were interested in unravelling the mysteries of our universe by expressing the inter-relationships between various elements and objects in nature (such as seasons, planets and sounds) in numerical equations. Essentially, they believed that a group of elements possessed a characteristic or vibration that could be mathematically represented.

Plato, for example (a philosopher who was a pupil of Socrates and later taught Aristotle in the 5th century BCE), associated each of the four elements – earth, air, water and fire – with a regular solid shape, the so-called Platonic solids. The number 4 related to a square – the most stable geometric shape – which suggested a stable vibration. Eventually, The Emperor (Major card number 4) imparted the vibration of stability, representing the characteristic of 'the builder', who created stability from nature's four elements.

Pythagoras, a mystic and philosopher credited with developing numerology, spent time in the Near East studying other number systems that were popular at the time, such as the Chaldean number system (used from 625 to 539 BCE), Zoroastrian philosophy, the Abjad system (developed by the Arabs by assigning a numerical value to each letter of the alphabet), the Jewish tradition of assigning mystical meanings to words based on their numerical value, as well as Latin alphabet systems and Chinese and Indian number systems. The writings on mysticism of St. Augustine of Hippo (354–430 CE) were influenced by Pythagoras. In turn, they influenced the development of Western philosophy and Western Christianity. Like Pythagoras, St. Augustine believed that "everything had numerical relationships and it was up to the mind to seek and investigate the secrets of these relationships or have them revealed by divine grace".

The Vibrational Meanings of Numbers

'Classical' numerology considers numbers 1 to 9 only. This is because any number larger than 9 can be obtained by adding other numbers to it (from 1 to 9). For example, 10 is the result of adding 1 and 9. Moreover, in modern numerology, the number zero carries special significance, although its value is nought. Zero is considered to contain potential of all other numbers. In personal numerology, the zero amplifies the potential of a person's life purpose, for example, or highlights innate abilities and calling. When the number zero appears after other numbers, such as 10, it amplifies the vibrational characteristic of the original number, making it a potential 'higher level'. For instance, the number 10 is the higher potential of the number 1 – on a higher octave, if you like. The following is a synopsis of the symbolic meanings of numbers 1 to 10, which will assist you in developing a clear knowledge of the vibrational meanings of numbers, attributed to the Tarot.

Major Cards Numerology

0: New Beginning – THE FOOL

At the beginning of the journey, The Fool carries the number zero, which conveys his lack of experience, wisdom and maturity. In his childlike innocence, he is unaware of the risks of this journey. Yet if he does not begin the journey, he will never find out what it will teach him. Zero is the vibration of potential. Moreover, zero will remain a static or dormant potential unless it intends to take a first step or action! The journey could be a success or a failure; caution is therefore necessary.

1: Inner Resources/Unity – THE MAGICIAN

The number 1 can create all other numbers. It expresses its own character through the vibrations of initiative, leadership and great mental inventiveness. The number 1, like The Magician, possesses the four elements required to successfully realize his dreams. The number 1 transforms potential into reality with skill, dexterity, logic, discipline and flexibility, much like The Magician. The infinity symbol over The Magician's head conveys the message, "Master your skills, and you can create endless possibilities."

2: Duality/Heightened Sensitivity – THE HIGH PRIESTESS

The number 2 symbolizes duality. It can see both sides of the coin, itself and the other. It has both an inner sense of logic and imagination. It possesses both an understanding of spiritual principles and the logical means to manifest. Two perceives both the visible and the invisible, expressed as The High Priestess; it vibrates the psychic potential of receiving messages from spirit, dreams or animals. It is aware of the subconscious communicating through dreams. It perceives both worlds: the spiritual and the physical. The number 2 must learn to regulate itself or its sensitivity would overwhelm it. Just like a sponge, it can absorb any type of water. It must learn to trust its own talents, become self-sufficient and carefully select its surroundings.

3: Creativity/Growth – THE EMPRESS

Three is the fruitful outcome of numbers 1 and 2, the initiate and perceiver. It symbolizes The Empress, who vibrates abundant joy and successful self-expression. Its cheerfulness makes it a joy to be with. Three understands the creative arts and has practical common sense. Like The Empress, the number 3 has an inner desire to create beautifully, give birth (figuratively and literally) and communicate. Three is a natural speaker, well-suited for occupations such as marketing and public relations. Three can transform a dream into reality because it is a creator (not a labourer). However, it requires the assistance of other numbers to manifest its creative vision.

4: Stability/Structure – THE EMPEROR

Because the vibration of the number 4 values space and time, its environment and routine must be in order to develop a stable legacy (its throne). To The Emperor, everything must be seen through to the finish – and he has the authority to make it happen! Four is a vibration of establishing rule and order, the result-oriented Emperor, the builder who is competent, fair and disciplined. Four develops long-lasting structures, processes and methodology. It understands routine, rhythm and process because it values time and meeting deadlines. It develops techniques to achieve its goals. When a person is overly disciplined, he or she may become obstinate or dogmatic, or micromanage details instead of focusing on the big picture.

5: Versatility/Freedom – THE HIEROPHANT

This is a powerful vibration of all that's new. Manifesting requires flexibility. The number 5 understands the cycles of change (destiny) and restless inner nature. It desires travel and discovery in all things. Fresh experiences bring about new understanding, which helps it evolve. Like The Hierophant, it has a strong connection to its inner senses as well as the awareness of its purpose, which give it the freedom of flexibility. It is also known as The Oracle, because of the connection to Spirit. Change, adventure, freedom of mind and action are all represented by the number 5. Its vibration is like a rolling stone that can take you anywhere – which can make it unstable. It moves quickly, absorbs knowledge like a sponge, and is ready to take the next risk.

6: Balance & Harmony – THE LOVERS

Six is a vibration of harmony. To attain this harmony, it needs balance as well as honesty, fairness, and the ability to give and nurture. The Lovers are the vibration of love that seeks to find harmony by uniting those who share desires and ideals. Six loves to build peaceful communities and families. It requires a purpose for its devotion. Happiness can only be achieved when these gifts are shared to help others. It learns, grows and heals through personal relationships. It learns how much to give and what not to offer. The number 6 has a strong affinity with youngsters, so it makes an excellent teacher. Six's challenge is not to make others emotionally dependent on it, or to become overprotective and possessive. It must, therefore, be aware of its motives to stay in balance.

7: Mastery/Victory – THE CHARIOT

Seven is the visionary mystic who masters inner and outer senses and resources. Like **The Chariot**, it is spiritual but not religious, an independent thinker and formulator of mindful strategy. By reflecting on its experiences and honing its skills, it is determined to conquer its dreams successfully. Solitude is required for self-analysis, deep thinking and exploring its inner mystical and philosophical nature; therefore, its gifts may not be obvious to others. The number 7 is the vibration of soul growth, and strategy before action. Only in silent exploration will the answer to life's problem come from within to guide others. Seven has a strong sense of self-control and a tendency to repress emotions as it builds a protective wall around itself. However, once it is acquainted with its inner gifts and surroundings, it overcomes its fear of 'stepping outside', and its charm is revealed.

8: Delicate Balance – JUSTICE

To balance its energies, eight is required to root its actions in the greater good, rather than acting from the ego, greed or personal gain. It is a powerful, fast-acting vibration that produces tangible results. Life can be a never-ending cycle of dramatic endings and beginnings until eight has learned its lesson. The number 8 represents a chance to reinvent and evolve, having learned from failures. Intentions and actions must be guided by the heart rather than the ego. Eight emphasizes the importance of evolution on all three levels of manifestation: physical, emotional and mental. It represents Justice, expressing that this delicate balance is required to reach the right verdict. It symbolizes karma in the sense that 'what goes around, comes around' – the effect of actions is experienced immediately. However, the upside is that the dramatic sensitivity of balance makes identifying the wrong action clear. As soon

as eight takes the right action, balance is restored just as quickly. Eight is unaware of its potency. It will spend a long time waiting and agonising over repeated failures before it expresses its brilliance. A modest step in the correct direction can lead to success, and the opposite is also true.

9: Fulfilment/Completion – THE HERMIT

The Hermit in the Tarot expresses the vibration of 9. It is the wise teacher who retreated into isolation to understand himself and discover a higher purpose in life. Experience, inner knowledge, intellect and compassion for humanity and spirituality are all vibrations of 9. Nine is likely to suffer alone until it realizes that suffering is ineffective and that the appropriate action taken without prejudice is. It is also the purest expression of love, because 9 can be deeply connected yet remain detached and stand back without loving possessively. Detachment, and maintaining objectivity, is the most difficult challenge for 9. Its compassion will radiate from the heart, touching everyone in its path.

10: Change – THE WHEEL OF FORTUNE

Ten is the number of ending a cycle and beginning a new one. It is the law of time:

what goes up, must come down as it allows renewal and evolution. Ten is 1 plus 0, or 1 reinventing itself, having learned from the vibrations of the preceding numbers. It expresses the culmination of all actions, thoughts and emotions, and in a sense sets the tone for the next cycle. If the current cycle is a downward trend, then the next will be an upward one. It heralds a quick change of circumstance, propelling one into the cycle of evolution on the next level.

11: Gateway to Evolution – STRENGTH

Eleven is known as a master number or power number because it represents double the potential of the initiator, which is 1, and has its own stand-alone interpretation. Eleven operates on the level of the common good, and is concerned with humanity, not just itself. Because it is an 'evolved' 1, its actions are from the heart and not from the ego. Eleven is like the antennae to the Higher Mind. Eleven is connected to guidance from Spirit, relates to animals, plants and humans, and can have telepathic or channelling abilities.

Furthermore, other numbers from 9 upwards are formed by addition. Twelve is formed by adding 1 and 2, which results in 3. If you are a numerology enthusiast, refer to Figure 1 for key interpretations of the

Major cards and Numerology. We suggest that you intuit your own interpretations of the vibrational qualities of the rest of the Major cards by considering the meaning of the card and its final vibration (3, in this instance). For example, how does The Hanged Man relate to 3, which expresses abundance and fulfilment? This might lead you to new insights. There are more tips on developing your intuition in a later section.

Minor Cards Numerology

ONE (Aces): The Beginning/Unity

One is the prime number from which all other numbers arise. It is associated with the power of creating, individuality and unity – The True Self (The Magician). In the Minor cards, 1 is represented by the Aces – the beginning of all things. One is the number of creative strength and potential. All the Aces convey a strong drive and force. They represent new beginnings of a vibrant, positive and intense nature.

TWO: Duality/Collaboration

The Ace has split into two opposing aspects of 'the self'. They must come together, or reunite, to bring balance and harmony, creating a new outcome to this collaboration. Thus, 2 is associated with opposites: day and night, sun and moon, revealed and hidden, material and spirit, masculine and feminine aspects, container and content, form and essence, logic and intuition, process and creativity, fixed and fluid, and so on. The result of the 2 'united' is indicated in the Minor cards that follow in each suit – either as balance, or as potential unfulfilled.

THREE: Creativity/Growth

Three represents expansion and development; 2 begets 3. It represents the threefold nature of being human: body, mind and spirit. In the Kabbalah, 3 represents the Great Mother, the Great Holy Father and the Source of Being. Three is the result of, or birth of, something new.

FOUR: Stability/Structure

Four represents order, logic, methodology, discipline and authority. It also represents material and physical reality – the manifestation of understanding processes to create the tangible. It associated with hard work and practicality. Four reflects building a solid foundation for a new project. According to kabbalists, 4 is the number of memory.

FIVE: Versatility/Freedom

Mercury's swift speed and fluidity are represented by 5. It is related to adaptability because it embodies the vibrations of all the elements working together and signifies shifts, unpredictability and freedom (the unexpected). Five is flexible and can easily adapt to keep the flow going. Represented by the five-pointed star, or pentagram, which portrays a human's head, arms and legs, it is also associated with human desires. The pentagram is a symbol of positive spiritual aspirations when it points upward (white magic). When the pentagram points downward, however, it represents materialism and evil (black magic).

SIX: Union, Balance & Harmony

Six represents balance harmony, compatibility, beauty, loyalty and personal love as well as love of humanity and service to others. It is associated with romantic relationships, marriage and 'mothering', requiring a harmonious union of opposites. Six also symbolizes the Seal of Solomon in Jewish spirituality, or the Star of David, the six-pointed star consisting of two intersecting triangles. An upward-pointing triangle represents the spirit and a downward-pointing triangle representing the material form, or Earth. It vibrates the delicate balance required to create 'heaven on Earth'.

SEVEN: Mastery/Victory

The frequency of 7 is that of soul development. Seven explores silently to allow solutions to life's problems to emerge. They are natural leaders, once they bloom. Seven is a vibration of self-mastery because it has a strong sense of self-control. It also has a predisposition to repress feelings as it constructs a protective wall around itself. However, once it gets acquainted with its inner gifts and surroundings, it overcomes its trepidation about 'going outside', and its appeal is revealed. Seven can master its mind and make effort appear effortless, which allows it to excel and be victorious. It is also the vibration of the visionary mystic who masters his inner and outer senses, resources and skills. It is spiritual but not religious, a self-contained thinker and creator of mindful strategy.

EIGHT: Delicate Balance/Justice

In numerology, eight is the most misunderstood of all! It is frequently connected with wealth, fame and success. However, its true strength rests in the delicate balance that it must maintain. Any mistake in judgement might topple its balance with disastrous tangible consequences. Because it is a vibration of **Justice** and righteousness, balance between the spiritual and the material must be maintained. Eight is the vibration of prudence. Creating without purpose might constantly tip the scales and result

in massive gains and losses, making a 'dramatic' vibration.

NINE: Fulfilment/Completion (the culmination of all other numbers)

Nine is the last of the primary numbers and symbolizes completion and fulfilment. Because it incorporates all other vibrations, there is no limit to what it may accomplish. However, for its potential to be realized, it must accept what its essence is. It is the culmination of all experiences.

TEN: The End of a Cycle

Ten represents the end of the cycle in the Minor Arcana, the result of a cycle. It symbolizes 'perfection through completion'. In the Kabbalistic Tree of Life, 10 is the final emanation from God, which is the physical world – The Kingdom of Spirit (see page 39). Ten is 1 + 0, symbolizing a return to unity or the renewal of self.

TAROT AND ASTROLOGY

The art of Tarot and the science of astrology have been deeply linked for six centuries and have an undoubtedly profound affinity. Each Tarot card represented an astrological association to a planet, sign or element. To deepen their practice and get more insights from the Tarot, many practitioners integrate Tarot and astrology. Astrologer and Tarot reader Annabel Gat remarks, "One of the most exciting things to me about divination is the correspondences between the systems." The two fields come together beautifully in the complex 12-house astrological spread, which you will learn about later.

Astrological associations are assigned to the Major cards. However, they varied across time. Three of our planets – Uranus, Neptune, and Pluto – were not discovered during Classical Greece or the Renaissance. However, they have been considered by modern Tarot writers. For example, you might see associations of Uranus with The Fool, Neptune with The Hanged Man, and Pluto with Judgement (quite appropriate!). However, even modern astrologers disagree about the planets and the fusion of the Tarot and astrology disciplines. For instance, some do not consider Pluto a true planet (it is only 1,440 miles in diameter); it may even get officially 'delisted' as a planet. However, in the table below you will also see the 'standard' corresponding planet that governs each Major Arcana, its number and its related zodiac sign; both contribute to the vibrational quality and meaning of each of the Major cards.

TAROT AND THE KABBALAH

Kabbalah means 'received tradition', a term previously used in other Judaic contexts. It is also the term used by Medieval Kabbalists for their own doctrine, to express the belief that they were not innovating, but merely revealing the ancient hidden esoteric tradition of the Torah.

The Ancients wondered about the nature of our universe. Several ideas were developed independently by different cultures throughout the ages, to understand the nature of the material (including man) and spiritual worlds. The Classical Greeks believed, for example, that the world is made up of four elements – air, earth, fire and water – a theme that is still depicted in the Tarot and differentiates or identifies the meaning and attributes of each Minor cards suit. Kabbalah is the esoteric interpretation of the 'sacred knowledge' in Jewish mysticism. The Judaic Kabbalah tree of life, known as Sefirot embodies how *Ein Sof* (God, The Endless One) manifests creation. Moreover, the word 'mysticism' is derived from the Greek verb meaning 'to close' or 'to conceal', dating to Ancient Greece.

In modern times, mysticism has come to refer to the desire for connection with the Absolute, the Infinite, or God – depicted by the transformed Fool at the end of his self-development journey as The World

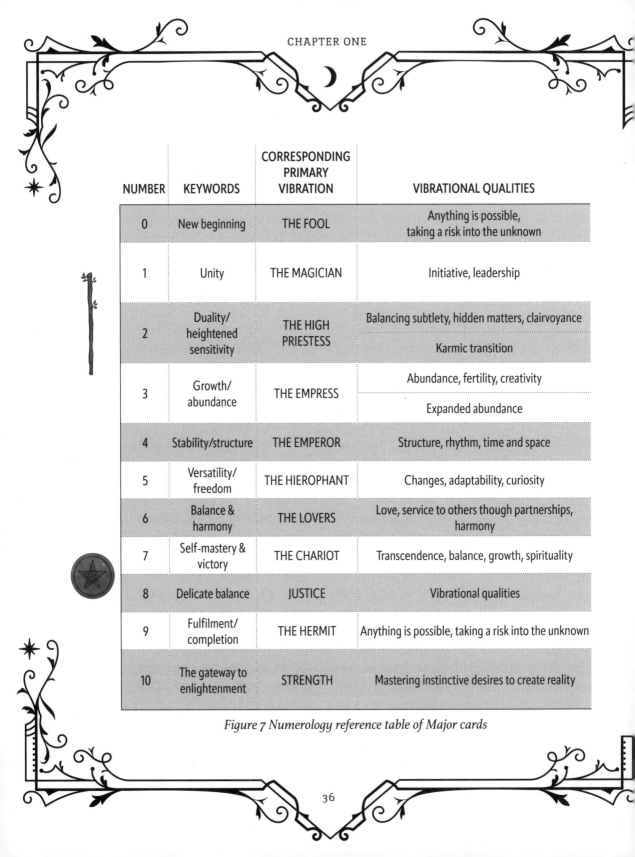

NUMBER	KEYWORDS	CORRESPONDING PRIMARY VIBRATION	VIBRATIONAL QUALITIES
0	New beginning	THE FOOL	Anything is possible, taking a risk into the unknown
1	Unity	THE MAGICIAN	Initiative, leadership
2	Duality/ heightened sensitivity	THE HIGH PRIESTESS	Balancing subtlety, hidden matters, clairvoyance / Karmic transition
3	Growth/ abundance	THE EMPRESS	Abundance, fertility, creativity / Expanded abundance
4	Stability/structure	THE EMPEROR	Structure, rhythm, time and space
5	Versatility/ freedom	THE HIEROPHANT	Changes, adaptability, curiosity
6	Balance & harmony	THE LOVERS	Love, service to others though partnerships, harmony
7	Self-mastery & victory	THE CHARIOT	Transcendence, balance, growth, spirituality
8	Delicate balance	JUSTICE	Vibrational qualities
9	Fulfilment/ completion	THE HERMIT	Anything is possible, taking a risk into the unknown
10	The gateway to enlightenment	STRENGTH	Mastering instinctive desires to create reality

Figure 7 Numerology reference table of Major cards

SECONDARY VIBRATIONAL REPRESENTATIONS	CORRESPONDING GOVERNING PLANETS	ZODIAC SIGN
Dormant potential	–	–
10 WHEEL OF FORTUNE (1+ 0 =1) **19** THE SUN (1+9 = 10 =1)	SUN	LEO
11 STRENGTH (1+1 = 2) **20** JUDGEMENT (2+0 = 20 = 2)	MOON	CANCER
12 THE HANGED MAN (1+2 = 3) **21** THE WORLD (2+1 = 3)	JUPITER	SAGITTARIUS
13 DEATH (1+3 = 4)	URANUS	AQUARIUS
14 TEMPERANCE (1+4 = 5)	MERCURY	GEMINI
15 THE DEVIL (1+5 = 6)	VENUS	TAURUS
16 THE TOWER (1+6 = 7)	NEPTUNE	PISCES
17 THE STAR (1+7 = 8)	SATURN	CAPRICORN
18 THE MOON (1+8 = 9)	MARS	ARIES
1 THE MAGICIAN **2** THE HIGH PRIESTESS	–	–

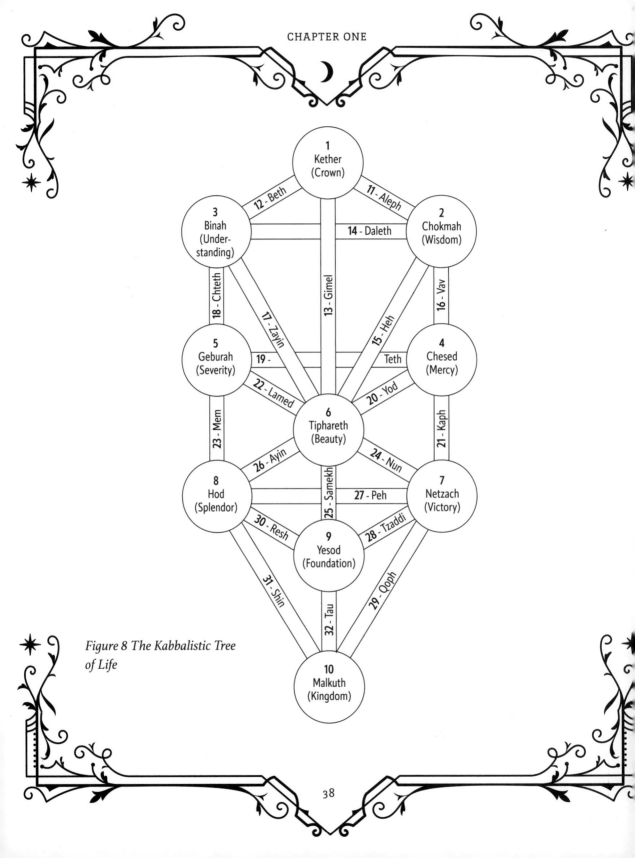

Figure 8 The Kabbalistic Tree of Life

card. (In the Rider-Waite-Smith deck, he is neither man nor spirit, but a well-balanced fusion of both – self-mastery.)

An academic study of Jewish mysticism by Gershom Scholem (*Major Trends in Jewish Mysticism* published in 1941) – a German-born Israeli philosopher and historian widely regarded as the founder of the modern study of Kabbalah – distinguishes between different forms of mysticism across different eras of Jewish history. Of these, Kabbalah, which emerged in 12th-century Europe, is the most well-known, but not the only form, nor the earliest to emerge.

The anonymous ancient mystical book *Sefer HaBahir* (which translates as *The Book of Brightness* or *The Book of Illumination*) is credited to Talmudic sage Rabbi Nehuniah ben HaKana, of Southern France, in the 1st century CE. It is considered an early work of esoteric Jewish mysticism that later became known as Kabbalah. Moreover, scholars (such as the authors of *The Tree of Life: From Eden to Eternity*, by John Woodland and Donald W. Parry, 2011 and Simo Parpola, author of *The Assyrian Tree of Life: Tracing the Origins of Jewish Monotheism and Greek Philosophy*, 1993) believe that the concept of a tree of life with several spheres comprising multiple aspects of reality originated in Assyria in the 9th century BCE; they also assigned values and numbers to their

deities, similar to those used later by the Kabbalah. The Kabbalistic teachings explain the cosmological origins of the universe and the symbolic elements of the creation process.

The Kabbalistic Tree of Life is a symbolic representation of God's nature and God's relationship to the created universe, showing the spiritual path of ascent by man, who is seen as a microcosm of Divine creation. The Jewish Kabbalah refers to this symbol as The Ten Sefirot (spheres). *Sefirot* also means emanations, representing the 10 attributes through which *Ein Sof* (The Infinite) is revealed and continuously creates both the physical realm and the higher metaphysical realms.

The ten Sefirot can be thought of as spheres of consciousness, which represent encompassing aspects of existence, God, or the human psyche. They are numbered 1 through 10; *Kether* is the first emanation, and the final step of manifestation is 10, *Malkuth*. Spheres that represent similar archetypes are arranged in a column. There are three horizontal columns and one vertical column.

The word *sefirah* is related to the verb *lesaper*, which means to tell, express, or communicate in Hebrew; therefore, the function of the *sefirah* is also to communicate an attribute. The name is also related to the word 'sapphire' (in Hebrew *sapir*), a gemstone recognized for its dazzling, glowing, light-giving properties. Apart from expressing the characteristics, another duty of the sefirot is to serve as vessels that bring or provide light.

The connections between the spheres are typically shown by numbered lines symbolizing the mystical pathways or conditions necessary to move from one sphere to the next. The Tree of Life has a total of 32 paths, the first 10 of which are the Sefirot (spheres). The remaining 22 pathways correspond to the energy lines or channels that connect the Sefirot. Each of these paths corresponds to one of the 22 letters of the Hebrew alphabet. The Hebrew alphabet is seen as essential heavenly code, a blueprint for the cosmos. The 13th-century *Zohar* (Book of Splendour) is replete with references to the Hebrew alphabet's significance, and many Jewish visionaries have emphasized that understanding the Hebrew alphabet allows an individual to attain supreme knowledge of the realm of matter.

The Meaning of the Ten Sefirot

The positions of the spheres on the Tree of Life help explain the nature of the sefirah. For example, *Kether* (the Crown) is at the top of the chart, while *Malkuth* (Kingdom) is at the bottom. *Kether* is thought to be the first

or primary connection between God and the world, and this is symbolized by placing *Kether* at the top. In contrast, *Malkuth*, the ultimate sefirah, represents the culmination or result of all the other spheres, which is the manifestation of humanity in the physical world, the physical cosmos, and everything it contains.

1. Kether (The Crown): spiritual transcendence or the experience of oneness is represented by this symbol. The word *Kether* means 'crown' and stands above all the other *Sefirot*, like a crown on the head. *Kether* is the *Sefirah* hat, standing above all the *Sefirot*.

2. Chokmah (Wisdom, the potential of what is): active intellect. It is often understood to express the masculine or father principle. It symbolizes the original idea and is frequently referred to as the first flash of intelligence, where all the specifics of an idea are contained but not yet defined. It is everything in its potential, and that potential has been compared to a dot, in which everything is contained but nothing has yet been actualized or defined. This is represented in the Tetragrammaton (the four-letter biblical name of the God of Israel in Hebrew and YHWH in Latin script) by the first letter, *yud,* which resembles a dot.

3. Binah (intelligence, understanding): passive intellect. *Binah* means to comprehend or extract one matter from another. *Binah* expands and develops the initial concept in both breadth and depth, making it more crystallized and clarified than it was in the Chokmah, when the idea was undefined. As a result, the preceding concept, which was in a condensed form, is now disclosed and understood as *Binah*. It signifies that the dot has grown in both breadth and length, symbolizing the feminine, or mother principle.

4. Chesed (love, kindness): active emotion; the serene face of the universe's ruler, as well as heavenly mercy and majesty. *Chesed*, which translates as loving-kindness, is the attribute that extends love and generosity to all without restriction. Creation is regarded as an act of *Chesed*. It also refers to the whole outpouring of *Shefa*, or abundance, and healing. *Chesed* is the divine quality that describes the function of expansion.

5. Geburah (power, strength): passive emotion. *Geburah* represents strength, judgement, law and power, and is the attribute of restriction since it has the power to limit and contract. While *Chesed* creates an outpouring of energy, *Geburah* controls, contracts, and limits the flow, maintaining an equilibrium between expansion and contraction. This is because judgement requires that *Chesed* be distributed justly and in proportion to the recipient's worth, rather than in an indiscriminate manner.

6. Tiphareth (beauty, compassion): the individual self. *Tiphareth* is located on the path to mystical enlightenment, halfway between the realm of everyday existence and the reality of ultimate spiritual transcendence. It represents the concept of spiritual resurrection or rebirth and is symbolized by the sun. It is the core balancing sphere of the entire Kabbalah Tree of Life, as it flows into all other spheres (except *Malkuth*), harmoniously integrates *Chesed* and *Geburah*, and is also known as (beauty) for its harmonic blending of all the sefirot. It symbolizes the synthesis of both *Chesed* and *Geburah* to achieve its overarching purpose, which is facilitating the development of human beings to their full potential. *Tiphareth* is the midpoint of the direct line flowing down from *Kether* to *Malkuth* on the Tree of Life, and hence is positioned on the tree's central balancing column. It is also known as *Rachamim*, which means 'mercy' or 'compassion' in Hebrew.

7. Netzach (victory): active action. The word *Netzach* traditionally translates to 'eternity', but in the context of Kabbalah it alludes to perpetuity, victory, endurance, conquering, and overcoming. As a result, *Netzach* is meant to reflect the concept of supremacy. For example, by giving in an unlimited manner, the receiver is overwhelmed – thus victory. It is regarded as an extension of *Chesed*.

8. Hod (splendour or majesty): passive action. *Hod* is the opposite of *Netzach* and is said to be an extension of *Geburah*, as it symbolizes a state of extreme strain to the point of submission. *Hod* is derived from the Hebrew word *Hodaah*, which means 'thank you', 'admit', or 'submit'. As a result, total submission denotes a *Hod* relationship, whereas total domination denotes a *Netzach* relationship. *Yesod*, the following sefirah, balances the *Netzach* and *Hod* by facilitating communication, and is said to reflect the world's foundation.

9. Yesod (foundation): ego identity. *Yesod* is the Hebrew word for foundation. It is related to the soul's ability or power to interact, connect and communicate with the outside world (represented by the sefirahh of *Malkuth*). It can be understood in a similar way to the foundation of a building, which connects, grounds or unites the structure with the Earth (*Malkuth*). The *Yesod* is also thought to correspond with the male procreative organ, and as such, *Yesod* serves as the basis for future generations. The ability to procreate is thought to be an expression of the infinite within the finite. As such, the *Yesod* is the link between the unlimited procreation potential that pours into it and its actual embodiment in man's offspring.

10. Malkuth (kingdom, sovereignty, Earth): this symbolizes everyday consciousness, the earth, crops, the surrounding environment and all living things associated with it. *Malkuth* means 'kingdom' in Hebrew. It is a summation of all the other spheres (also referred to as nodes) that precede it – if you like, the ultimate gathering of all spheres, the result of one's labour, and the final revelation of the entire process of creation. In the Kabbalah, it is described as 'having nothing of her own'. The book of *Zohar* compares *Malkuth* to the moon, which has no light of her own. All the spheres emerged to manifest *Malkuth*. As a result, *Malkuth* is both the recipient and the consummation of giving.

The 10 emanations of the Creator fall into three groups. The first three spheres address the idea emerging in the mind. The second group are concerned with the emotional aspect, where an idea is assessed or evaluated. And the final group symbolizes action, which brings the idea into form in physical reality. The last sphere, *Malkuth*, is the manifestation of creation.

Exercise: What similarities can you identify between The Tree of Life and the Journey of The Fool? What Major Arcana cards would you correlate with each sphere and pathway? Contemplate the Tree of Life and lay the Major cards that you feel are associated with each sphere and pathway in front of you. What interpretation can you draw from each card according to the corresponding 'house' or sphere? Keep your remarks in your Tarot journal. You might just be inspired to create a Tarot spread of your own!

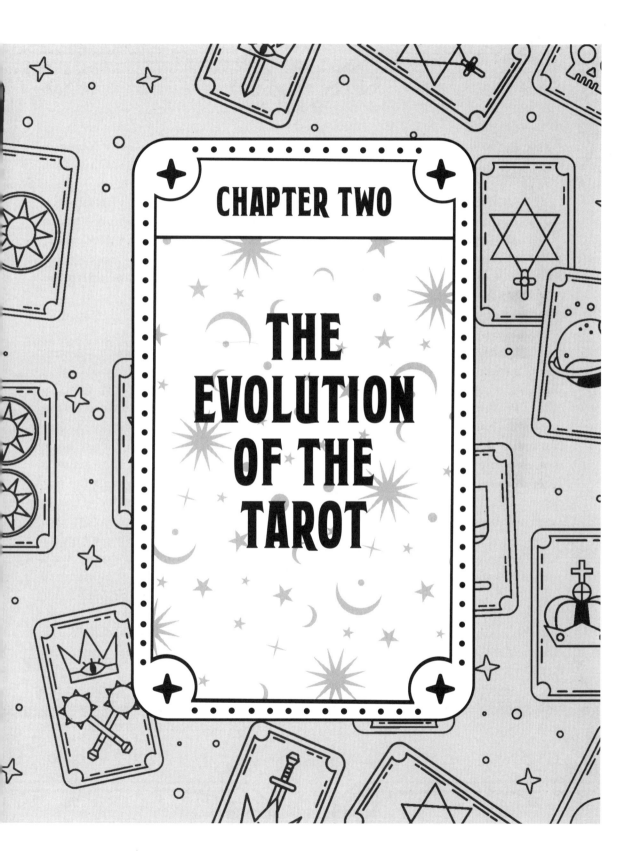

CHAPTER TWO

THE EVOLUTION OF THE TAROT

In this chapter, you will gain a fresh understanding of Tarot symbolism within the framework of its evolution. Hopefully, it will serve as a springboard for your own interpretation when reading the Tarot. As Arthur Edward Waite said, "The true Tarot is symbolism; it speaks no other language and offers no other signs."

Standard modern Tarot decks are based on *The Tarot de Marseilles*, which was based on the earlier Italian *Tarocco Piemontese* (Tarot of Piedmont). This deck is considered part of Piedmontese culture and was the standard Tarot pack of the Kingdom of Sardinia. It is worth pointing out that what is often overlooked in most books on the Tarot are four significant historical turning points, which have shaped the Tarot we came to know and love:

1. The origins of the Tarot in China, as a deck of entertaining playing-card games.

2. The four suits of the Minor cards, and the influence of the 13th-century Islamic Mamluk Sultanate of Egypt (1250–1517); this shaped the composition and symbology of the four suits of the Minor cards, which remain almost unchanged in modern Tarot decks.

3. The role 15th-century Italy played in developing what became the Major cards.

4. The role of the Hermetic Order of the Golden Dawn in the late 18th century in establishing the Tarot as an esoteric tool.

The above turning points gave birth to the Tarot we know today.

I. China

The Tarot was created in 9th-century China as a set of playing cards to amuse the Tang Dynasty, owing to the invention of woodblock printing. Su E, a Tang dynasty writer, wrote the *Collection of Miscellanea in Duyang* in the 9th century; it is the first known work containing a possible reference to card games. In 868, it mentions Princess Tongchang, daughter of Tang Emperor Yizong, playing the 'leaf game' with members of the Wei clan, the princess's husband's family (reported by A. Lo in his 2009 book *The Game of Leaves: An Inquiry into the Origins of Chinese Playing Cards*). The cards were printed on complete sheets and then cut into money cards to symbolize play money, such as Monopoly money, in the 11th century. "The first cards may have been actual paper currency that doubled as both gaming tools and the stakes being played for, like trading card games," wrote William Henry Wilkinson in his book *Chinese Origin of Playing Cards* (1895). Wilkinson served as Consul-General for the United Kingdom in China and Korea and was also a playing-card collector and card-game enthusiast. "Paper money was impractical and risky, therefore play money, often known as money cards, was substituted."

Playing cards quickly gained popularity and expanded throughout China. According to David Parlett's article *The Chinese 'Leaf' Game,* the first recorded instance of a card game occurred on July 17, 1294, when "Yan Sengzhu and Zheng Pig-Dog were caught playing cards (a game called *zhi pai*) ... wood blocks for printing them had been impounded, together with nine of the actual cards" (2015).

Madiao, another trick-taking game from the Ming Dynasty (1368–1644), was the first game for which rules were documented. It was played with 38 'money cards' divided into four suits, according to 15th-century scholar Lu Rong: nine in coins, nine in strings of coins (which may have been misinterpreted as sticks from primitive illustrations), nine in myriads (or multitudes) of coins or strings, and 11 in tens of myriads (a myriad is 10,000). To signify their rank and suit, the two latter suits were marked with *Water Margin* characters (*Water Margin* is one of the oldest Chinese novels in vernacular Mandarin) rather than pips in Chinese. The suit of coins was organized in reverse order, with the 9 of coins as the lowest card and the 1 of coins (Ace?) as the highest. This could be the start of the Minor cards.

The addition of *Water Margin* characters to the playing cards might be seen as an important evolution of the Tarot, as figures began to emerge on the cards. *Water Margin* is credited to Shi Nai'an, a Chinese writer from the Yuan and early Ming Dynasties (1296–1372). "Shuihu Zhuan (translated in English as *Water Margin*) is one of the four great classical novels of Chinese literature," according to Bill Findlay's 2004 book *Frael Ither Tongues: Essays on Modern Translations into Scots.* (It is also translated as *Outlaws of the Marsh* and *All Men Are Brothers* in English). In 100 chapters, it relates the tragic story of Song Jiang, a historical hero from the 12th century.

In the story, the hero starts off as a fugitive who eventually evolves into a superhero with the help of his 108 rebel allies. The supreme deity banishes them all together, turning them into spirits (36 Heavenly Spirits and 72 Earthly Demons). After being mistakenly liberated from incarceration beneath a dragon-tortoise god, they were reincarnated as heroes who came together for the sake of justice. A Han dynasty historian, Sima Qian, regards the protagonists in this tale as a dramatization of the period's Chinese knights, describing them thus: "Their words were always true and trustworthy, and their acts were always fast and resolute. They always kept their promises, and they would rush into dangers threatening others without regard for their own safety." (Could this have been the rise of the Court Cards, notably the Knights?)

Playing cards began to incorporate illustrations of characters from this popular novel and were separated into four suits, one of which is still in use today: Coins. To put it another way, the cards evolved in lockstep with their users, reflecting the culture of each region they spread to. Furthermore, despite local authorities banning the production of cards (a repeated theme in 14th-century Italy), their appeal has never faded. By this time, we can already trace emerging Tarot themes including storytelling, heavenly and earthly aspects, spirits, knights, justice, outlaws to heroes, card ranking, coin symbols, four suits, and major 'face' characters.

2. The Mamluks

The card game grew in popularity rapidly and expanded westward through the Middle East, finally reaching Egypt's Islamic Mamluk Sultanate in the 13th century. It was divided into four suits, numbered 1 through 10, known as pip cards, as well as three Court Cards known as *malik* (king), *nā'ib malik* (viceroy or deputy king), and *thānī nā'ib* (second or under-deputy). There are no 'face' images on the Tarot deck yet. The Tarot remained a very popular card game for nearly 1,000 years, before it eventually made its way to Italy through the Mamluk Sultanate around the late 14th century. What are now known as the Major Arcana cards first appeared in the Tarot in Italy. Countless decks with wonderful artwork were created to delight the royal houses, while a black-and-white counterpart appeared to entertain the public. The polo sticks (originally symbolizing the sticks used in polo, which was a prominent sport in Central Asia, where the Mamluks descended from) were a mystery to Europeans. They were reassigned as batons (read more about this in the evolution of the Minor cards section).

3. Italy

Fifteenth-century Europe, particularly Italy, saw a boom in designing Tarot decks for card games – one of which, *Tarocchi* (from which the name Tarot is derived), became popular. Depending on the designer, various pictures were arbitrarily added and removed from the cards over the years. The Major Arcana cards, often known as face cards at the time, began to appear in pictures. There were no pictures on the first deck of playing cards. Court Cards were created from the newly incorporated drawings, which ranged from the allegorical to pictures of court life and personalities. The order of what became known as the Major Cards, on the other hand, remained consistent, emphasizing the importance of the story presented by the cards and their numbers.

A deck of cards was invented in Italy in the 1430s to play *Tarocchi*, according to historical evidence. A fifth suit was added to the pack's existing four suits during that time. A fifth suit of 21 specially illustrated cards known as *trionfi* (triumphs, later known as trump cards) was added, as well as an odd card known as *il matto* ('The Fool'). The trionfi cards were dubbed 'face cards' to distinguish them from the rest of the deck. Each trionfi card depicted a different metaphorical illustration instead of the usual symbols representing each suit at the time. The illustrations for the new fifth suit were medieval re-enactments of Roman triumphal processions, like floats in a modern festival parade. The new trionfi suit did not come with a number at first. It was critical to remember the order of the cards.

The Tarot travelled across Europe to France, where Marseille, which was under Italian administration at the time, became the centre for printing them. By 1736, the famed Marseille printer Chosson had manufactured the first uniform pattern of Italian-suited Tarot pack with 78 cards. It was based on the Tarot of Piedmont.

SUIT				
English	Clubs	Cups	Swords	Coins
Italian	Bastoni	Coppe	Spada	Denari
Spanish	Bastos	Copas	Espadas	Oros

Figure 9 Suits of the Tarot

4. The Birth of Esotericism in the 18th Century

The significance of the new suit's sequence is likely what influenced the 18th-century scholars who founded the Western Esoteric Schools of Enlightenment. The sequence was thought to represent The Journey of The Fool's Enlightenment because numbers were added to the superior, or face cards. The Major Arcana, or secrets, were the face cards. 'Minor cards', or 'lesser secrets', were the names given to the pip cards.

Furthermore, Arthur Edward Waite (1857–1942), the creator of the Rider-Waite-Smith Tarot, the first fully illustrated deck, was a serious student of all things occult. He was also influenced by the works of Éliphas

Lévi Zahed, a French esotericist, whose *Book of Hermes* is regarded as the beginning of the 19th-century British occult group, The Hermetic Order of the Golden Dawn. It was founded by Samuel Mathers, William Woodman, and William Wynn Westcott, and it attracted several notable figures of the time, including Edward Munch, August Strindberg, Rider Haggard, Aleister Crowley, William Butler Yeats, Bram Stoker and others. According to Jason Ānanda Josephson Storm, author of the 2013 book *God's Shadow: Occluded Possibilities in the Genealogy of Religion*, "Lévi incorporated the Tarot cards into his magical system, and as a result the Tarot has been an important part of the paraphernalia of Western magicians." Under the strict supervision of Waite, Pamela Colman Smith, a fellow member of the Order of the Golden Dawn, designed the 70 cards, encapsulating several age-old symbols in her illustrations, including the four elements.

The aforementioned academic Michael Dummett, author of *The Game of Tarot*, states that the Tarot was only used for playing games until the 18th century. And so, The Etteilla deck, the first Tarot deck specifically designed for occult purposes, was published around 1789 and included an instruction booklet on how to use it. The Major cards addressed the questioner's spiritual challenges and Major life trends. In the Minor cards, wands are associated with business and professional goals, while cups, swords, and coins are associated with relationships, money, and material comfort. The fortune-teller shuffles the Tarot deck before arranging a few cards in a spread pattern (either chosen at random by the questioner or dealt from the top of the shuffled deck). The significance of any card varies depending on whether it is turned upside down, where it is in the spread, and which cards are adjacent to it.

According to Dummett, the belief in the cards' divinatory meaning is linked to a belief in their occult properties, which was popularized by prominent Protestant clerics and freemasons in the 18th century. The occult Tarot rose to prominence in the late 1880s not only in France, but also throughout the English-speaking world. In 1886, Waite published *The Mysteries of Magic*, a collection of Lévi's writings that was the first significant presentation of the occult Tarot to be published in England. The esoteric Tarot was not established as a tool in the English-speaking world until the Hermetic Order of the Golden Dawn was founded in 1888.

During the late 18th and 19th centuries, the Western mystery tradition, or esotericism, saw the Tarot as a tool for greater spiritual insight. In *The Game of Tarot,* Dummett writes, "It was only in the 1780s, when the practice of fortune-telling with regular playing cards had been well established for at least two decades."

The term esotericism first appeared in Europe in the late 18th century, around 1789. Esotericism is a broad term that refers to a variety of Western ideologies and traditions. It was regarded as a separate school of thought from mainstream Christianity, representing a hidden heritage. The first European schools of Western Esotericism to evolve and influence what the Tarot cards represented were Hermeticism, Gnosticism and Neoplatonism.

As a result of various intellectuals combining pagan theories with the Kabbalah and Christian philosophy during the Age of Enlightenment in the 18th century, esoteric groups such as Christian Theosophy arose (which refers to a variety of Christian viewpoints that focus on attaining direct, unmediated knowledge of the nature of divinity as well as the origin and purpose of the universe, according to Boaz Huss' *Forward, to the East: Napthali Herz Imber's Perception of Kabbalah*, published in 2013).

According to Dummett, the belief in the cards' divinatory meaning is linked to a belief in their occult properties, which was popularized by prominent Protestant clerics and freemasons in the 18th century. The occult Tarot rose to prominence in the late 1880s not only in France, but also throughout the English-speaking world. In 1886, Waite published *The Mysteries of Magic,* a collection of Lévi's writings that was the first significant presentation of the occult Tarot to be published in England. The esoteric Tarot was not established as a tool in the English-speaking world until the Hermetic Order of the Golden Dawn was founded in 1888.

In the 19th century, new esoteric thinking tendencies, now known as occultism, emerged. In that century, the Theosophical Society and the Hermetic Order of the Golden Dawn, of which Arthur Edward Waite was a member, were both influential. Mystical philosophies were the name given to their newfound ideas. According to *Encyclopaedia Britannica*, mysticism is usually associated with becoming one with God or the Absolute, but it can also refer to any type of ecstasy or altered state of consciousness that has a religious or spiritual value. It can also refer to the search for ultimate or hidden truths, as well as personal growth aided by various techniques and experiences.

The three most popular esoteric Tarot decks were the Tarot of Marseilles, the Rider-Waite-Smith Tarot cards, and the

Thoth Tarot deck. Marseilles, in southern France, was once a major centre for playing-card production. Modern paganism, which includes religious movements like Wicca, arose from occultism. The 1960s counterculture and subsequent movements were influenced by esoteric beliefs, resulting in the New Age phenomenon of the 1970s. Éliphas Lévi Zahed's work as a member of the Golden Dawn order influenced Arthur Waite (whose original name was Alphonse-Louis Constant). Lévi began his career as a Catholic priest before becoming an esotericist and poet. He wrote over 20 volumes on magic, Kabbalah, alchemy, and occultism in the 19th century.

He founded The Hermetic Order of Golden Dawn by writing *The Book of Hermes*. In the book, he claims that the Tarot predates Moses and that it is a universal key of knowledge, philosophy, and magic that can unlock Hermetic and Qabalistic principles. As a result, astrological and Hebrew symbols were included in the Rider-Waite-Smith Tarot illustrations, as well as the numbering of the Major arcana cards to emphasize their numerological significance. The order of the Major Trump Cards, on the other hand, had to be remembered in the 15th century.

Even though such stories helped popularize the Tarot, Tarot historians have yet to discover any evidence that the Tarot meaning was founded in ancient cultures or civilizations like ancient Egypt or The Holy Kabbalah. What's important to remember is that Tarot was the catalyst for the emergence of all those schools of thought. The Tarot was specifically mentioned in the Hermetic Order's founding document, the *Cipher Manuscripts* (a collection of 60 folios containing the structural outline of a series of magical initiation rituals corresponding to the spiritual elements of earth, air, water and fire).

The Fool was placed before the other 21 trumps when determining the Kabbalistic correspondence of the Major Arcana to the Hebrew alphabet, attributing the Hebrew alphabet correspondences to pathways in the Tree of Life, swapping the positions of the eighth and eleventh arcana (Justice and Strength), and reassigning Qabalistic planetary association. This manuscript served as the foundation for Tarot interpretations by the Golden Dawn and its immediate successors. The letters of the Tetragrammaton (derived from Greek, a tetragram is a four-letter word that transliterates as YHWH, the name of Israel's national god) were assigned to each of the Court Cards. As Ronald Decker and Michael Dummett noted in their 2002 book *A History of the Occult Tarot: 1870–1970*, the

Golden Dawn also linked the Court Cards and suits to the four classical elements and linked each of the 36 cards, ranked from 2 to 10, inclusive, to one of the 36 astrological decans (subdivisions of a sign, in astrology).

Academics have questioned Westcott's story's veracity. The documents' age and contents have been the subject of much debate. According to Carroll Runyon's 1977 book *Secrets of the Golden Dawn Cipher Manuscripts,* the authenticity of the manuscripts contributed to the Golden Dawn Order's first great schism in 1900. "They were capable esoteric scholars, with access to works on the Qabalah, Hermeticism, and Egyptology in Masonic libraries, to have combined it all into the form followed by the Golden Dawn," she wrote. The Cipher Manuscripts' true origins are still unknown.

Nonetheless, by the 18th century, the Tarot had established itself as a means of preserving and communicating this sacred knowledge: the path to self-awareness and enlightenment, a system of guidance told through The Fool's journey. The enigma that surrounds the Tarot as a 'keeper of ancient knowledge' is not diminished by revealed information and studies on the Tarot in the late 20th and early 21st centuries. It may even demonstrate how far people went to attribute significance to it throughout the centuries by involving ancient ideologies and civilizations, such as ancient Egypt, as well as other disciplines. Indeed, several modern Tarot decks have emerged in the last decade or so, interpreting the Tarot with new graphics and meaning, and these are quite different from the original divinatory decks from the 18th and 19th centuries.

EVOLUTION OF THE FOUR ELEMENTS OF THE TAROT

The pre-Socratic Greek concept of four essential elements – air, earth, fire and water – survived throughout the Middle Ages and into the Renaissance, profoundly affecting European thinking and culture. The four elements (and later ether) were proposed as classical elements to describe the complexity of nature that constituted the material world and all matter. It was known as cosmology, which is a discipline of philosophy. Plato connected air, earth, fire and water with regular solid shapes (a cube, octahedron, icosahedron and tetrahedron, respectively). Similar views were held by ancient cultures in China, and India. Local languages might refer to air as wind, and the fifth element as 'void'. (Plato later added a fifth element, ether, which he interpreted to represent the unseen material "which made up the heavens".)

While the classification of the material world in ancient India, Hellenistic Egypt and ancient Greece into air, earth, fire and water was more philosophical, medieval Middle Eastern scientists used practical, experimental observation to classify materials during the Islamic Golden Age (8th to 12th century), which became known as alchemy. Medieval alchemy was originally developed by the Arabs and is mostly attributed to Jabir ibn Hayyān (who died around 806–816). Hayyān published a wide range of writings on cosmology, astronomy, and astrology, as well as medicine, pharmacology, zoology, botany, metaphysics, logic and grammar.

The Greek traditions were translated and developed further by Ibn Hayyān. Like the Platonists, Ibn Hayyān considered the four elements as having properties such as heat and cold (the active force) and dryness and moisture (the recipients). He called these properties the 'natures' of the elements, or *ṭabā˘i* in Arabic. He went on to say that the components are made up of these 'natures', as well as a fifth element, an underlying 'substance' known as *jawhar*, or essence. He hypothesized that by changing the nature of one metal, a different metal would emerge. This, he argued, would necessitate the presence of a catalyst, an *al-iksir* – the elusive elixir that could bring about the transformation. In European alchemy it became known as the philosopher's stone (Arabic: *ḥajar al-falāsifa*).

The Islamic Golden Age saw the establishment of theoretical frameworks in alchemy and chemistry, giving birth to a flourishing tradition of Latin alchemy in Europe and playing a significant role in the development of early modern science (particularly chemistry and medicine), which was subject to experimental verification in the 1600s during the scientific revolution. Nineteenth-century mystics, including Waite, Lévi and many more, were influenced by the philosophies of those who preceded them in seeking truth about the nature of the universe.

The Tarot, as a system of divination, encapsulates this influence and includes several aspects of ancient philosophies. The following table demonstrates in a small way how humans strived to understand the world and the meaning of life. Ideas or philosophies arose independently, in separate cultures, evolved over time and eventually poured into the reservoir of knowledge that influenced the 18th-century European mystics who developed these ideas further, ascribing their own meaning and interpretation of the Tarot. As you have a better understanding of the Tarot, you will

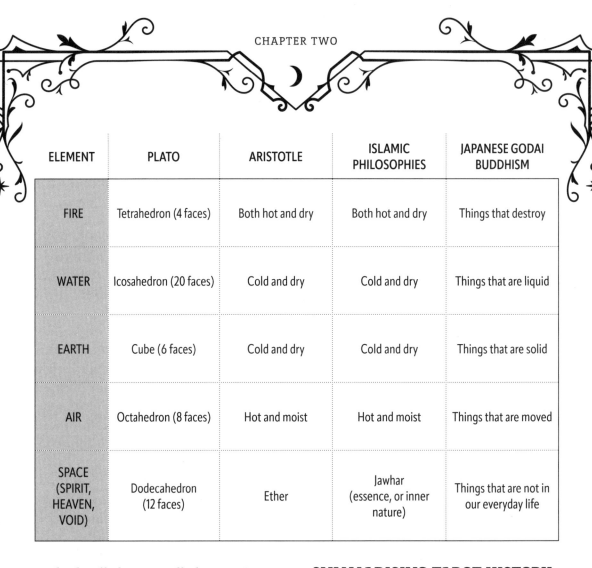

ELEMENT	PLATO	ARISTOTLE	ISLAMIC PHILOSOPHIES	JAPANESE GODAI BUDDHISM
FIRE	Tetrahedron (4 faces)	Both hot and dry	Both hot and dry	Things that destroy
WATER	Icosahedron (20 faces)	Cold and dry	Cold and dry	Things that are liquid
EARTH	Cube (6 faces)	Cold and dry	Cold and dry	Things that are solid
AIR	Octahedron (8 faces)	Hot and moist	Hot and moist	Things that are moved
SPACE (SPIRIT, HEAVEN, VOID)	Dodecahedron (12 faces)	Ether	Jawhar (essence, or inner nature)	Things that are not in our everyday life

undoubtedly be compelled to continue to innovate on the meaning of their symbols.

Nowadays, a traditional Tarot deck consists of 78 trump cards, as they were referred to in the past. The 78 cards are divided into two distinct types: 22 Major Arcana (Greater Secrets) cards and, 56 Minor Arcana (Lesser Secrets), which resemble modern playing cards.

SUMMARISING TAROT HISTORY

It's fascinating to see how, as the game spread around the world, each culture and civilization adapted the deck, adding their own symbols, cards and hierarchies to the game. As you will see, this evolution influenced what we now know as traditional Tarot. As you consider each Tarot card, give it the time it deserves. Note which symbols

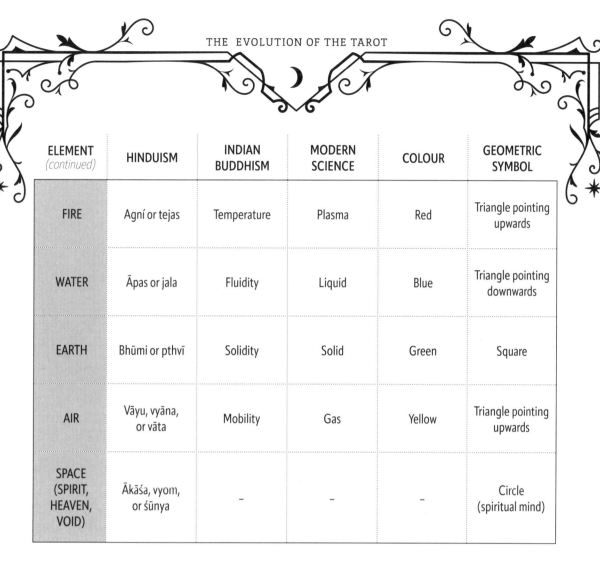

ELEMENT *(continued)*	HINDUISM	INDIAN BUDDHISM	MODERN SCIENCE	COLOUR	GEOMETRIC SYMBOL
FIRE	Agní or tejas	Temperature	Plasma	Red	Triangle pointing upwards
WATER	Āpas or jala	Fluidity	Liquid	Blue	Triangle pointing downwards
EARTH	Bhūmi or pthvī	Solidity	Solid	Green	Square
AIR	Vāyu, vyāna, or vāta	Mobility	Gas	Yellow	Triangle pointing upwards
SPACE (SPIRIT, HEAVEN, VOID)	Ākāśa, vyom, or śūnya	–	–	–	Circle (spiritual mind)

speak to you. You will most probably be struck with your own insights, adding to this wealth of knowledge. We hope that by reading this book, you will be inspired to develop your own intuitive interpretations. One day, you might decide to make your own deck! That is the Tarot's true power.

Figure 10 Philosophical interpretation of the elements

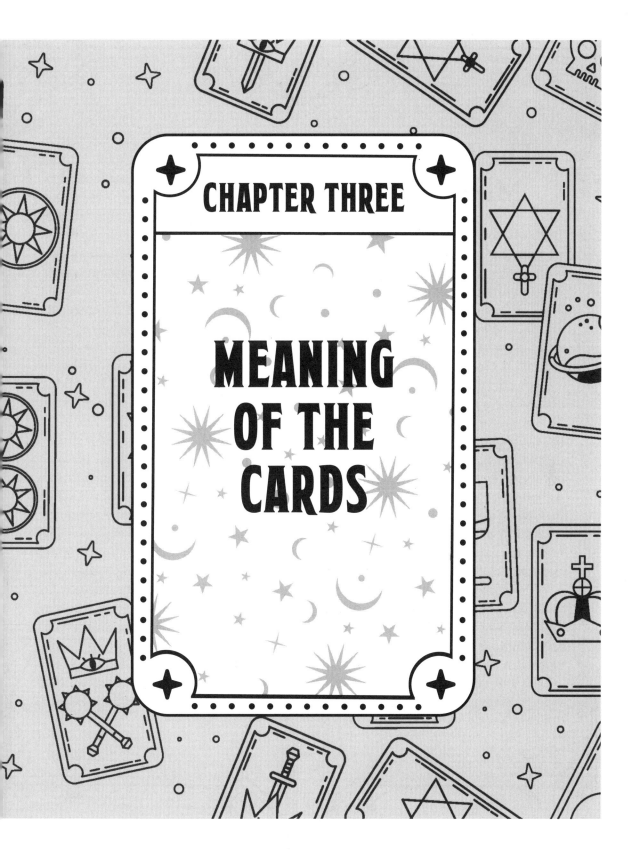

CHAPTER THREE

MEANING OF THE CARDS

The Major and Minor Cards

The Fool is chosen by the Tarot to recount the story and provide the way to self-awareness. He goes through multiple lessons to help him fully integrate the various facets of being a spirit in human form. The Fool finds his place in life at the end of this journey and becomes a completely integrated individual, capable of achieving any goal.

Along the way, he learns how to express himself in a way that is different from how he was raised. Each card teaches him a lesson or points him in the direction of what he must resolve to discover his particular talents, abilities and ways of self-expression. Although the 'lessons' appear to be similar, they are on a different level since The Fool is urged to go deeper within himself and bridge the gaps each time. The Tarot can assist us in understanding and realizing our own life's ambitions and goals. You'll notice parallels between your own life and that of The Fool. The Tarot tale encourages you to reflect on your life while seeking direction to live in a way that is rewarding to you.

The journey teaches us that not every event in life is pleasant. Some of them are difficult, but they are also necessary for us to grow and establish our own path in life. The Fool's journey teaches us that understanding life's experiences offers us a fresh perspective, and hence knowledge. It aids in emotional healing, allowing new opportunities to develop. In effect, we can progress through life with joy and ease. We hope you'll come to your own conclusions regarding The Fool's journey and the significance of each card that represents a step closer to discovering his real self-expression. To identify the process of self-development The Fool underwent, we have divided it into three phases: 'The Making of a Hero', 'Inner Alchemy', and finally the 'Fulfilment' phase.

The Fool, on the other hand, is clearly not a fool! He is a fearless explorer who has experienced both losses and wins in his life and continues to take risks. He does not succumb. As a result of his perseverance, life rewards him. He develops resilience and learns how to re-invent himself and his life, thereby further empowering himself. He attains a level of 'self-mastery' that enables him to keep his alignment and manifest from the spirit into the physical realm. The Fool masters his instincts, evolving into a wiser, more fulfilled individual who has conquered his emotions and mind, and has learned that the magic to making anything happen is taking the first step!

On the following pages, you will meet the Major and Minor cards as characters and situations that shaped The Fool's character and helped him integrate his inner skills, knowledge, self-control and wisdom. You will encounter different aspects of The Fool in each suit, as the Page, Knight, Queen and King.

THE MINOR CARDS

Underneath each Major card, the corresponding Minor cards are presented, to help you build a more complete picture of the Tarot secrets. For example, the Court Cards represent the developing stages of The Fool's personality: the Pages represent an aspect of The Fool's evolving character. The Knights are an older Fool who becomes The Magician.

The Queens relate to The Empress Card and correspond to developing the feminine aspect of The Fool; and finally, the King Court Cards relate to The Emperor, whom The Fool becomes, having integrated the feminine aspect. Like The Fool, the Court Cards are not numbered.

Moreover, as the Minor cards that follow the Court Cards are numbered, they each depict or express that development within the context of their suit. For example, Wands represent the developmental cycle of The Fool's skills, Cups depict his emotional development, Swords express his evolving thoughts and mastering his mind; and Pentacles express the tangible result of The Fool's developing personality – the culmination of the previous three aspects. In this way, you can begin integrating the meaning of each card, or step of development; as it is expressed first as the Major card, then again as the Court Card, and finally as a step, or number of steps, in the daily situations-cycle of the numbered pip cards.

The Tarot can serve as a source of inspiration for you. A modern interpretation, an exercise and a helpful visualisation are included with each card to help you develop your intuition and get better acquainted with the Major cards. Have fun on your journey!

PHASE 1: EXPERIENCING OPPOSITES (CARDS 1–7)

We encounter the characters who helped form and prepare The Fool during his childhood and youth in the first phase of the Tarot story. It represents the groundwork that will allow The Fool to make his first decisions on his own, conquer his first conflict, love, and prepare for bigger conflicts. New experiences will aid him in realizing his full potential and, ultimately, achieving his life's objective. The Fool represents the start of self-actualization as well as the pinnacle of wisdom or experiences garnered along the way.

THE FOOL

0 – The Fool: A New Beginning

The Fool's adventure begins with separation or leaving the past behind. He leaves his family and everything familiar behind, packing all his worldly things in a little pouch that he carries lightly on a staff over his shoulder (is he truly prepared for the journey?). He wanders carefree under the sun, dressed in bright colours, with a crimson feather in his cap symbolizing his ambitions and a garland of flowers around it. He is about to take a leap from a cliff, dreaming about the new prospects that await him. The Fool's faithful companion, the white dog, attempts to warn him by barking at his feet, but The Fool remains unconcerned.

The voyage starts with a young man who appears innocent, happy and full of promise. He is preparing to go on an adventure into the unknown. This trip necessitates understanding the fundamental principles symbolized by the little pouch in which he keeps all his belongings. His gaze is fixed upwards, oblivious to the dangers that await him. Even though his trusty dog barks to alert him of the danger, he remains unconcerned and determined. Although you might think that The Fool is unprepared for this part of his life, the fact that he has chosen to embark on it indicates that he is bold and courageous.

The Fool is also a symbol of everlasting youth and innocence. We see him poised to take a step off a precipice and into the unknown void below. He holds a white rose in his left hand, symbolizing spiritual longing, and a wand in his right hand, symbolizing the duality of the spiritual and material worlds, respectively. A small pouch dangles from the wand's end, containing only the necessities for the voyage – the four elements of air, earth fire and water, with which he will learn to realize his aspirations. His dog, a companion and guide, is attempting to warn him about the danger, but he ignores it. He's standing on the edge of a cliff, daydreaming, and gazing upwards into the sky. The Sun is beaming brightly above his head, symbolizing his optimism and faith in life's process.

Moreover, the snow-topped mountains in the distance hint at the terrain of the journey – or the size of the challenges he is about to encounter. This contrasts with the shining sun, symbolizing the fluctuating cycle of seasons (bad and fair weather) on the journey. Nonetheless, he is thrilled to embark on his new adventure. As a result, The Fool displays entire trust in life, believing that it is worthwhile to live and worthy of his trust. He isn't foolish but naive, and it is his innocence and openness to life that keeps him going and provides him with delight. Because he represents every one of us at every stage of our lives, The Fool archetype is profound and significant. Life continues to give up new situations in which we feel vulnerable, at risk, and unknown, no matter how old or experienced we are.

The Fool is leaving his home and his parents behind, taking a risk that symbolizes the first step toward self-actualization. Through the experiences he is about to have, he will be changed and transformed. In many respects, he is a juvenile version of an alchemist (The Magician), who begins with simple components and masters them to change his existence into a rewarding experience. Alchemy is a sophisticated process in which opposites are mixed and destroyed to produce a new outcome on a higher level – a purification process through separation and reunion, if you will. The effort gradually and painstakingly proceeds, through trial and error, toward actualizing the best form of The Fool through recurrent steps of separation and reunion, of letting go and accepting challenges. Then he would have accomplished his life's goal.

Upright Meaning: The card represents sudden opportunities and a decision to embark on an adventure. There's a choice to be made as a new life cycle begins, for the journey cannot begin without a decision. A decision is the first step. This card expresses the need to let go of old habits and begin something new and unexplored. Anything can happen, but there must be a beginning step. It denotes someone who is unconventional, courageous, and daring. It can also symbolize a new opportunity,

meeting someone new, or beginning a new cycle or scenario where you may feel inexperienced or unprepared, depending on where it appears in the spread. The outcome is determined by how effectively you manage yourself and retain your balance. Nonetheless, it is the experience gained from this new opportunity that will enrich your life, not the outcome that The Fool represents. When The Fool appears in a spread, it denotes risk-taking and trusting one's instincts. Also, surprising influences are around the corner. Now is the time to think beyond the box and believe in yourself and your ability. It heralds the beginning of an exciting mental, physical or spiritual adventure.

Modern Interpretation: Someone with a great deal of potential; a disruptor of a business or field. A young businessperson. A unique and unexpected chance that has the potential to open doors. You'll get an answer if you take a step forward.

Reversed Meaning: A hasty decision or connection that could end badly. Before you take the plunge, make sure you've done your homework. Pay attention to your gut instincts and don't take unnecessary chances.

Exercise: The Fool's image contains a plethora of smaller symbols. How many do you think you can find? Meditate on this card in your Tarot journal and write down the symbols you notice and the meanings that come to mind (hint: notice the feather on his head, and his lavish attire).

Meditation: This meditation will help balance your emotions and create open-mindedness. Whenever you are on the verge of something new, hold The Fool card and gaze into it while you breathe deeply a few times. Relax your eyes and imagine or pretend that you are moving into the image on the card. Have a sense of the place, and the environment. See the the latter in high definition – make it as real as possible. Imagine or pretend that you meet The Fool. Have a conversation about your new opportunity or circumstance. When you feel it is time to leave, bring your awareness back to your body, and to your feet onto the floor. Pick up a pen and write down any thoughts or impressions you receive before you forget them. You will find that your mind has cleared, and you feel neutral and open.

Court Cards – Pages

The Pages in each Minor card suit represent a younger 'Fool'. They illustrate everyday happenings and the developmental stage of The Fool. Each Court Card suit highlights a different facet of The Fool's developing personality.

Meaning: Pages are youngsters or adolescents who, depending on the suit to which they belong in a reading, reflect youthful potential, dreams and other characteristics. They encapsulate the tender qualities of a young Fool, which must be nourished for them to mature. Pages are messengers who announce the timing and seasons, as well as news of any type. In a reading, take note of the Page's corresponding element to get ideas for an event's timing.

Page of Wands is a youngster or personality who is lively, creative, restless or hyperactive, and warm. It also refers to springtime, which is characterized by frenzied activity, new beginnings, inspiration, innovation and expansion. It tells you to make wise choices in the future, since you will reap what you sow.

occurs in a spread, this card encourages you to develop your creative side rather than being lazy or daydreaming! It's a call to action to make your dreams a reality right now.

Reversed: An overly emotional youngster – or the reader's current state.

Page of Swords is a bright, athletic, but possibly difficult young person. They are witty and intelligent. Their actions may be hasty, but they are intellectually curious

PAGE OF WANDS

Reversed: When this card is reversed in a spread, it denotes a troublesome youngster who has most likely been neglected. They are seeking attention to express their creativity and be acknowledged. As a result, they might behave in an excessive manner. They can be hyperactive and lack concentration.

Page of Cups represents a child's imaginative, emotional and poetic character. The Page of Cups is a sensitive, sympathetic individual who is easily hurt. When it

PAGE OF CUPS

and fast to pick up new information. They have the potential to be introverted. This is a child who appreciates sports and active games. This card also represents polishing one's abilities and skills to advance in life.

Reversed: Indicates a significant mental state, or the need for professional assistance to address one's mental state.

Page of Pentacles: This card represents a young individual who is studious or financially savvy. If you've just started a project, it could also mean profit or minor winnings. This is a youth who is inquisitive and has financial intelligence.

Reversed: A child, or someone who acts childishly, and has personality issues because of their serious nature. Interacting with others is tough for them.

PAGE OF SWORDS

PAGE OF PENTACLES

THE MAGICIAN

1 – The Magician: The Initiator

The archetypal achiever is The Magician. The card describes The Fool's first lesson. Early on in his journey, The Fool learns that no matter what his goals are, he has a natural potential to enhance his abilities, skills and talents. These he must cultivate to achieve his goals. The Fool must learn to channel his creative force into the tools and equipment represented by the four elements on the magician's table. We see The Fool transforming into a skilled 'magician' who masters his inner resources and abilities.

Essentially, to fulfil his goals and get results, The Magician taps into universal powers, bridging his inner resources with the universal or spiritual power of inspiration. By doing so, he is integrating unconscious desires and the cognitive awareness of how to make his goals a reality. The Fool has matured into The Magician, who realizes that he must maintain balance by reconciling Spirit and materialism. By seeking inspiration and gaining techniques to actualize goals tangibly, he represents both the feminine and masculine principles. The Magician exhibits this balance by raising one arm to the skies and holding a white wand that represents purity of intention and spiritual awareness, while pointing one finger down to the Earth with the other hand, which represents logic, practicality and earthy skills.

However, for his aspirations and ideas to come true, he must retain a sense of balance throughout his life journey – but first, he must act. In front of The Magician, the four elements of creation are represented by a cup that represents water, a pentacle or a desk that represents earth, a wand that represents fire, and a sword that represents air. These are qualities that must be developed and mastered to express his talents and achieve his goals. It takes four 'seasons' to achieve a result. In other words, as the four elements suggest, there is a cycle for growth. Emotions, thoughts, and actions must be oriented toward that goal in order for it to become real. The Magician's red robe and white garment underneath symbolize his pure intention, his focused mind, and his will to see his intentions through to completion – and he develops a plan to do so. This card represents the limitless possibilities we are born with, as well as the necessity to learn new abilities and hone our inner resources to achieve our goals.

Furthermore, the red roses in front of the Magician contrast with the white lilies, which indicate passion and spiritual inspiration, as well as abstract contemplation. This is the result of logic and intuition working together. When The Magician appears in a Tarot spread, it means you could act and make decisions, that you have inner abilities to deal with any situation. You are balanced between intuition and reason, and you can connect the inner abilities and outer expression. It represents a person who possesses both creative and logical abilities. Furthermore,

it denotes having the energy and inspiration to overcome doubts by taking an initial act. Objectives will be realized. This card demonstrates great leadership talents as well as creative thinking.

The Magician is unafraid to take risks. He believes in himself and is willing to stake his reputation on it. He also knows what he wants to achieve and why he wants to do it. He does not hesitate because he is fully aware of his circumstance. The Magician can concentrate with a single-minded determination. He remains the perfect conduit for miracles if he remembers the heavenly source of his power. The Magician suggests in a reading that you have access to the fundamental forces of creativity if you can claim your power and act with awareness and concentration. This card is a call to action, and it is time to act now if you know exactly what you want and are determined to achieve it.

Upright Meaning: This card represents the use of reasoning and a thinking process or methodology to achieve one's goals. If you are upright, you have willpower, a strong intellect, initiative, flexibility and physical/mental focus. The Magician predicts that you will be able to complete your plans and that your project will take off. You are self-assured, clever, expressive and at ease in any situation. This card represents a writer with a creative touch, a sharp, creative business-oriented person, and a future leader.

Modern Representation: The Magician represents a creative person such as a novelist, architect or engineer. A charismatic politician is someone who has a good balance of logical and creative qualities, who speaks well and expresses their ideas clearly, and is well-suited to journalism, marketing or public relations.

Reversed Meaning: Confusion, loss of concentration, worry, and failure to carry ideas to an acceptable finish are all signs of learning difficulties. Plans that were once good are now being abandoned. Revisit your goal and take steps to achieve it, such as creating a strategy and a procedure, and then hone the abilities you'll need to make it a reality.

Exercise: List four attributes that inspire and empower you in your Tarot journal. What exactly are they? Do you have a hobby, a talent or a passion that you have neglected, or you are not nurturing? What would you do if anything was feasible, and money was not an issue? Examine your response and ask yourself, "What four elements do I need

to cultivate in order to make this happen?" To make your goal a reality, what skills do you need to hone or learn? What is the first move you can do right now to make this a reality?

Meditation: If you have an idea for a project or goal, use The Magician card to meditate, for inspiration and clarity of mind. Lay the card in front of you, or hold it in your hands, and gaze upon it calmly. Imagine or pretend that you enter the garden of The Magician. Smell the roses and the lilies. Look at The Magician's table and ask, in your mind, "What do I need for my plan to manifest?" Gaze upon each element for a few moments and start writing down your thoughts. Once you are done, read what you wrote; you might just be surprised!

Court Cards – The Knights

The Knights represent a stage in The Fool's development as he progresses from a Page to a Magician, and then to a King (or Queen.) They represent energy and action, and symbolize the creative, emotional, mental and tangible results The Fool achieves as the four aspects of his personality evolve. In a reading, they represent youths, older than Pages, who are on the lookout for ways to express themselves by identifying their innate strengths and capabilities.

KNIGHT OF WANDS

Knight of Wands: This Knight depicts a lovely young man galloping across the desert, symbolizing the promise for expansion (from a desert to a garden or forest). Over his suit of amour, he wears a cape embroidered with salamanders. He exudes purpose and assurance as he effortlessly holds the reins of the horse in one hand, suggesting confidence, and a wand in the other, symbolizing creative force and drive. This young man has brilliant ideas and a keen sense of adventure; he is a generous and warm friend or lover, yet he can be impulsive, inconsistent and hasty in his decisions. He has a terrific sense of humour and will go to any length to have a good time. This knight may also indicate foreign business connections.

Upright: This card represents an occasion or an event, such as a change of location, a long journey or even immigration to a new country.

Reversed: Business activities not going as planned, not very helpful, causes problems, project muddled, unfinished.

Knight of Cups: Soft, sensitive poetic, creative, dreamer. This card depicts an artistic, caring and amorous young man. The Knight of Cups is frequently a fair-haired man. Despite being as handsome as the Knight of Wands, the Knight of Cups has a much kinder disposition. Consider his appearance and the horse he rides. Unlike the confident gallop of the Knight of Wands, his lovely white horse bows coyly and moves gently and deliberately. His spiritual goals are symbolized by his winged helmet. And his clothes are embellished with the fish of creative imagination. A stream passes across the terrain in the background of the scene, between the hills and the valley, implying

KNIGHT OF CUPS

Reversed: Unfaithful, led astray, emotional problems.

Knight of Swords: Consider the way this Knight is rendered in comparison to the previous ones. Notice the horse and the scene's background. The Knight of Swords appears to be racing across the card, leaning forward in his saddle, sword drawn and ready to attack. Take note of how far the horse's legs are extended and how its mane is blowing in the wind. Both

the thin line that separates conscious and unconscious sentiments. He represents a sophisticated, high-principled creative youth, an idealist, and a seeker of perfection and emotional truth.

Upright: This card usually denotes a marriage proposal, a project in the realm of art, or even a love arrival. It signifies an arousing caution when it appears in a spread. While you may admire the romanticism, be careful not to be led astray by this romantic type.

KNIGHT OF SWORDS

how its mane is blowing in the wind. Both images convey movement and quick action. In the corner, you will notice the cypress trees in the background, which represent grief or hardship; these have been bent by the force of the wind.

The Knight of Swords is an odd mix: an enticing, fascinating personality that easily draws others' attention and affection. However, he has a ruthless streak, and while he is not malicious, he tends to harm others in pursuit of his own ambitions. He doesn't offer emotional support, since he doesn't think about it. He does, however, possess a sharp mind and a strong business sense, and he excels in his field.

Upright: This is an assertive young man or personality who moves quickly and makes his presence felt. Enthusiastic. As a situation, he may represent an event that begins with a flurry of excitement and then fades almost as fast as it began, leaving chaos in its wake.

Reversed: Troublemaker, deceitful, can be violent (if card appears in a spread with The Tower + The Devil). Argumentative.

Knight of Pentacles: The Knight of Pentacles differs from the other three Knights in a significant way. His horse

KNIGHT OF PENTACLES

is pictured patiently studying their surroundings in a recently ploughed field (results are emerging). The image is serene. This Knight possesses boundless patience and tolerance! Furthermore, he is nice and trustworthy, and will complete a task no matter how long it takes. He never fails to achieve his objectives because he never gives up. Others seek out his attributes of endurance and capacity for honest effort.

Upright: This is a finance-oriented, analytical and slow-moving dark-haired young man, someone who is methodical, reliable and logical. This person is sensible, systematic and stable in his approach, and he can be trusted. In a spread, he signifies a happy outcome of a situation, particularly business ventures that have gone on for a long time or appeared unfruitful at first.

Reversed: This represents someone who cannot be trusted with money, is too focused on it, or has financial/career troubles.

Minor Cards – The Aces

The Ace, or number 1, represents the start of everything. One is the number of creative potential and power. It is the starting point from which all other numbers develop. The Aces show a tremendous burst of energy. They represent new beginnings that are essential, positive and forceful. All Ace cards depict a hand appearing from the clouds hanging over the element of the suit. This seems to suggest that manifestation of all things arises from one aspect: an idea or a thought, since clouds represent the air element, leading up to The Ace of Pentacles, which denotes the beginning of realizing tangible, physical results – the end of the four-season cycle of The Fool creating his own reality.

Ace of Wands: Growth of New Ideas

The image on the card is of a strong hand firmly clutching a budding wand as it

ACE OF WANDS

emerges from a cloud. A castle on a hill in the distance represents the goal to be attained, and what the future may hold. Wands correspond to the element of fire, creativity, inventiveness and vitality. The Ace of Wands denotes a fresh start, as well as new ideas or projects. Aces symbolize energy in its purest form. The Ace of Wands thus expresses pure creativity.

Upright: This card can represent a new commercial enterprise, a fresh endeavour, a new foundation and creative ability – all of which have a lot of promise and aspiration to succeed.

Reversed: Projects and ideas are experiencing creative stumbling blocks or delays. Things are not likely to get off the ground right now.

Ace of Cups: New Strong Emotional Connections

The Ace of Cups shows a hand emerging from a cloud, suggesting a new opportunity that appears out of nowhere. The five senses are represented by five streams of

water that spring from the cup and descend into a pond of lilies. The water lily is a metaphor for emotional development. Spiritual principles are symbolized by the dove diving into the cup. The cups are associated with water, the element that governs feelings and emotions. As a result, the purest part of emotional energy is represented by the Ace of Cups.

Upright: It denotes the start of a new relationship, the reawakening of strong emotions, love, marriage, motherhood, and a great joy or satisfaction derived from a loving partnership. If The Lovers card appears in the same spread as The Hierophant or Justice, it implies a marriage proposal.

Reversed: Emotional turmoil. Happiness isn't long-lasting, and love's energy is dwindling.

Ace of Swords: Inevitable Powerful Change (for the better)

The two-edged sword on the Ace of Swords indicates that it can cut both ways. It is a card of enormous power, force and strength. All thoughts and actions have either a positive or a negative consequence. The crown on the sword is a symbol of attainment – winning the prize. Two leaves

ACE OF SWORDS

situation. In other words, what appears to be a hopeless situation can turn out to be quite promising. This card has a sense of inevitable powerful change. Moreover, you have the strength needed to overcome the situation, but first you must decide to defeat it. The decision establishes the mind-set to overcome this powerful cycle of change.

Upright: The Ace of Swords signifies strong forces at play, which may herald problems. However, the message of this card is also: you have the ability to overcome obstacles; the right mind-set is essential. It's a time for making decisions and moving in a new direction.

Reversed: A phase or cycle of tension.

hang from the crown; on the right is a palm leaf, representing victory, and on the left is an olive branch, symbolizing peace. Either victory over a conflict or peace can be attained by the sword. This suit is associated with the element of air, and is symbolic of the intellect, reason or strategic thinking. They also denote conflict and difficulty, such as a confused or conflicted mind. The Ace of Swords is a card of perseverance in the face of hardship, and it frequently signifies that something good will emerge from a bad

Ace of Pentacles: Receiving a Large Sum of Money

In this card, a golden pentacle is offered by the hand coming out of the cloud, denoting positive results for hard labour. This is mirrored by the image of a well-kept garden underneath the pentacle. The Pentacles represent the earth element, which represents the body, matter and all material achievements. It expresses earthly prosperity and accomplishments, as well as financial security and fortune

ACE OF PENTACLES

THE HIGH PRIESTESS

in life. The Ace of Pentacles indicates a successful start and financial security from any financial venture. It can also refer to a lump-sum payment received unexpectedly as gift or a bonus, as opposed to borrowing money.

Upright: The Ace of Pentacles represents a fresh opportunity or venture that you must seize and put your skills to use; or receiving a large sum of money.

Reversed: Indicates a difficulty with the tangible world. Smaller sums of money are received.

2 – The High Priestess: The Unseen/Intuition

The Magician may have imagination, a process and logic; what he lacks is intuition, which is represented by The High Priestess.

Here The Fool (now The Magician) is faced with the unknown. He must learn to acknowledge and develop his psychic instinct. Astrologers associate The High Priestess with the moon, the ruler of the night; the card also depicts the subconscious. The High Priestess sits on a throne between two white and black columns, symbolizing nature's duality: the two aspects of good and evil, or positive and negative forces, the conscious and unconscious, the essence and the not-yet-manifest form, darkness and light, and the dual nature of the feminine, birth-giving or destructive. A veil decorated with pomegranates (representing fertility) hangs between the pillars, through which water may be seen, flowing toward a crescent moon lying at her feet.

She sits passively in plain blue robes, hands clasped gently, holding a scroll with the inscription Torah, the law of natural wisdom. If the letters were to be rearranged, the word could almost read Tarot, which refers to the Tarot's inherent wisdom and law. Her ethereal aspect contrasts with The Empress' earthly wealth and fertility. Yet the two combined form the feminine principle, or the nature of spiritual and earthly mother. Too much emphasis on one leads to an imbalance. And, as you have seen so far, the Tarot emphasizes balance and wholeness in all levels of the

personality, seeking to achieve integrity of being. The feminine nature contains both positive and negative aspects, creative and destructive, benevolent and malevolent, fruitful and barren.

The ethereal quality is a metaphor for unrealized potential. The treasures of the unconscious mind are brought to consciousness through The High Priestess. She can also signify a link to the occult and the esoteric, as well as heightened hearing or mediumship. The unseen or unknown alludes to hidden talents and potential that must be revealed. All life began in darkness, whether it was the blackness of the womb or the darkness of the soil. As a result, a period of gestation is required for the formation and birth of a new life. The foetus developing in the darkness and secrecy of the womb until the time comes for it to be born into the light is an illustration of this.

The waxing and waning Moon is represented by the silver crown on her head, with the full orb in the centre. Her blue-and-white cloak cascades over her shoulders to the ground, resembling a glistening torrent of water. The glimpse of water behind the curtain represents the treasures hidden in the depths of the unconscious mind, as well as the changing lunar cycles and emotional sensitivity guided by the phases of the Moon. She wears a solar cross on her breast to symbolize the union of male and feminine duality, the hidden and the revealed.

Upright Meaning: The spiritual celestial mother and heightened feminine perceptive nature are represented by this card. When this card occurs in a spread, it means that something hidden or unknown is about to be disclosed. It also represents unconscious beliefs, fear or emotions, as well as the ability to seek advice through dreams. It represents mediumship and psychic abilities as well as a curiosity in mystical and esoteric studies, and the development of feminine abilities of intuition and natural insight. This card urges you to explore your unconscious, and the meaning of your dreams. As an outcome card, it indicates that the future or outcome is undetermined; be patient and wait for the proper timing. Furthermore, it can signify a pregnant woman, depending on where it occurs in a spread.

Modern Interpretation: This is a sensitive person who is greatly awakened. Artist, channeller, musician, medium, healer or mental healer are all terms used to describe people who work with their higher mind. A diplomat or peacemaker, they enjoy a higher sense of perception and gentleness, and have the ability to perceive the wants and needs of others. Also, it represents someone who makes an excellent counsellor.

Reversed Meaning: Negative psychic influences, self-delusion. Using psychic abilities to manipulate; drug and alcohol overuse. In a reversed position, The High Priestess might suggest mental illness, a muddled mind, and suppressed or neglected intuitive feelings, as it relates to clairaudient and clairvoyant aptitude. It can represent hidden influences, someone who is working against you, or that you are surrounded by shallow, superficial individuals, depending on where it appears in a spread. This card warns you to be cautious, and to keep your own counsel.

Exercise: Say the following affirmation to the back of your hand, a few times. Afterwards, notice any sensations or feelings. Write them in your Tarot journal. *"I am open to the divine wisdom of The High Priestess. I share her secrets and knowledge for the highest good. I am a vessel for Divine intuition."* Now ask yourself which aspects of your feminine principle need nurturing or balance.

Meditation: The High Priestess card can help you clarify your mind and uncover the subconscious meaning of dreams. You can simply write down a question before going to bed – something about which you seek clarification. Then put the card under your pillow and note any feelings, impressions or dreams when you wake up.

The Minor Cards – The Twos

Positive and negative, male and female, spirit and matter, ego and higher purpose, conscious and subconscious, and so on are all examples of complementary opposites represented by the number 2. To achieve balance and harmony, The Ace's pure energy is split into two opposing forces. The duality of the twos is expressed in the Minor cards that follow in each suit. It might signify either a balance of forces or unrealized creativity.

Two of Wands: A Choice of a Collaborative Partnership

Wands signify ambition and initiative. The man in the image stands atop the castle's foundations, his wands firmly planted on the ground, indicating everything he has already accomplished. He has a small globe in one hand that shows future expansion possibilities. He seems to be deliberating over his next move. The pattern on his castle battlements, white lilies, signify pure thought, while red roses reflect desire and ambition. The card's essence is further

potential that is yet to be realized, even though the combination implies a well-balanced disposition.

Upright: This card suggests a new outlook on a situation, high ambitions and goals, a desire to travel or foreign connections. It denotes success as well as expansion based on strength and vision. Taking initiative can help you overcome obstacles.

Reversed: There are issues with your partnership, or it is not working.

Two of Cups: Love Affair, Relationship Development, Good Friendship

In this card, the number 2 is symbolized by a balance of two opposites: a man and a woman swapping cups. The cups represent love and emotion as well as the pure energy that emanates from The Ace of Cups, which is now divided between two people. Both of their interests and intentions must be considered. This marriage of opposites, symbolized by the intertwined snakes, reflects spiritual and physical love, and brings healing and support.

Upright: This card represents the start of a good and balanced relationship or friendship. The two spouses share their sentiments and create a balanced environment based on harmony and cooperation. It symbolizes the emotional balance needed in order to achieve goals. It denotes a commitment or engagement, a marriage proposal, or the resolution of a fight or dispute.

Reversed: Separation, or an emotional imbalance in the relationship.

Two of Swords: Strained situation, A Decision is Required Between Two Alternatives

The blindfolded seated woman in the Two of Swords represents a stalemate in which the figure is unable to see a way out. She appears to be holding both blades in balance for the time being, but the future is uncertain. She's sitting on the edge of the water, oblivious to the breaking waves (her emotions) against the rocks (the hard reality of her predicament) behind her. It represents the necessity for courage to overcome this state of fear. This impasse will be broken by confronting the facts and deciding.

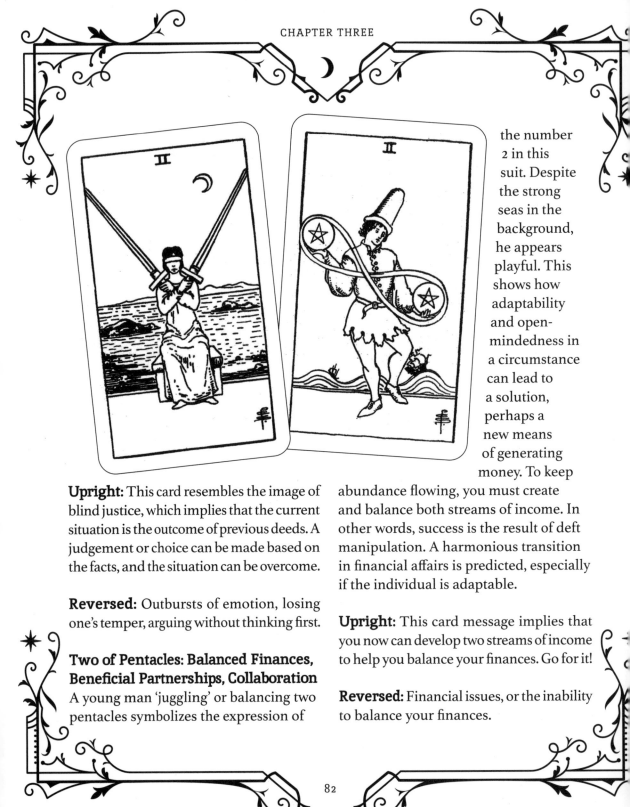

the number 2 in this suit. Despite the strong seas in the background, he appears playful. This shows how adaptability and open-mindedness in a circumstance can lead to a solution, perhaps a new means of generating money. To keep abundance flowing, you must create and balance both streams of income. In other words, success is the result of deft manipulation. A harmonious transition in financial affairs is predicted, especially if the individual is adaptable.

Upright: This card resembles the image of blind justice, which implies that the current situation is the outcome of previous deeds. A judgement or choice can be made based on the facts, and the situation can be overcome.

Reversed: Outbursts of emotion, losing one's temper, arguing without thinking first.

Two of Pentacles: Balanced Finances, Beneficial Partnerships, Collaboration
A young man 'juggling' or balancing two pentacles symbolizes the expression of

Upright: This card message implies that you now can develop two streams of income to help you balance your finances. Go for it!

Reversed: Financial issues, or the inability to balance your finances.

THE EMPRESS

3 – The Empress:
Growth and Abundance

In the Major Arcana, The Empress and The High Priestess are the two parts of the female archetype. The Empress is a representation of the fertile, life-giving mother who rules over nature's bounty and the Earth's rhythms. All the delights and joys of the senses, as well as a profusion of new life in all its forms, flow from her. The Empress encourages you to develop your connection to nature – the source of our existence. Often, seeking fake appearances and materialistic pleasures can make us forget our roots in the natural world. The Empress serves as a gentle reminder to keep your feet firmly planted on the ground.

A lovely, calm garden and forest serve as The Empress' backdrop. She is a representation of fertility and abundance. She wears large, colourful robes hinting at pregnancy or what is yet to come. This implies that a promise has been realized – the realization of consistent effort. The pomegranate represents conjugal love, while the sheaf of corn represents fertility. The 12 stars on her crown signify the 12 months of the year and the 12 zodiac signs. Infinite cycles of time are made finite and represent the 12 hours of the day and night. The Empress symbolizes the natural rhythm of the cycles or seasons of life: from seed, to flower, to fruit and, finally, decay. The water pouring into a pool in front of her represents the union of male and female merging to produce and nurture new life, while the forest represents natural abundance, depicting different growth cycles throughout the year. The astrological sign of Venus, ruler of Taurus, the sign linked with nature, is shown on the heart-shaped shield by her feet. Everything about the imagery of The Empress indicates natural growth cycles.

Moreover, The Fool learns all about women, their nature, and how to care for and nurture his own and others' bodily needs from his earthly mother, The Empress. The Fool learns about natural growth as well as the cycles of death and rebirth, and the cycles that men and women go through in their relationships. The Empress is a symbol of happiness and stability in partnerships. Her enigmatic smile represents the realization of one's potential in all forms of abundance: love, marriage and motherhood.

In a reading, The Empress can represent any nurturing aspect of motherhood. As a Major Arcana card, her qualities transcend the particulars of motherhood to its essence, which is the giving of life (to ideas, projects or business as well as children) and nurturing it through loving care and attention. She is a reminder of the seasons, of the time needed to reap the fruits of one's efforts and labour. Furthermore, The Empress can represent wealth and abundance in any form. In a reading, The Empress suggests financial reward, but only until you understand that wealth comes with a generous and open heart.

Upright Meaning: This card represents timing, the changing rhythm of nature, and taking the right action at the right time to realize ideas, nurture them, and reap the fruits of consistent efforts to sustain them. It is a positive card that gives a message of success and materialistic fruition. It denotes abundant living and caring for one's physical health to fulfil one's life mission. In a Tarot spread, it can indicate a pregnant woman. It also heralds news of births, happiness around an occasion or an event (such as the launch of a creative endeavour), fulfilment, fertility, pleasure, love affairs and marriages. If the card falls in the house of career, it denotes a career associated with beauty, or a business or product connected with women. In describing a person in a reading, it represents a warm, loving, sensual person with a nurturing nature.

Modern Interpretation: Successful female/feminine business, art dealer, event organiser, wedding planner, content creator, nurturing mentor.

Reversed Meaning: Overindulgence in pleasure and material things. Sterility or miscarriage (of ideas or children), the end of a love affair, inharmonious influence, an unhappy woman. An Empress reversed symbolizes blocked creativity, material discomfort, sexual ties without love, pleasure-seeking nature, an unwanted child or an abortion.

Exercise: How much of your personality represents the hidden aspects of The High Priestess and the revealed, or expressed potential of The Empress? In other words, have you given birth to your talents and abilities? In which form have they been expressed? In your Tarot journal, write down the qualities you admire about yourself, and talents you have not explored. Identify which activities bring you pleasure, and what can you do to bring them into the light. When is the right time for you to start planting and growing seeds?

Meditation: How do you feel about abundance? Are you nurturing your plans consistently? What can you do to bring your ideas, talents and life goals to fruition? Gaze upon The Empress, visit her in her garden, take in the fresh smell of the flowers and vegetation, listen to the sound of flowing water. Imagine dipping your bare feet into the cool pool at her feet. Feel the connection with Mother Earth and start writing answers that inspire you in your Tarot journal.

Court Cards – The Queens

Queens represent older authoritative women, symbolizing their personality or profession. They denote the feminine creative aspect of one's personality. Queens and Kings do not tend to represent timing of events, like the Pages and Knights. When they appear in a spread, they depict the personalities of people. Generally, they are depicted as noble-looking women sitting on a throne reflecting their authority and abilities.

Queen of Wands: The throne of the Queen of Wands is adorned with flaming lion motifs. She wields a wand in one hand and a sunflower in the other, symbolizing her strength and power. The black cat sits at her feet, symbolizing the Queen's status as the creator of her life at home. She can successfully run a house and a family while still finding energy and motivation to pursue her own passions and aspirations. She is well loved by those around her and always helps her friends without getting distracted from what she values most. However, if she is ever crossed, she fights back fiercely, like a lioness! Her unwavering adaptability is a desirable trait.

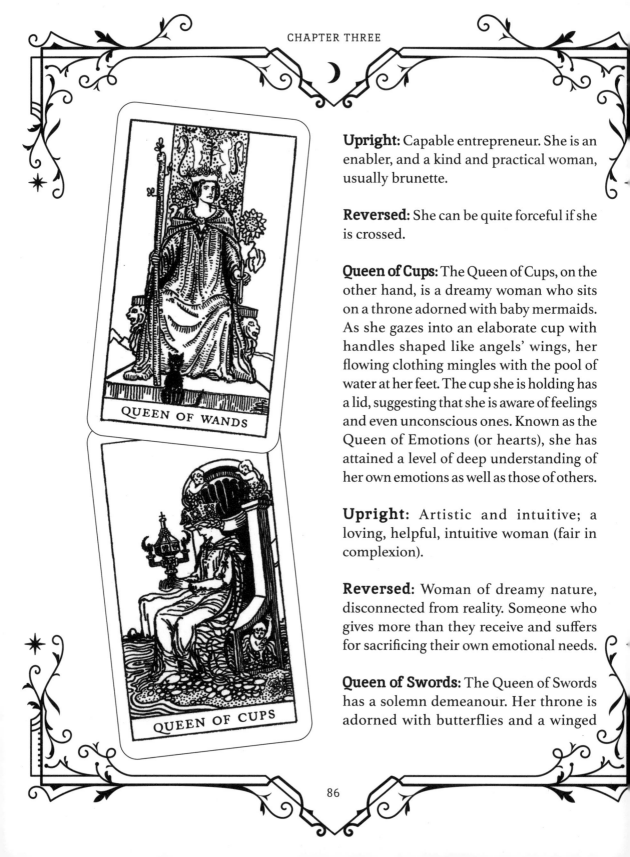

QUEEN OF WANDS

QUEEN OF CUPS

Upright: Capable entrepreneur. She is an enabler, and a kind and practical woman, usually brunette.

Reversed: She can be quite forceful if she is crossed.

Queen of Cups: The Queen of Cups, on the other hand, is a dreamy woman who sits on a throne adorned with baby mermaids. As she gazes into an elaborate cup with handles shaped like angels' wings, her flowing clothing mingles with the pool of water at her feet. The cup she is holding has a lid, suggesting that she is aware of feelings and even unconscious ones. Known as the Queen of Emotions (or hearts), she has attained a level of deep understanding of her own emotions as well as those of others.

Upright: Artistic and intuitive; a loving, helpful, intuitive woman (fair in complexion).

Reversed: Woman of dreamy nature, disconnected from reality. Someone who gives more than they receive and suffers for sacrificing their own emotional needs.

Queen of Swords: The Queen of Swords has a solemn demeanour. Her throne is adorned with butterflies and a winged

QUEEN OF SWORDS

a queen. The Queen of Swords represents a tenacious and strong-willed woman, someone who can cope with whatever life throws at her and make the best of it. In times of loss and grief, she is supportive and helpful.

Upright: Lonely; a mentally capable woman who overcomes obstacles.

Reversed: A person who is not facing the reality of their situation. Overcome with grief or feeling sorry for herself, she can be cruel and selfish. Can indicate muddled thinking and a narrow or limited perspective.

Queen of Pentacles: The Queen of Pentacles sits contentedly on her throne, surrounded by a lush, fertile background brimming with the earth's bounty. Flowers and rabbits, which represent fertility, are framed on the card. The goat's head on the armrests represents Capricorn, the earthy sign. She is shown as a pragmatic woman who appreciates material possessions and is skilled at obtaining them, since she appears to be enjoying herself. She understands exactly what she wants and is happy when she gets it. This also means that she accepts responsibility for her judgements and is

angel. In the background, notice the storm clouds and the darkening sky. Her cloak is decorated with little clouds representing her pensive nature and mental acumen, symbolized by holding the sword firmly. Her straight sword and stern face shows her determination. She depicts a woman who has suffered loss, and may be alone; she could be a widow, divorced or separated. She has loved and lost, but she knows the cycles of life. For now, she must wait, but she knows she will discover love again. She faces her pain patiently and courageously – like

QUEEN OF PENTACLES

Reversed: This card reversed can indicate a materialistic, selfish personality, someone who takes more than they give. Moreover, someone who is unable to manage their finances or business and is heading toward failure or bankruptcy.

Minor Cards – The Threes

The number 3 represents The Empress as well as progress and expansion. The number 2 represents the two partners who collaborate (on a proposal or a project); the number 3 sees the collaboration through to completion. It represents the initial completion and achievement of the first phase.

Three of Wands: The man who featured in The Two of Wands reappears here. This time he is looking over a much larger horizon. This is symbolized by the three Wands he had already planted firmly in the ground. The decision he made after contemplating in The Two of Wands has taken him to the next set. His consistent efforts have been rewarded. He is ready to move beyond what he has achieved. The card's message is this: the person who works relentlessly toward his objective will cross the finish line – and beyond. Moreover, the next phase of growth will come quickly.

fair and wise in business; the reason she is affluent is due to her hard work. She represents a helpful friend or employer with a generous personality and the ability to provide realistic advice.

Upright: This card describes a well-off, realistic and supportive woman who may also be a professional or a businessperson. The Queen of Coins would make an excellent business adviser or mentor. She is an abundant, helpful businesswoman (with dark skin/hair), and is supportive, practical and wealthy.

Upright: Success and expansion. This card indicates that although much has been achieved, there is more success and expansion to come. Rejoice!

Modern Interpretation: Expansion of business through more branches, franchising, overseas branches or international growth.

Reversed: When this card appears reversed in a spread, it indicates that one has lost an opportunity or missed out on a collaboration that could have led to growth and success.

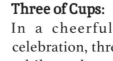

Three of Cups:
In a cheerful celebration, three maidens dance while each carries her cup. This indicates a celebration that is shared by a family, a household or a group. Flowers and fruits are plentiful around the feet, indicating the extent of the celebration and reaping the fruits or rewards of the happy union or collaboration of The Two of Cups. This card can represent a marriage or a birth as well as emotional growth, happiness and accomplishments. It also denotes recovery from emotional wounds. Although it is a wonderful and exciting moment, like with The Three of Wands, it is merely the beginning. Emotions and emotional reactions must be maintained and balanced for more happiness to come.

as swift as the swords are, a flash of insight might occur, allowing the person concerned to put this disappointment and sorrow into perspective and begin to heal. Even though this is a sorrowful time, there is a sense of clearing the ground or the beginning of something new. Swords are symbolic of a person's thinking and perception and therefore imply that challenges in a relationship, or a degree of disappointment and sorrow, can be overcome if confronted with honesty.

Upright: Celebration. Birth of a child. Celebrating the success of a new business or joint venture.

Reversed: Lost opportunity or pregnancy, or an occasion celebrated too soon.

Three of Swords: This card's picture makes it self-explanatory. The background is gloomy, indicating stormy weather ahead. Together, the heart and the swords indicate profound emotional and mental turmoil. As a result of this disappointment, there may be quarrels or separations. However,

Upright: Emotional quarrels and separation. Love affair ends due to one of the partners being unfaithful.

Reversed: The person is hanging onto the sorrow without facing the facts of the situation or deciding to move on and get a new perspective on it. An end leads to a new beginning!

Three of Pentacles: Three people, or craftsmen, are depicted in this image;

they appear to be discussing plans. This implies that one stage has been achieved, and plans for the next phase are being made. Furthermore, it signifies that the foundation of the project or business was a solid one, and that material gain was achieved successfully because of the efforts made. In otherwards, strategy and execution were on par.

Upright: Commercial collaboration outcome and planning. This card describes the abilities and talents that will help you succeed. Joint collaborations with others will be a success. Financial affairs will prosper. Also, skills you already have can lead to a successful business if you apply them.

Reversed: Pentacles have to do with tangible achievements and material gain. When this card appears reversed, it indicates problems with a project at hand, delayed success or unnecessary anxiety over business. A rest or break is needed to maintain balance. It can also indicate sudden opportunities and the need to develop (more) skills to achieve success. Finances are currently blocked – need to activate your skills to create money flow. The help of other collaborators needs to be acknowledged.

THE EMPEROR

4 – The Emperor: Authority and Structure

The Emperor represents The Empress' masculine side. As The Fool's earthly father, he is the complementary role model to The Empress. The Fool learns about authority, reason, power and structure from The Emperor. After learning about

The Empress' yielding, intuitive and giving nature, The Fool now learns about balancing it with structure and leadership aspects.

The Emperor signifies material stability and big, worldly achievements that necessitate focus, determination, hard work and dedication. It also indicates the difficulty of adhering to principles and making a solid commitment. The message of this card is: things do not come easily, but they will surely happen.

The Fool leaves behind the natural, nurturing softness of The Empress to learn from his earthly father, The Emperor. The challenge is striking a balance between worldly desires and what is important in life in the long run. The Emperor strives to build long-lasting structures – a legacy. Notice that his throne is made of solid, grey and everlasting stone, the opposite of the luscious and colourful throne of The Empress. His red robes signify his drive, determination and commitment to consistent efforts. In contrast to the feminine aspect of nurturing, The Empress, The Emperor appears stern in adhering to his commitments. He knows that higher ambitions take more time to be realized, and that building a solid foundation is essential. The Emperor is the essence of leadership in devising plans, structure, methodology, overseeing the implantation of ideas to the end, and holding people accountable for their respective responsibilities.

Note The Emperor's armour, disguised by his red cloak. It implies his inner constitution and power that lie beneath enormous strength, which is available to him at any time. The jewels on his head signify his financial prosperity and rank, while the orb he holds symbolizes his rational grasp of the laws that must be followed by man. The sceptre is a symbol of masculine power and inventiveness. The image conveys a strong sense of authority, power and material prosperity. The Emperor instructs The Fool on matters of authority, leadership, administration, rules, and moral and ethical behaviour. The Emperor's posture is strikingly close to that of Justice, which embodies similar traits; the balance of justice must be upheld.

The Emperor's essence is a representation of spiritual creative forces channelled into dynamic force, creating solid and functioning ideas. He represents the desire for ambition, power, riches and fame. In contrast to his consort, The Empress, whose feminine energy is receptive and caring, he communicates in a straightforward and strong manner. The Empress and The Emperor's connections offer the complete and crucial lesson to The Fool about the dual nature of each person. An excess of either masculine or feminine attributes can be damaging. An equation involving two opposites needs to be balanced. While The Emperor strives for perfection, The Empress is content with the best that can be achieved within the constraints of earthly reality. Both elements of The Emperor and Empress are necessary in life; without them, harmony and balance of any goal cannot be materialized. Nevertheless, it is important to recognize when a compromise is necessary between what is ideal and what is functional or can be practically attained.

Upright Meaning: Represents structure, power and wisdom. A man with authority who can build stability and has achieved worldly success. It also represents dealing with an authority figure, like a boss, or someone who prefers to be their own boss. Can symbolize a man who has difficulty expressing emotion or is unwilling to let defences down (note the other cards in the spread).

Modern Interpretation: CEO, architect, just leader; someone who works in the armed forces, or a politician.

Reversed Meaning: Immature, selfish, domineering man. Hatred of authority or about to lose authority. Feeling threatened, drained, vulnerable, lacking in ambition. Overshadowed by dominant parent. A man who is exploiting his authority by acting foolishly. The latter can also be advice given to the seeker, depending on the purpose of the spread.

Exercise: How do you wield power in your life? Meditate on The Emperor card, and write down your thoughts on the following questions: How do you feel about this card? Is it a positive or negative image for you? Are you a leader or a follower? How can The Emperor represent both strength and weakness? How is your relationship to authority figures – your dad, your boss, etc? If The Emperor were a tree, what tree would represent him best? Once you have decided on a tree, close your eyes and hold the image in your mind. Mindfully walk toward it and sit under it, absorbing its energy and qualities, and balancing your own. When you feel wholesome, see the image disappear. You can invoke that mental image any time you need to.

Court Cards – The Kings

Kings are the male counterparts of Queens, and in readings represent men. They, like Queens, represent authority in each respective suit. You might notice that the Queens appear more relaxed on their throne, while the Kings are poised for action with respect to their suits. This enforces the traditionally-held view of feminine principle being one of flexibility, passivity or openness, while the masculine is about action and accountability (actions have consequences). These historical archetypes are an invitation to integrate both aspects harmoniously. Both are needed and complement each other.

KING OF WANDS

King of Wands: The fiery king appears to sit forward on his throne, poised for action. This is a vivid image of a king, whose clock and background are decorated with lions and curled salamanders. A real salamander stands alongside him, preparing for action as well. The salamander has long been associated with fire as an animal. Some salamander species, such as those associated with the element of fire, exhibit a vivid orange colour. After it has rained and the earth is still damp, we frequently spot them in the woods or on pathways. These peaceful, harmless creatures appear on the forest floor like curls of flame, and we must tread cautiously so as not to step on them. The salamander's sinuous physique, with its ability to bend and twist with stealthy ease as it creeps across the earth, suggests not only the element of fire but also charm and sexual appeal that can be magnetizing. Its wet skin reminds us that fire frequently needs the element of water to cool down!

The King has wit and charm. He is friendly and generous, with a wonderful sense of humour and a great desire to have a good time. Because he is entertaining and upbeat, he can persuade anyone to do anything. He never runs out of fresh ideas or visionary insights, and is ready to decide on difficult matters whenever they arise. However, he can easily overlook minor details and become agitated, or lose his optimism when met with the reality of details. He follows his instincts and surfs any obstacles toward success, unfazed by setbacks.

Upright: Successful entrepreneur. Important, kind, interested in business. Strawberry blondes, freckles, brown hair.

Reversed: Represents an impractical person, someone who might overvalue their looks or charm in the face or practical achievement. In other words, promises a great deal, but without tangible results.

King of Cups: The King of Cups, on the other hand, sits atop a throne, seemingly uneasy, as he overlooks stormy seas. A fish leaps over the waves in the distance; however, he is oblivious to it. The golden fish around his neck represents his creative imagination. It seems to be a hollow token compared to the vibrant imagination behind him. His feet do not contact the water, implying that he wants to connect with his unconscious emotions – unlike his Queen, who effortlessly blends into the waves. Despite being the master of emotions, his frequent mood swings (symbolized by the stormy water under his throne) imply that he is not fully connected to his element, that he is somewhat troubled

KING OF CUPS

by expressing his emotions and feelings, or is duty-bound to make others happy. Masculinity is generally associated with conscious cognition and intellect. However, this King seems uncomfortable in the world of emotions. Rather than express his true feelings, he tends to pay lip service to them. If the King of Cups appears in a spread, it represents an aspect of the private personality behind the image. It indicates that the man concerned is having difficulty connecting with his genuine feelings.

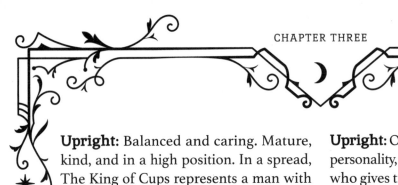

Upright: Balanced and caring. Mature, kind, and in a high position. In a spread, The King of Cups represents a man with light hair or a light complexion.

Reversed: The person concerned may be a romantic, charming talker; often his words are hollow, without any genuine feelings. It represents an unreliable, unfaithful, two-faced man.

King of Swords: The King of Swords looks calmly straight ahead, wearing a purple cloak symbolizing wisdom, while he holds his sword upright, unfazed by the stormy clouds building up – a common sight in the suit of Swords. The air appears to be still; we see the cypress trees standing erect. This King exudes inner strength, self-assurance and a strong sense of conviction. The Sword represents the mind and the air element; it emphasizes a desire for truth and justice. Can you find the parallels between this card and a Justice card? A pleading for forgiveness or compassion will not influence The King of Swords. He might be tough in his judgements, but he is always fair. He's always been feared and revered. He tends to be too suspicious and over-cautious, on the negative side. However, his sense of justice and fairness are admirable as long as they can be modified with a little compassion.

Upright: Older man with an authoritative personality, vision and experience. Someone who gives truthful advice or fair opinions, although they may seem harsh.

Reversed: Whenever it appears reversed, this card represents a manipulative, uncompassionate or mentally violent man or boss.

KING OF SWORDS

King of Pentacles: The King of Pentacles, like The Empress figure, or his counterpart, The Queen of Pentacles, is surrounded by wealth and fruits of the earth. His throne is adorned with a bull's head symbolizing the earth sign of Taurus – the love of material possessions, maintaining a warm and nurturing homelife. He is depicted casually resting his hand over the pentacle, whereas most figures in this suit hold the pentacle underneath. This indicates that he has mastered creating his physical reality with confidence and is therefore not obsessed with material gain. Notice the majestic castle behind him, which symbolizes his earthly achievements.

He is a man who adores money and wealth and is content to amass and enjoy it. He's a bit of a financial whiz when it comes to business. He is not, however, corrupt in his love of money. Quite the opposite – he is patient and earns money the hard way, through ethical business practices. He is generous with what he has and willingly shares the results of his labour with others. This card's message, or the lesson he offers The Fool, is to be satisfied with what you have. Enjoy your wealth, but remember that as much as you cherish it, you need to work hard for it.

Upright: Financial wizard, wealthy. Dark skin/hair. Financial security. Honest. It refers to an older, mature man on whom you can rely. He is compassionate, self-made, and extremely successful or affluent in business. He is helpful, but he has high standards for others.

Reversed: An unethical businessman, someone who can be thrifty and overly possessive.

KING OF PENTACLES

Minor Cards – The Fours

A square with equal sides is represented by the number 4: reality, logic, reason and structure. It is also man's threefold nature – mind, body and spirit – that is brought to the material plane, making a square that symbolizes 'stable manifestation', having understood the law of Spirit.

Four of Wands: The two central characters in the background, carrying bouquets high over their heads, herald the news of a celebration. It also reflects that it is time to rest, to enjoy the fruits of labour (or have a vacation). The bridge over the moat and the castle behind it represent success, and the act of crossing the bridge to get to your destination. The flower garland that adorns the four wands in the foreground represents the success that is about to be celebrated. If you look closely, you will notice a mix of fruits, flowers and lilies that represent the fruits of labour while upholding spiritual values. The Four of Wands represents the characteristics of the Wands, which result in productivity and contentment.

Upright: Enjoyable collaboration, a restful break, or a vacation.

Reversed: Problems with a project or business. Delayed success, or unnecessary anxiety over business or work. A rest is needed. The end of a career, or forced change.

Four of Cups: A young man sits cross-legged with his arms folded because of the turbulent emotions that are overcoming him. He seems unhappy, looking at three cups in front of him while ignoring or denying a fourth cup offered by a hand emerging from the cloud. He looks to be conflicted about his views and deeds. The steadiness represented in number 4 is not embodied. This is because an important

Four of Swords: This image depicts the effigy of a Knight resting over his tomb. Although it seems threatening, as three swords are hanging over him and a fourth is fixed to his tomb, it denotes a much-needed rest after a long and tiring struggle. It indicates healing, resting and convalescence to gather energy and recharge. The three hanging swords over him are not touching him, perhaps indicating that he is too worried about the need to fight; but the fourth sword, underneath him, indicates that it is time

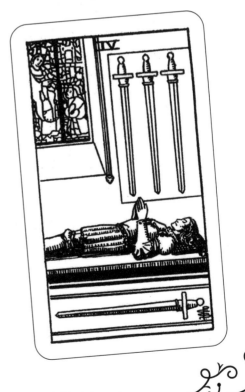

component is missing: an understanding of the situation's wisdom. This card represents a call to take a fresh look at life and examine the current circumstances.

Upright: Boredom. Re-evaluating emotional affairs or connections. Indulging in an emotional state and ignoring present opportunities.

Reversed: Lack of enthusiasm, fear of being alone or overindulging in disappointment to the point that one is missing new, unexpected opportunities.

Four of Pentacles: In this image, a man is seen clutching the gold he has earned. Another gold coin hangs over the crown on his head, indicating thoughts he has or is considering for future monetary gain. This card represents both the number 4's strength of purpose and the pentacle's monetary aspect. "Save half of what you make while investing the other half wisely" is the card's message.

Upright: Doing well financially. Financial matters are currently your top priority, and you are well positioned to excel in that area. Remember to set aside money for savings as well as some to reinvest in your business.

Reversed: A spendthrift or miser.

to rest. Notice the stained-glass window in the top left corner, depicting an angel or saint, with a halo around its head, blessing the kneeling figure. The halo seems to spell out PAX, which means 'peace' in Latin. The message of this card is that getting control over our thoughts and worries brings peace.

Upright: Rest is needed. Stop worrying!

Reversed: Enforced rest, feeling alone.

THE HIEROPHANT

5 – The Hierophant: Versatility and Freedom

The Fool learns about accepting his intuitive nature and maintaining a connection to higher wisdom by acknowledging his strong sense of knowing. He upholds his core values and moral responsibilities. The Hierophant, or pope, is the carrier and transmitter of spirituality and wisdom. He represents an 'evolved' mind.

The celestial, or spiritual, parents are The Hierophant and his counterpart The High Priestess. By learning from both, The Fool's personality is integrated. His connection to Spirit is encouraged through developing his inner sense of knowing and intuition. He is now encouraged to find a higher purpose to his existence – his destiny. While The High Priestess represents secret or hidden knowledge, or the ethereal world, The Fool must now obtain the revealed knowledge and wisdom of The Hierophant to fulfil his earthly desires.

Between the celestial parents, The Fool's personality is now balanced, integrating the feminine receptive side with the masculine action side. On another level, The Hierophant symbolizes the wisdom of connecting with a higher spiritual purpose that is behind materialistic human ambitions, and a deep sense of knowing since all secret knowledge was revealed to him. The Fool's ability to maintain the flow of abundance, while realizing his destiny by touching the lives of others he encounters on his journeys, is due to integrating the two opposites, hidden and revealed knowledge.

The Tarot frequently emphasizes both themes: balance and the integration of opposites. The known and the unknown, the hidden and the exposed, the feminine and the masculine, perceiving and acting are all in balance during this phase. In other words, The Fool gains a sense of knowing through balance. When he falls in love, he is a little wiser, and ready to make his first decision as a young adult on his own.

Although religious in essence, this image serves as a symbol for all types of initiations (note the two figures in front of The Hierophant, and his hand raised toward them). Youngsters in any culture are taught to abide by society's customs and become a part of a certain worldview. The Hierophant represents all structures within a society, such as schools, clubs, teams and companies. Moreover, this card symbolizes The Hierophant initiating The Fool to find his own way, his own expression, and follow his inner calling or destiny.

Upright Meaning: Conventional learning as well as intuitive knowing. Spiritual marriage ceremony when coupled with The Lovers card and Justice. It also denotes a gifted 'teacher' imparting experience and knowledge, or an old friend or older person who gives sound advice. The Hierophant symbolizes a high level of consciousness, a natural teacher,

diplomat, or counsellor from whom you might seek advice. It describes a wise person, someone who has knowledge and deeper wisdom and applies it to make his vision a reality. When this card appears in a spread, it indicates that one's destiny is about to be fulfilled.

Modern Interpretation: Lateral thinker. Inspirational speaker, a person in the diplomatic corps, a mediator or charismatic actor. Someone with high moral standards.

Reversed Meaning: Materialistic. Unorthodox. Rebellion against establishment. If seeking advice from an accountant or lawyer, get a second opinion. Do not rush into new agreements. They might prove disappointing!

Exercise: What higher knowledge, wisdom or understanding needs to be revealed to you now? Contemplate this question while you breathe steadily and easily, holding this card or gazing upon it. Soak in the red colour of The Hierophant's robes and imagine or pretend that you are being initiated by him. You are now ready to hold your pen and start writing any inspiration you perceive in your Tarot journal.

The Minor Cards – The Fives

Five represents flexibility and openness, the opposite of structure and conformity. It is also the midpoint of the cycle from 1 to 10, and represents changes of circumstance, and any struggle or obstacles that may arise. Change brings new circumstance, so the fives are about adapting or modifying behaviour, plans, thoughts and feelings. Although lack of structure brings uncertainty, flexibility is required because it allows for adjusting behaviours, actions, thoughts and feelings to achieve what we yearn for and fulfil our destiny. In other words, fives in the Minor cards imply change; a situation is not permanent, but is open to negotiation and can develop. It represents a minor cycle of change within the Tarot theme of evolution and progress.

Five of Wands: This card depicts five young men carrying large wands. It suggests a conflict in life (business or love). This card also represents little temporary annoyances and roadblocks in communication and plans. When these obstacles are overcome, the situation can improve. However, at the moment, nothing appears to be working out.

Upright: Negotiations and competition.

Reversed: Backstabbing or legal disputes.

Five of Cups: Three cups of wine are spilled, and a person in a dark robe is mourning the loss. However, there are two other upright cups remaining behind him, but he does not see them. He can only think about what has been spilled. The card symbolizes remorse over previous actions. Something has been lost, yet something remains. Because the two upright cups are full, the person must consider what may be saved. Despite the loss, there are two new possible options.

Upright: Disappointment. Something good is about to happen.

Reversed: Unhappiness is a short phase and will end quickly. Be hopeful but cautious.

Five of Swords: Clouds and water together are recurring themes in the Swords suit. Emotions and thoughts are inextricably linked. When anxiety rises, it elicits strong emotions, which can lead to wrong actions.

This card represents a victorious person who appears to be invincible, and the other men are forced to surrender their swords to him. The message of this card is to swallow one's pride and accept one's limitations before progressing upwards and onwards. The victor stood his ground and won. It also represents that one must give up fighting the wrong battles and try standing one's ground for something that can be won. Currently, he is banging his head against a brick wall, and might be taking on something far too massive. The card's advice is to acknowledge limitations and move forward in a new, more beneficial direction.

Upright: This card represents an unexpected bad omen (similar to The Tower). However, the situation cannot be avoided. It can imply, for example, the repossession of a home (check the 4th House in the 12-card astrological spread). Underhanded tactics, lies, gossip or malice could be the cause of your struggle. As such, this card advises you to review your situation and adjust your thoughts or perspective on the matter.

Reversed: Strained times are ending soon.

Five of Pentacles: This is the opposite of the customary good luck that comes in the pentacles suit. Here we see two beggars pass beneath an illuminated church window. Five pentacles are shown in the stained-glass window. They are walking in the snow (out in the cold); one of them is lame and feeling ashamed, with a bell hanging around his neck, symbolizing the stigma attached to poverty. The other looks to be homeless and destitute. Because they are hunched down in despair, they do not appear to notice the light over their heads. There may be financial stress or anxiety, which is a sign that temporary financial difficulties are on the way.

However, the message might be about more than a shortage of funds. The beggars in this card may have lost their spiritual awareness, as symbolized by their inability to find solace and shelter in the church they are passing. The card advises the seeker to pay close attention to the small things in life. Money, success, material gain and happiness are all manifestations of the spiritual understanding needed to create them. Being poor does not equal being spiritual (and spirituality is not about dismissing material wealth). Everything is achieved in balance, and is also transient. When anything of significant value is not handled with care, it may be lost.

Upright: Serious financial problems. If you have just lost a job, you are capable of regaining control of your finances, and finding another one. Your skills, efforts and hard work will be rewarded.

Reversed: Finances can be restored through hard work and getting back into balance.

THE LOVERS

6 – The Lovers:
Collaboration and Service to Others

The Fool's first lesson in making his own decisions and balancing his duality is represented by this symbol. He receives his first lesson in making his first decision after being nurtured by his parents, The Empress and The Emperor. To do so successfully, he must learn to balance the male and female elements in himself, as well as how to share the journey with others in a harmonious manner.

The Fool's initial decision-making challenge is represented by The Lovers card. The image depicts a couple standing naked and exposed in a lovely garden, beneath an angel. The Fool is facing the woman, who is looking up at the angel. It implies that the male principle of intellect needs the emotional, 'passive' feminine principle of intuition to connect with Spirit. The relationship's endpoint – the mountain peak – can be seen in the space between them.

The Lovers picture shows that love is more complicated than it appears at first! If the relationship is to reach new heights, it will require honesty, vulnerability, venturing out of their comfort zone (the garden) and learning to make many decisions jointly. The Angel is there to assist them in maintaining harmony in their relationship. The Lovers show The Fool that joining forces with another person is a conscious decision that will have an impact on his life's path. The success of the voyage requires a companion with complementary attributes, which is why emotional encounters are crucial for growth. By partnering with others and achieving his goals, The Fool learns to master his ideas and decisions. This card signifies a harmonious union of two people, as well as the courage to be one's genuine self to find true love (or the right partner).

Upright: Love, romance, and emotional, spiritual and physical union – soulmate. Choices are not crystal clear; use your intuition. If it occurs alongside The Hierophant, it can represent religious marriage, or civil ceremony if the Justice card also appears in the same spread.

Modern Interpretation: Making an important decision that will affect the rest of your life. This card also describes a humanitarian, activist, support-group leader, or someone who specializes in mergers and acquisitions.

Reversed: It is a warning to the seeker to make the proper choice when choosing a partner. It also represents adultery, sex without love, or relationship difficulties. It indicates a disrupted sex life or jealousy. Moreover, you might be making an irrevocable choice regarding a romantic or work relationship (depending on where the card falls in a spread) – so take your time and think carefully.

Exercise: What important decisions do you face in life? Consider your goal as the mountain in The Lovers card. It may seem out of reach, but it does require you to be courageous and honest in facing the issue and realizing that you might need the help of another person. Are you truthful with yourself? Can you identify your motive and your intention regarding your issue? Write down your answers in your Tarot journal as you contemplate The Lovers card. Consider the angel floating above the Lovers. What or who is your source of inspiration? What do you value about your relationship or the issue you are deciding on? Keep your writing flowing, without stopping, until you feel you have nothing more to write. Get up and take a break, then go back to your journal and read what you wrote. You will find the answer there somewhere!

The Minor Cards – The Sixes

Six is a number that represents balance, harmony and equilibrium. The six-pointed star is made up of two triangles, one pointing up to the sky, or heaven, and the other down to the body, or Earth. This represents a healthy balance between the two as well as the integration of the two aspects. Six also represents romantic and professional relationships. It represents love for another individual as well as love for humankind. Because each decision to do with a relationship will have long-term consequences, the balance suggests that prudence and awareness are required while making decisions, and the necessity to be guided by Spirit or higher values. Moreover, it also represents opposites coming together for the greater good or the highest good. It also represents the sharing of values that allows two people or a group of people to cooperate and work together.

Six of Wands: A man is depicted on a horseback, wearing a laurel wreath, signifying victory and achievement (does this image remind you of the Knight?). His wand has another wreath tied to it. People swarm around him in awe, celebrating his accomplishments. This card represents achievement, the fulfilment of aspirations and wishes, bravery, a successful job, triumph in love, and an overall sense of gratification. Others provide recognition, and success is rewarded with acknowledgment. It denotes a promotion for exemplary work or a prize for putting up effort in favour of a worthy cause.

Upright: Stability and triumph in manifesting or achieving material and creative goals.

Reversed: Indicates losing to the other side (the competition, or other parties). It also indicates trouble at work.

Six of Cups: A little boy presents a flower-filled cup to a young girl, symbolizing friendship (or budding romance). There are five additional cups filled with flowers in front of the two figures. A charming landscape of a village, a thatched cottage, and greenery can be seen around them, evoking warm recollections of home and youth. The Six of Cups indicates a reunion with an

connecting with one's inner child or becoming childlike. Meeting old friends from childhood.

Reversed: Loss of innocence or childhood, loss of a childhood friend, letting go of opportunities, cutting binding cords that hold you back.

Six of Swords: The Six of Swords, a suit that frequently shows striving through hardship, represents the delicate balance. A ferryman transports a distraught mother and her infant (the consequence of a broken relationship?) across the sea to a distant land. It's worth noting that the water on the right side of the boat is turbulent, while the water on the left is calm. This denotes a shift away from troubles and into a more serene period. This card can represent a literal voyage, a shift to more attractive surroundings, or the urge to embark on an inner journey. It denotes the release of tension and anxiety following a time of pressure. Harmony and balance will be re-established. Six is a number associated with assisting others. This card also represents the need to seek

old friend or childhood acquaintance, the reappearance of an old sweetheart, or the revival of a love affair with roots in the past. This card might also indicate that something from the past is being reconsidered. The Six of Cups, if misplaced in a spread, might indicate that the seeker is too caught up in the past, or is too sentimental to be practical, and needs to focus on current and future prospective relationships.

Upright: A time of nostalgia and recalling happy times. Reliving childhood memories,

Six of Pentacles: This card represents six as a harmonious number. A trader is meticulously weighing gold to distribute it to the needy. It indicates that money owed will be paid back, or that you will receive what is rightfully yours. Moreover, a kind friend, company or boss may provide financial assistance. It is a good omen if you are seeking a loan or mortgage. Your financial situation may remain steady for a time. It also suggests sharing your good fortune with others who need financial help or support.

assistance, when trapped or suffering, to go forward in life. Furthermore, it is necessary to stop feeling sorry for oneself. A break, a change of scenery, or stepping back from the issue will provide a fresh perspective.

Upright: Travel across water, away from troubles. A vacation. Time or opportunity to restore harmony and balance.

Reversed: Disappointment, such as a cancelled journey. Tenacity and guts are required to resolve your situation.

Upright: Financial help or gift. Generosity from friends or acquaintances. Unexpected financial assistance. Also, it is a message that you've met your financial goals and are encouraged to share your good fortune with others. Giving time and money to good causes brings a great deal of happiness.

Modern interpretation: Successfully securing a loan or a mortgage.

Reversed: Represents a mean or greedy person, stingy behavior or material loss, such as money or a property.

VII

THE CHARIOT

7 – The Chariot:
Mind Mastery and Transcendence

The Chariot might be the most mystical card of the Tarot. Within its symbols so many secrets are revealed!

Having made the first personal decision about love and relationships, The Fool must now learn to regulate and balance opposing energies within himself to run a steady course and overcome other types of hurdles and conflicts in life. Having learned about his dualistic nature through The Lovers card, The Fool realizes that life is a cycle of strife and victories, he must now learn how to resolve larger challenges and conflicts. To overcome outer conflicts, he must master inner conflicting forces within himself first, namely his mind over his ego.

In contrast to The Lovers card, where he was naked and vulnerable, we see The Fool heavily armoured, upright in his vehicle of battle, implying the need to keep the ego in check and connected with an inspired mind, symbolized by the eight-pointed star crown over his head, the blue four-pillar star-spangled canopy. The chariot and the four pillars represent the four elements and the seasonal cycles of change. The star canopy represents the heavens. The Fool appears like the Greek god of war, symbolizing the effort exerted in maintaining integration of spirit and matter as a human.

Moreover, his chariot is drawn by two opposing sphynxes, one black and the other white, which pull the chariot in opposite directions (the result of the union of opposites in The Lovers card). His main task is to keep them under control, symbolizing man's struggle in balancing opposing desires, feelings and thoughts within himself, as well as the conflict between staying with what is familiar and moving forward. However, no change creates stagnation. Moving forward brings evolution. The Chariot card represents fortitude, which is required to move forward in balance. 'Conflicts', or cycles of change, are necessary to bring about change and growth in life.

Furthermore, look closely and you will notice that there are no reins attached to the sphynxes. They are masterminded by The Fool, who seems to be cemented in his chariot (from the bottom down). And, although the chariot is made of heavy stones, it has somehow crossed over water onto land, as if it hovered over it. Additionally, The Fool's (or charioteer's) garment is embellished with several mystical symbols: secret writings and an enigmatic sash across his torso denoting full control over his instinctual desires. The focus is on the intellect and the mind, symbolized by the white shining square across his chest; the two crescents on his shoulders, pointing to heaven, symbolize his receptive intuition to spiritual guidance. This is further enforced by the red bolt on the chariot's shield, with a winged disk on top.

He is in control and balanced, as he holds the wand of The Magician in his right arm. All refer to the mystical knowledge he received from each of the characters we've met so far. Intuition and logic, creativity and methodology, feminine and masculine, spiritual and material aspects are all integrated and in balance. This card signifies The Fool's triumphant crowning for his achievements so far. He has transcended the duality and constraints of the nature of man.

Upright Meaning: At this point in life, you must be practical and regularly apply your developed skills as well as mental focus to overcome any problem or struggle you may be experiencing. This card represents triumph. Hard work is about to be rewarded. Overnight success, material gain. News or friends from afar. Consistent effort is needed to overcome your struggle. Your inner gifts are about to emerge. Don't fuss – get on with it!

Modern Interpretation: Strategist, high-level problem solver, visionary, innovator, specializes in overseas expansion.

Reversed Meaning: Lack of discipline, situation out of control. Addiction, envy, avarice. Afraid to use abilities. Arrogance or lack of self-confidence. Burying head in the sand. Warning against overwhelming ambition, burnout or wasting resources.

Exercise: When you need the strength and determination of The Chariot, place the card in front of you and meditate on it while gazing intently into it. Breathe in the vastness of the starry skies, as well as control over the ego and its desires. Feel the energy rising your spine in a straight line from the centre of the Earth to your crown. Know that you have the necessary skills and experience, as well as the motivation, to complete your task successfully. Now, repeat the following affirmation while holding the card at arm's length and rotating it clockwise and counterclockwise until you feel all resistance leave you as you breathe out: "I am confident in my ability to fully express myself and live up to my full potential. I have an abundance of endurance and stamina."

Minor Cards: The Sevens

Seven is the number of wisdom, as well as the completion of a cycle or phase within a cycle. It represents completion,

completeness, safety, victory and rest after achieving a meaningful ambition or a milestone. It is also a mystical number that represents wisdom and spiritual growth. There are seven notes on a musical scale, seven colours in the rainbow and seven planets in traditional astrology. We are in a state of extreme happiness and balance when we are in 'seventh heaven'. It's like the feeling of relief after a long exhale.

Seven of Wands: Purpose and value are two attributes of the number 7 – both of which are depicted on this card. The Seven of Wands depicts a brave man with a wand fighting six other wands that rise to attack him. It symbolizes competition and conflict that appears overwhelming at first. However, the man stays focused on his mission or purpose, and triumphs. The card indicates that a successful career change is likely; however, strength and determination are required to achieve success. It is also possible that stiff competition will be confronted in business, but perseverance and courage will triumph in the end. This card represents knowledge and incorporates skills. It can represent an excellent teacher, training, lecturing or writing.

Upright: When success is followed by stiff competition, it is time to show perseverance and courage to overcome any opposition and difficulties. Success is assured (if you persevere).

Reversed: Time to retreat and wait for an opportune moment; opportunities thrown away due to fear.

Seven of Cups: The Seven of Cups represents a man who has a vivid imagination! Seven cups appear from the clouds floating before him. He stands perplexed, unsure which one to select: the castle, the jewels, the victory wreath, the dragon, the curly-haired woman or the snake. However, draped in the centre is a figure with a halo in a cup. This represents his true self, which is yet to be revealed. The card suggests that a decision must be made with great care and consideration. Otherwise, his dreams and ideas will remain castles in the clouds. Unless one of the cups is chosen and worked with, nothing will be achieved. It's a time when the imagination runs wild and soul options seem numerous. Confusion over the decision is accompanied by an abundance of creative and artistic talent and energy that can be directed in a positive way.

Upright: There is a lot of creativity and talent around this situation, but there is also a lot of confusion. Decisions about creative and relationship matters must be made, no matter how difficult they are. You are confused because there is so much choice. This is not the time for daydreaming; your imagination is too vivid. Need to be realistic.

Reversed: Loss of opportunity; dangerous delusions.

Seven of Swords: A man appears to be fleeing from a camp in the background with a bundle of five swords. Two swords remain embedded in the ground behind him. As he sneaks away, there is a guilty expression on his face, and he looks over his shoulder. This card represents the need for caution and staying away from temptation to achieve your goal. Direct or aggressive tactics will be ineffective. Diplomacy and charm will be potent. If the card is badly placed, a flight from a dishonourable act is advised.

Upright: Now is the time to think carefully, tactfully and diplomatically. Aiming for goals aggressively will not work, nor would being overly hostile. However, caution must be taken because deception is likely.

Reversed: Take professional advice otherwise you may will lose out. Be cautious of burglary and superficial contacts.

Seven of Pentacles: A young farmer is depicted leaning on his hoe. He seems to have the necessary skills to gather his harvest and has done good, solid work. The seven days of labour are over, yet he pauses from work, assessing his harvest and dreaming about what needs to be done, wondering if it is good enough. This card indicates a pause of a business or an enterprise and warns against stopping for too long. Previous efforts will only be successful if they are consistent.

Upright: Financial choices and decisions. Fortitude is required. You u are about to enter a challenging period, but don't give up! Do not lose hope; instead, pick yourself up and make the required changes after a brief break. The pause will help you find a new avenue to pursue.

Reversed: Giving up easily, or constantly worrying about money or career without acting. Has skills but won't work. Discipline, focus and consistent practical work is advised.

PHASE 2: INNER ALCHEMY (CARDS 8–14)

The Fool has now grasped the concept of complementary opposites. He's also learned that he can achieve his goals by honing his own skills, collaborating with others, and mastering his ego and mind. Instead of successfully overcoming conflicts, The Chariot teaches him to apply mental mastery of his ego and connect with his higher purpose.

The Fool's next stage of growth entails confronting the complexities of being human. It entails delving deep into his inner world to find balance, control, maturity and a higher purpose in his life. In addition, he begins to understand the impermanent nature of life, short cycles of unexpected change and unavoidable transitions. Choices have consequences, and he must learn that stepping away to reflect on life is necessary before continuing his journey. If he doesn't, life will force him to!

8 – Justice:
Balance and Legal Matters

Despite the universe's apparent randomness, its structure contains a certain justice or fairness that reflects the need for balance and harmony in our lives. The Justice card underlines The Fool's karmic lesson: actions have consequences for which he must take responsibility. Any decision has an impact. With Justice, inner transformation begins as the ego, or the personality, aligns with the intentions and higher motives of the consciousness when one makes decisions that invariably impact others.

The Justice card implies that opposing viewpoints are always present. The scales represent the feminine principle of passive evaluation, while the sword represents the masculine principle of decision and action. Justice's message is that when opposing forces work together, the right decision can be made. Choices also have consequences because they cause change. Justice teaches The Fool that making the right choice entails making a dispassionate decision based on facts after weighing all the factors involved. Justice was reassigned to number 8 by Waite in the second edition of the Rider-Waite-Smith pack. Can you see how this is relevant to Justice?

Justice indicates that, even though circumstances may be dictated, mastering and balancing emotions is critical to making the best and fairest decision. The Justice figure is an androgynous-looking, unbiased figure who exhibits a dispassionate but discriminate and fair intellect. The purple veil behind Justice represents the wisdom of making fair decisions. To achieve harmony, balancing opposites necessitates a well-balanced mind.

The choice must be made fairly by balancing heart and mind, as symbolized by Justice's red and green robes and the everlasting solid stone throne on which he sits.

The red circle inside the white square around his neck denotes passion and spirit, respectively – the result is balance and harmony. If you look closely at the card, you'll notice that Justice's right hand is pointing upwards, towards Spirit, while his left hand, which is holding the scale, is pointing downwards, towards Earth, symbolizing spiritual wisdom applied practically to material life on Earth (a mature older Magician). The one foot of Justice sticking out from beneath the robes, pointing to material life, embodies higher wisdom applied to everyday living.

Upright Meaning: The message of this card is that when opposing forces are in harmony, the appropriate decision can be made; nonetheless, choices have consequences since they cause change. You are advised to consider that making the right decision requires a dispassionate evaluation of your situation, using your intellect, and facts – not emotions. The situation requires you to be honest and fair. Have courage and connect with your conviction before making any decisions. Being resolute and grounded is required, integrating conscious and subconscious. It also denotes a generous and fair-minded person, or a favourable settlement of legal matters, contracts or negotiations. It can indicate choice or decision – logic. Balanced, fair, clear-sighted view of life. Indicates accountants, judges, lawyers and people who make laws.

Modern Interpretation: Legal (if The Hierophant appears in the same spread, and The Lovers) and civil marriages (The Lovers). Signing of contracts, a legal battle that ends fairly, signing of legal documents to establish a contract or a business.

Reversed Meaning: If making unreasonable demands, you may get less than you hope. It indicates complications in legal matters, injustice, imbalance and delays. Major adjustments are needed to balance life. A divorce or separation, dissolution of partnerships.

Exercise: Reflect on decisions you made recently; write down your observations in your Tarot journal. What were the consequences of those decisions? How did they impact your life? Were they fair? Did you weigh facts and emotions? What could you have done differently for your decision to have beneficial, fair results? What was missing?

Meditation: Take a few breaths, relax and imagine or pretend that you are sitting on the throne of Justice. With your eyes closed, consider your robes, the sword you are holding in your right arm, and the scales in your left hand. How do you feel? Focus on a point above your head as you consider a decision you need to make. What guidance are you receiving from Spirit? Take a few moments before you bring your attention to the scales and your right foot resting on the steps. What practical matters and facts do you need to consider? Are your emotions in check? If not, ground your emotions in facts – consider the details of the situation and recognize that you are reconciling emotions, facts and inspired guidance together until you feel balanced within yourself. When you achieve 'neutral', wiggle your toes, open your eyes and write down your experience. We hope that your decision is a clearer now.

Minor Cards – The Eights

The number 8 represents regeneration and the balancing of opposing forces. It symbolizes the death of the old, which is evil or wrong, and the birth of the new, which is pure and just. It enables situations to be modified, as well as addressing what was out of balance, unfair or unjust. The number 8 acts as a thruster. Decisions will have a cascading effect that will be felt almost immediately. To grow in wisdom, one must die a little each day, letting go of old ideas, habits and ways of thinking as they become obsolete.

Eight of Wands: The Eight of Wands depicts a dramatic image of eight wands flying across the sky, passing over the peaceful countryside below. This card represents the need to get up and do something. It's a time for new beginnings and activities. It indicates the end of a period of delay or stagnation and the beginning of initiative and action. A busy and exciting time lies ahead, indicating travel and relocation.

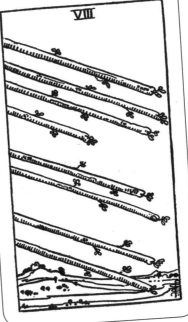

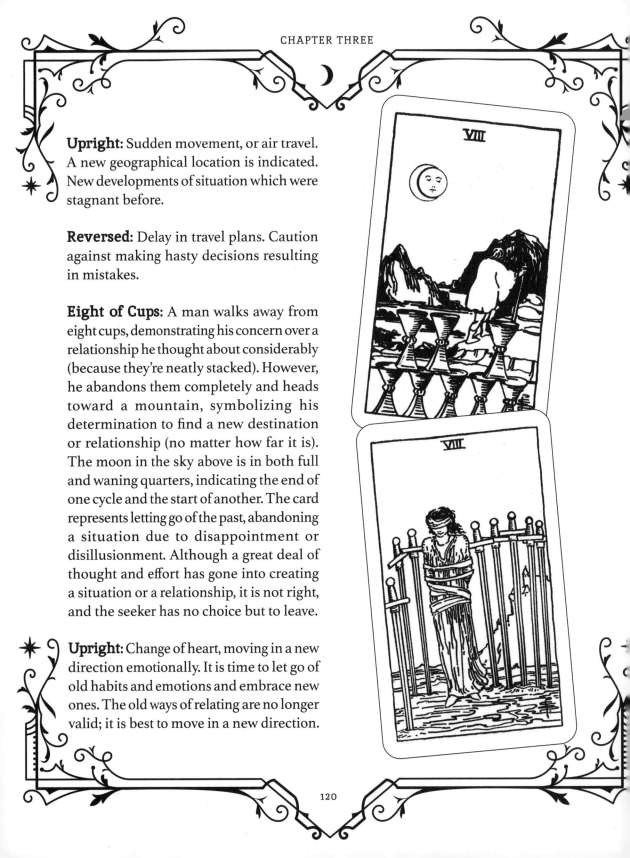

Upright: Sudden movement, or air travel. A new geographical location is indicated. New developments of situation which were stagnant before.

Reversed: Delay in travel plans. Caution against making hasty decisions resulting in mistakes.

Eight of Cups: A man walks away from eight cups, demonstrating his concern over a relationship he thought about considerably (because they're neatly stacked). However, he abandons them completely and heads toward a mountain, symbolizing his determination to find a new destination or relationship (no matter how far it is). The moon in the sky above is in both full and waning quarters, indicating the end of one cycle and the start of another. The card represents letting go of the past, abandoning a situation due to disappointment or disillusionment. Although a great deal of thought and effort has gone into creating a situation or a relationship, it is not right, and the seeker has no choice but to leave.

Upright: Change of heart, moving in a new direction emotionally. It is time to let go of old habits and emotions and embrace new ones. The old ways of relating are no longer valid; it is best to move in a new direction.

Reversed: A person following a fantasy, not seeing the reality of their situation but rather indulging in emotions. Situation can lead to depression. Stagnating due to indulging emotions without rational thinking and considering facts.

Eight of Swords: A woman appears to be stranded on a marsh, surrounded by eight swords planted in the water. Behind her, a large castle can be seen in the distance, symbolizing a better place where she would be safe, dry and protected. The card appears bleak, but it is her fears, her refusal to confront the situation, and her inability to make decisions that keep her imprisoned or limit her movement. The card's message is to be brave when faced with problems and to face them head on in order to solve them. You can't be paralyzed by your fears forever.

Upright: Stalemate situation, or trapped conditions. The constraints and limitations that this card implies are frequently self-imposed and persist due to fear and indecision. Positive action has the power to end the stagnation.

Reversed: Gradually seeing light. Getting answers, or releasing fear, anxiety and indecision.

Eight of Pentacles: Pentacles are being carved out by an apprentice craftsman. He appears to be pleased and enthusiastic about his work, the results of which are nailed to the block of wood in front of him. When the energy of the eight is combined with this card it symbolizes talent and skills. It can indicate the possibility of turning a skill or talent into a profession, or the possibility of earning money through such a skill. Although things are still in the apprentice stage, do not let that hold you back. There is the possibility of new employment in the skilled field. Hard work and practical ideas are the solid foundations for establishing a new and lucrative career, both emotionally and financially.

Upright: Skills will bring financial rewards. Patience. A new project has begun. This card represents learning and mastering new skills, which can lead to a new means of earning income or pursuing a new project. You are honing your skills in preparation for a new and challenging project. On the other hand, financial prosperity is predicted, and now is the time to maintain your composure and faith in your talents. Also, you are ready to head in a new direction or start a new project, business or career.

Reversed: Indicates disorganisation and problems in a project, a business or finances. Overwhelmed by having too much to do.

THE HERMIT

9 – The Hermit: Withdrawal and Reflection

The Hermit is the wise spiritual mentor or teacher. A lone traveller who illuminates the route for other travellers. He promotes The Fool's growth by digging further into spiritual understanding beyond personal gain. Larger life decisions necessitate a period of seclusion, meditation and withdrawal. Before continuing his quest, The Fool must confront his own insecurities. The Hermit requires patience, as opposed to Justice, who must act quickly and equitably. This signifies that wisdom is achieved via the use of a clear, thoughtful mind. After some time alone, The Fool realizes that there is more to life than what happens in the hectic, distracted outer world.

The Hermit symbolizes The Fool grown up. The Hermit is typically depicted as an elderly man with a long white beard, cloaked and hooded, and carrying a lamp. It represents the archetype of the wise elderly man; in the Tarot, he is, in fact, The Fool who is getting older. The Hermit bridges youth and old age. In his youth, The Fool leaps off the brink of a cliff in broad daylight, his face elevated and his staff lightly held. The older and wiser Hermit has learned many valuable lessons, and now walks with caution and relies on his staff (Wand) for support. He is frequently shown carrying a lantern, figuratively illuminating the darkness for others as his eyes are closed (in confidence). As he continues his solitary journey over snow, his heavy cloak and hood protect him from the cold.

Hermits typically reside in monasteries or hermitages; however, in the Tarot, The Hermit is frequently seen in a landscape,

implying that he is still looking for a spot to rest. This also represents the never-ending pursuit of knowledge, understanding and wisdom. The journey here is an inner one of reflection rather than a physical one – in other words, withdrawing from society to gain enlightenment within. Furthermore, alchemical thought is frequently used in the quest for personal transformation and enlightenment. The first half of our life journey is usually about achieving security and worldly gain, while the second half is a search for self-knowledge and self-reflective contemplation that begins with The Hermit. Today's fast-paced lifestyle makes it difficult to devote time to the process of inner knowledge. We are increasingly pressed to find immediate solutions. While our outward world is continuously changing, our internal reality is not.

Upright Meaning: Travelling allows you to gain experience. There is always something new and fresh to discover about life. This card also asks you to withdraw into isolation to reflect on and learn from your previous experiences. The wisdom of life's obstacles will be revealed if you take time to reflect and understand. You'll have a better understanding of your life and be able to share your wisdom with others, enlightening them. It indicates the need for withdrawal to reach higher realms of consciousness and wisdom. The Hermit is a call for discovering the truth within. Worldly affairs can be distracting, so use caution and take your time when deciding on issues that matter – discreetly. It also indicates that you may feel you have accomplished everything you set out to do, and are wondering what's next. However, more knowledge or experience is required.

Reversed Meaning: Enforced loneliness. Immaturity and superficiality, life full of empty chatter. Do not reject advice given to you. Pig-headedness, refusal to listen. Wasting of time. Examine your life and preoccupations. Reconnect with friends.

Modern Interpretation: Professor, researcher, philosopher, mentor, specialized publisher, historian, experienced therapist, wise intellectual.

Exercise: Use The Hermit card for a visualisation exercise whenever you need to step back from the hustle of life and gain insights into a situation. Relax your mind by taking few deep breaths with your eyes closed, letting go of worry and concern as you breathe out. When your breathing has steadied, open your eyes and gaze upon the image of The Hermit. Imagine or pretend

that you entering the picture, putting on the robes of The Hermit and walking in his footsteps while carrying the lantern. How do you feel? Is the environment around you noisy or quiet? Can you hear yourself thinking? As you reflect on your situation, what thoughts are you guided by? Continue walking until you feel your mind has cleared and you have a better idea as to how to handle your issue. Once satisfied, write your thoughts in your journal, and read them later.

Minor Cards – The Nines

Before starting a new cycle with the Ace, you must complete nine rounds. It denotes the end of one phase and the start of a new one (Ace). The number 9 represents resurrection, and things that need to be gathered before completion. It also represents the culmination of all previous stages, such as preparation, knowledge-gathering, and skill-honing. It represents laying a solid foundation before the tenth step, which is the final completion.

Nine of Wands: This is a card of determination and strength. As if defending his territory, a man stands ready. He has already fought, as is evident by his bandaged head, but he is still willing and ready to fight for what he values. It implies that even when

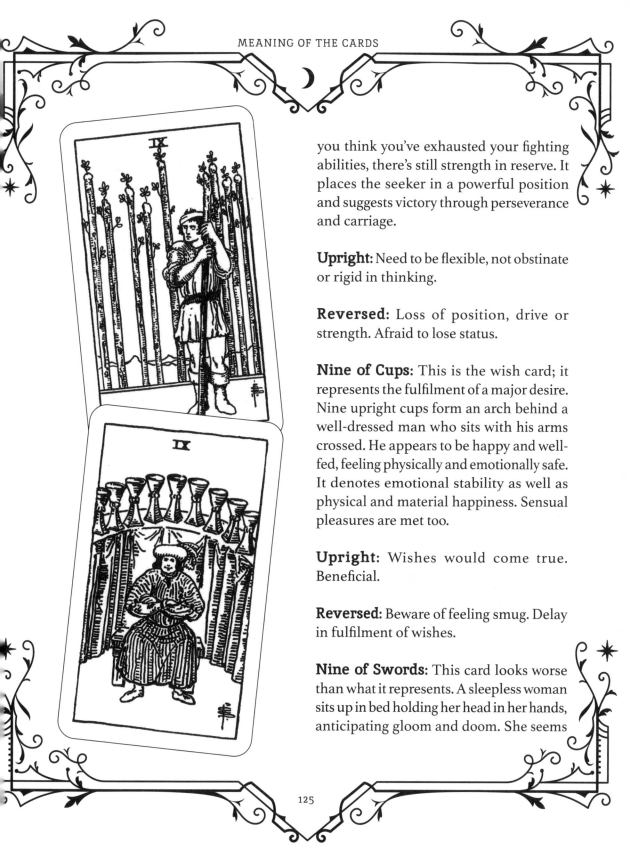

you think you've exhausted your fighting abilities, there's still strength in reserve. It places the seeker in a powerful position and suggests victory through perseverance and carriage.

Upright: Need to be flexible, not obstinate or rigid in thinking.

Reversed: Loss of position, drive or strength. Afraid to lose status.

Nine of Cups: This is the wish card; it represents the fulfilment of a major desire. Nine upright cups form an arch behind a well-dressed man who sits with his arms crossed. He appears to be happy and well-fed, feeling physically and emotionally safe. It denotes emotional stability as well as physical and material happiness. Sensual pleasures are met too.

Upright: Wishes would come true. Beneficial.

Reversed: Beware of feeling smug. Delay in fulfilment of wishes.

Nine of Swords: This card looks worse than what it represents. A sleepless woman sits up in bed holding her head in her hands, anticipating gloom and doom. She seems to be in despair. Next to her, nine swords are suspended, and on her bed panel two swordsmen are fighting. The signs of the zodiac embroidered on her quilt indicate that she has been feeling this for a long while. However, the swords do not touch her, indicating that her fears are unfounded, and are perhaps caused by her negative thinking or state of mind. Covering her eyes, she indicates that she is not facing her situation. Her fears about her difficulties are worse than the reality of the situation.

Extreme stress is indicated, and that is making her lose sleep. Nonetheless, no matter how difficult a situation seems, she must face her fears and decide as quickly and swiftly as the swords, because her worries are paralysing and far worse than the outcome.

Upright: Distress, mental stress or illness, nightmares, fear and anxiety due to overthinking and worrying, which might lead to feeling oppressed.

Reversed: Lessening of situation. Light at the end of a dark tunnel.

Nine of Pentacles: This card represents someone who can enjoy wonderful things in life while in solitude. In a blooming vineyard, a well-dressed woman stands alone in the garden of her manifested reality. The falcon on her gloved hand denotes that her thoughts are under control. A manor house in the background represents material wealth and the vastness of the land she owns. The card represents delighting in physical comfort and financial achievement. It does not suggest that the person is literally without relationships.

Not only does the person love her own company, but she is also at peace with herself, grateful to enjoy what she already has; she does not necessarily require companionship to feel content or complete. Moreover, notice the snail in the foreground. It symbolizes slow, methodical and consistent effort, which yields results. There is no attachment to material gain, rather enjoying the fruits of her labour. Financial and material advantages are anticipated and cherished.

Upright: Material prosperity. Windfall. Comfortable retirement. It's a wonderful life! You are about to start a new phase of your life, one in which you have attained financial independence and security. You no longer need to work. This card portends that your hard work and dedication will be rewarded shortly.

Reversed: Self-absorbed, and consequently suffering financial risks.

THE WHEEL OF FORTUNE

10 – Wheel of Fortune: Unexpected Change of Fortune

The Fool learns from The Wheel of Fortune that much of life appears to be random, with unanticipated, quick changes and opportunities. There are many ups and downs in life. He recognizes that the one constant in life is change.

All situations will ebb and flow continuously. He learns to respect the seasons and the cycle of life, and therefore the right timing for action. Moreover, he learns to persevere in hard times, for these too will come to an end. In other words, there are forces beyond his control.

Moreover, The Fool learns about the fast-paced natural cycles of change through The Wheel of Fortune. Therefore, it represents both stability and change. As a result, The Fool must be willing to accept and adapt to change, which builds his personal and emotional resilience. This is a significant step in his inner transformation. The period of seclusion and introspection rapidly gives way to a period of progress and development. Consequently, caution is required to be attentive and in the present moment, ready to adapt and act in response to forthcoming developments. Like The Moon, the wheel is round and ever-changing.

Although this card appears as a light-hearted bringer of good fortune, it is perhaps the card that contains the most alchemical symbols, emphasizing the cycles of self-transformation on various levels. Waite asked for his Wheel of Fortune card to be illustrated with a blend of Egyptian and biblical figures, emphasizing the notion of death and rebirth. The snake on the left represents Seth, the Egyptian god who introduced death to the Earth and assassinated the noble king Osiris. Anubis, the jackal-headed figure on the right, is a guide to deceased souls and a bringer of new life. On top, a sphinx representing Horus, son of Osiris and god of Resurrection, is depicted. The zodiac is another wheel depicting the cycle of death and rebirth – gain via loss and vice versa. The four animals in each corner appear to be inspired by Ezekiel's biblical vision (*Ezekiel* 1:10). They also reflect the astrological fixed elements of Taurus, Leo, Scorpio and Aquarius, which symbolize earth, fire, water and air, respectively.

Another depiction of a vast, ever-revolving wheel that indicates a passage through time by season is the zodiac. The elements represent those used in alchemy, and the symbols on the wheel's spokes are similarly alchemical. From top to bottom, clockwise, they read: mercury, sulphur, water and salt. The combination of the four elements results in a perfect fifth – continuity and flow.

The card's message is that through constant renewal, and cycles of death and rebirth, the inner self evolves and transforms to create a perfect state of harmony between heaven and Earth. The Wheel of Fortune also depicts the inner driving force that is formed when the cycles of time turn. The Wheel of Fortune informs us that, while changes are vital for growth and moving life forward, it is up to us, the individual, to adapt, change and evolve.

The hub of the wheel remains stationary as the rim rotates, depicting time marching on, year after year, season after season. The Sun, Moon and planets are always revolving, circling around the zodiac wheel, yet the wheel itself is always the same. Life is made up of cycles of change that symbolize opposing aspects such as day and night, expansion and contraction, blossom and decay. In the second stage of metamorphosis, The Fool has begun to experience those profound cycles. This card's message is also indicating the necessity of change to bring about transformation.

If you will, it is our deep, or unconscious, personality that frequently invites a change of situation in life. Although we may not always like change, we can typically perceive the opportunity for growth that it entails or seek to blame life! As a result, the more you learn about your inner self, the more freedom you will have in directing the course of your life. In a reading, The Wheel of Fortune represents a shift in circumstances. We may or may not want it, but it is critical that we respond to change. We can either move with the current in a favourable direction or blame fate. Whatever we do, the wheel turns The Chariot's triumph into misfortune, and then back into victory in a never-ending cycle.

Upright Meaning: Fortunate coincidences, quick changes, external influences, fortunate meetings and lucky breaks shape your life currently. The wheel has turned, and you are beginning a new cycle; unexpected opportunities are likely. Although it is a positive card, matters are in a state of flux, and you may feel confused. It is important not to resist this phase, and when the dust settles, you may find new friends, career, an unexpected new home or income. The Wheel of Fortune represents influences that can change the outcome of a circumstance. Regardless of the constraints, this card represents a breakthrough or unexpected swift change, such as moving residences, meeting someone new or obtaining a job offer, depending on where it falls in a spread.

Reversed Meaning: Bad luck dogs your path. Be patient; the wheel is always in motion and fate will smile once again. It's a bad time to initiate new projects or gamble on things going in your favour. Unexpected delays. Change is usually positive at the end. Expect the unexpected.

Exercise: Use a piece of string with some thickness to represent your life from birth until the present. As you reflect on your life, pick up one end of the string and tie a knot marking your birth. Leave a bit of space, then tie another knot that represents the next change or event, whether good or bad. Keep going until you reach the present (or run out of string!). When you have finished, place the string in front of you, and colour each knot using chalk or pens, assigning green, for example, to good memories or fortunate events, and red to negative ones. Pin down the end that represents your birth and join the other to it, forming a circle. What do you notice? Write down your remarks in your Tarot journal, describing how you felt, and the emotional and physical impact of each 'knot' on you. How did you respond? Was change easy, or did you resist? What happened when you resisted, and what was your attitude? Finally, what did you learn from your cycle of life?

Minor Cards – The Tens

The number 10 is associated with completeness and perfection. A ten-step procedure was required for the number 9 cycle to finish. In the number 10, one represents the beginning, and zero represents the spirit, before returning to a new cycle of one again. Ten allows the current cycle of preparation to finish. In the Minor Arcana of Cups and Pentacles, ten represents the pinnacle of bliss and happiness, whereas the Swords and Wands represent trial and tribulation.

Ten of Wands: A young man walks awkwardly and uncomfortably toward his home in the distance, grasping a large bunch of ten blossoming wands. He appears to be physically exhausted, but he continues to walk steadily, plodding toward his objective. This card indicates

that a load is about to be lifted or that an issue is about to be solved. Oppression, on the other hand, is frequently self-imposed, and the seeker can do a lot to lighten his load. The weight can be physical, mental or emotional, but there is something that can be done to help ease the strain. This card indicates excessive initiatives taken to the point of self-burdening. The point of the lesson The Fool is learning from this card is that, regardless of the difficulties he carries alone in life, there are times when it is beneficial to listen to others' advice and seek the assistance of those he trusts. Take time to examine your life, when your personal burden becomes unbearable, to ensure that you are still on the right track.

Upright: Avoid neglecting physical limitations; if you don't set clear enough boundaries, you risk being overburdened. Too much pressure can lead to sickness. Movement with responsibility. This card also represents the burdens of ambition.

Reversed: End of a period of hard work. Welcome new responsibilities that will lead to a promotion.

Ten of Cups: A young married couple stands arm in arm, holding hands and raising their arms to heaven in joy. Ten gleaming cups form

an arch above them, resembling a rainbow in the sky. Two children are joyously dancing together nearby. Over the hills, we can see the family home, which is surrounded by trees. The number 10 represents perfection, and this card represents a beautiful family life and long-term contentment. As the cups are made in the heavens above, their happiness stems from emotional security as well as spiritual connection. This card indicates that you are at a high point in your personal relationships and that you are experiencing harmony and integration

in all areas of your life. Your personal wishes and ambitions have been realized. It might also signify the start of a new cycle. Recognize the work you and others around you have done to achieve your goals, but also remain open to new possibilities so that your happiness can be long-lasting and continuous.

Upright: After a long period of hard work, this is a time of contentment and fulfilment. Good luck because of perseverance. A special happy event (marriage, childbirth, child's birthday), or lasting happiness.

Reversed: Feeling let down, or not getting the success you expected. Emotional reversals, or disruption of happiness.

Ten of Swords: A man lies dead on the ground, his back gravely wounded by ten swords plunged into it. The tragedy is heightened by the dark and ominous sky above. The dying man's right-hand fingers are bent over and touching each other in a ritual gesture that suggests completion. Even though this card initially appears to represent a violent death, it is actually about deep and profound loss. If this card appears in a spread, you may be feeling a loss in your personal life or work; however, there is another interpretation.

Perhaps a part of you has died suddenly, but you're now receptive to something fresh and energizing. The number 10 represents completion, but also growth on a higher level – just as death also represents rebirth. Your lower ego self must die for your higher self to experience spiritual awakening. This marks the end of one chapter and the start of a new one in your life. Before you can progress, you must let go of old, outdated patterns of thinking.

Upright: Disappointment, disillusion and false hopes clear the decks for a fresh outlook, truth and clarity of understanding. Deception, treachery or stress may lead to physical illness when understanding is lacking.

Reversed: Recovery from illness. Negative thinking must change. Change your attitude – it is holding you back.

Ten of Pentacles: A well-dressed, elderly man – the family patriarch – sits, with two loyal dogs at his knee. An adjacent archway bears his coat of arms, and two more members of the family, a young man and woman, greet each other joyfully nearby. The image appears to be one of clan or family unity, based on many years of tradition. The spheres of the Kabbalistic Tree of Life are superimposed on this mediaeval family setting, reminding us that we are members of both a family and a community, and that while we seek physical well-being and prosperity in our daily lives, seeking spiritual fulfilment is also important. This card represents long-term success based on spiritual wisdom and understanding. The card's message is that acquiring material gain through a balanced attitude lasts for generations.

Upright: The formation of sturdy foundations for families or businesses is indicated by this card. The purchase of a home, for example, or the establishment of a tradition, are symbolic of life's security, stability and permanence. Family money (legacy). Renewal. Financial comfort. You will get used to living in luxury but be careful not to grow complacent and overindulgent. Long-term prosperity and material contentment have been achieved, according to this card. You are at ease in your own house and will be in a position or have the potential to leave a wonderful legacy to your descendants.

Modern interpretation: A store, boutique, restaurant, department mall, business headquarters, office or luxurious home.

Reversed: Laziness, or a person who is lazy. Too much luxury stopping you from making real achievements. Family money or financial misfortune.

VIII

STRENGTH

11 – Strength: The Healer

This card, Strength, represents the female aspect of The Hermit, the wise feminine 'sagess'. She advises The Fool to trust his inner power, increase his confidence and use his limitless inner resources to oppose human cravings. Desires of the lower ego, or of the personality, must be kept under control. He learns to control his higher mind over his lower appetites, as well as tame his wants while remaining spiritually connected to his bigger purpose. The Fool learns how to lovingly discipline and control his inner cravings as he meets his feminine spiritual mentor, Strength, the counterpart of The Hermit. She is symbolized by Strength gently taming the masculine lion, which also represents masculine drive. The lesson is that true strength and power come from being gentle, and in command of our instinctual cravings and sexual desires. Inner strength necessitates a gentle integration of spiritual intuition over brute force, self-control and endurance.

There is no use of undue force or aggression about this strength. It's all about the feminine charm and tenderness. Strength teaches The Fool spiritual alchemy or self-transformation on a higher level, as The Empress did with gentle and caring love. Now that The Fool's inner and exterior resources (skills, abilities and talents) are in balance, he is poised to achieve greater heights. This is achieved by surrendering his 'old self', as he learned from The Wheel of Fortune and will learn from The Hanged Man. He must deliberately give up his old methods of perceiving, thinking and acting for The Wheel of Fortune to turn in his favour.

The image of a human battling the King of Beasts appears in several Tarot decks, and it represents man's fight to control his animal impulses. Strength can refer to both inner and physical strength. It echoes the conflict between man and lion, portraying the feminine aspect of dealing with the opposing lions portrayed by The Chariot – the struggle between instinctual desires and the conscious mind. In The Chariot card, the masculine aspect is represented by The Fool wearing a talisman 'skirt' around his genitals to control his ego and physical urges, which could impede or distract him from winning his battle. He is on high alert, summoning all his physical might and abilities to win. In the Strength card, by contrast, a woman is wearing a floral garland around her waist that cascades down to the ground, spiralling across her abdomen as she gently seals the lion's mouth. This is higher-level personal alchemy, or self-transformation.

Both cards suggest that our higher spiritual nature can triumph over earthly wants by conquering the lion. The woman wears flowers in her hair and is taming the lion and laying a garland around its neck in the Strength card. The woman, like The Empress, has lovely golden hair and wears a white gown to symbolize spiritual purity. Note how she is taming the lion with ease, demonstrating the power of spiritual intuition over sheer force. In the second phase, it means that The Fool has undergone a more profound metamorphosis, symbolizing control over any remnants of the animal soul that may still exist in a person's consciousness. The maiden, who represents the moon and femininity, is depicted beside the lion, who represents the sun and masculinity.

So far, we got a glimpse of The Fool's youth as we went through the Major cards. He had his first training from The Magician; we met his earthly parents, The Empress and The Emperor, and then his spiritual guides or heavenly parents, The High Priestess and The Hierophant. We learned about The Fool's struggles and vulnerability when he fell in love in The Lovers card, and he mastered his thoughts and feelings to find balance and continue conquering opposites in The Chariot card. When he gets to Justice, he has to do more than just act and respond. He needed to think about things objectively. The Hermit urged him to look for meaning in his own life. With The Wheel of Fortune, his mind-set shifts even more, as he realizes that he remains vulnerable. He could rise and fall, but it is out of his control because such are the cycles of life. Now he needs Strength to provide him with the self-control, dignity and courage he needs to confront the next phase of the journey to the underworld.

Strength helps him undergo an even more profound transformation, but in a gentle manner. The Tarot path does not ignore sensual or sexual urges as it intensifies. The Fool learns the ability to regulate, discipline and weigh those components within himself that will bring healing and unification of man and spirit. This is further enforced by the infinity sign The Magician also had over his head, symbolizing the endless process of self-alchemy. Strength teaches The Fool that love and intuition are stronger and more enduring than hatred, sheer force or antagonism, and that not only courage and perseverance will help him conquer his challenges. Drawing this card indicates that you have triumphed over fears or anxieties you may have had in the past. Now is the time to master your resources and energies in preparation for the next chapter of your life's journey. Moreover, future success will be realized more easily and effortlessly through evolved understanding, love and compassion (towards other people and sentient beings, including animals) in your everyday life.

Upright: Better times are on the way! This is your chance to prove your inner strength and wisdom. You will prevail over life's hardships if you have the fortitude to endure. A beloved animal could enter your life. If you have relationship difficulties, open your heart, forgive and forget. Besotted with an older woman. Recovering from illness.

Modern Interpretation: Healing on a deep level. A person who has healing abilities. Animal communication skills. Someone who specializes in conflict resolution. Accomplished personality. Woman of substance and impact, who is charismatic, self-assured and grounded. A mentor.

Reversed: Fear and weakness are barriers to success. Your inner strength will help you overcome difficult situations. Will succeed if overcome fear of failure. Someone who is not in control of their instincts and sexual desires.

Exercise: Take out your Strength card and use your intuition to guide you into the image. Consider the difficulties you've faced in the past. Ask yourself, more significantly, where your inner power comes from. Where do you find your sense of personal power and strength? Consider a time when you overcame a challenge and achieved your goal. How did you manage to do that?

Consider the internal process that happens when you realize something you really desire. How did you reconcile your inner conflicts and find a comfortable middle ground? Was it effortless?

THE HANGED MAN

12 – The Hanged Man: Surrender and Sacrifice

The Fool learns from The Hanged Man that certain answers can be found if one stops looking for them, surrenders and accepts his current predicament. The Fool can see things from a fresh perspective by hanging upside down! To be set free from suspension, The

Fool must give up his previous way of life to be enlightened. The Fool recognizes the need to let go, to separate from the materialistic rut he created for himself, to fully understand the spiritual wisdom that lies beneath his 'suspended' state.

The Hanged Man represents another form of death, change or transformation; this time it is forced upon The Fool to help him prepare for the next phase. He must mature by giving up the childish ways and attitudes of earlier life. Effectively, he is learning to give up his personality ego, and be guided spiritually to a more meaningful existence. The 'incarceration' is forced upon him to teach him the lesson of voluntary sacrifice. He must reach a state of deeper self-awareness, depicted by the halo around his head, and recognize that the past must change. A new cycle of growth demands a renewed attitude and maturity.

Traitors were sometimes killed upside down by the Italians in mediaeval times. In Renaissance Italy, people used a type of graffiti known as 'shame paintings'. If they didn't like a local ruler, they would create an upside-down cartoon of him on a wall, often hanging by one foot. The card is known as The Traitor in several Italian decks, and depicts a person contorted with pain, arms outstretched and bent, as if flailing. Coins occasionally fall from his pocket.

However, if we consider the nameless and unnumbered card from the Visconti-Sforza Tarot of 1450 – probably the earliest version of Major Arcana cards we know of – The Hanged Man is depicted as an elegant young man with his hands behind his back and a calm expression on his face. The card depicts tranquillity rather than pain. Traditionally, the image of The Hanged Man in the Tarot is represented by an unusual figure hanging upside down by one foot. Despite his awkward position, his face is calm and composed, giving the image a soothing effect.

The card implies that The Fool must take this particular upside-down position at this point on his journey to gain fresh perspective on life (not punishment) and therefore attain a new degree of spiritual and psychological insight. The Fool has fought the lion, his shadow-self, with the Strength card. He realized that he could identify with more than simply his conscious self. He is now aware that he has an unconscious side that he is only beginning to understand. The Hanged Man signifies the start of his journey into the unconscious (the third phase) as well as his preparation for the next and last stage of his development and fulfilment.

Moreover, the illustration of The Hanged Man portrays a man suspended from a tree trunk, with leaves spreading across the two ends, implying a dynamic image of growing life – not an end of growth, or a punishment, but a continuous evolution. The Hanged Man is hanging in the middle of the trunk, signifying the delicate balance he must strike between two opposing forces: the conscious and unconscious mind. His crossed leg forms an inverted triangle, pointing downwards towards the unconscious. The Fool sees the world from a whole different perspective when he is upside down. The card represents yet another opportunity to bring opposites together to achieve enlightenment. The Fool must sacrifice control of his conscious ego and surrender to the unknown territory of his inner world.

When The Hanged Man appears in a reading, it's a period of personal choice. Something of great personal value must be given up, achieving something of even greater value. Because there is no assurance of outcome for what The Fool might leap into next, this sacrifice requires faith. As a result, the sacrifice must be done without the expectation of a reward – only the hope that it will be worthy.

Upright: The Hanged Man denotes inability to move forward in life due to a period of temporary pause or suspension. However, other people's input and behaviours are also a part of the delay (others had tied The Hanged Man to the tree trunk). The card's message is that this is not the best time to decide; there will be some delays. So patience is required as well as a revaluation of your intentions. Moreover, you will need to 'sacrifice', or voluntarily give up your old ways, to evolve and reinvent yourself. Something must be lost before you can make your way forward; otherwise, this status quo will continue.

The Hanged Man urges you to make a conscious decision to let go of the past (yourself or habits), which no longer benefits your life cycle, because something better is on the way. This card imposes the need for a moment of rest and reflection; this is in contrast to The Hermit, who gently urges you to reflect and prepare for a new cycle of regeneration. By trusting your higher wisdom and letting go of old habits and beliefs, you can overcome the source of your delay. In other words, if you are not self-aware, life will force you to stop and reflect!

Modern Interpretation: Opportunity to reset your life. You will emerge from this period with renewed energy.

Reversed Meaning: Warning against selfishness and materialism. The person in the reading might have neglected their spiritual growth and their unconscious programming or actions, and is preoccupied with material life. Holding on to the past and failing to grasp new opportunities. Bad investments, loss of belongings and reversals of fortune. Stop and think. Do not let others pressure you into getting involved.

Exercise: Allow your imagination to wander freely over the associations connected with the image of The Hanged Man in your chosen deck. Consider instances when you have had to give up something in your life, whether in a relationship, financially, professionally or with friends and family. How did it feel, and what did you gain as the result of giving up past perspectives or patterns? What was the difference in your feelings when you deliberately gave up something versus when you were forced to do so? How simple or difficult is it for you to take a step back and look at your life from a new perspective?

Consider using the following affirmation after you've written down your ideas and feelings in your Tarot journal:

"In stillness, I peacefully reflect on my life and receive higher perspective. I am willing to follow life's guidance and let go of what no longer serves me."

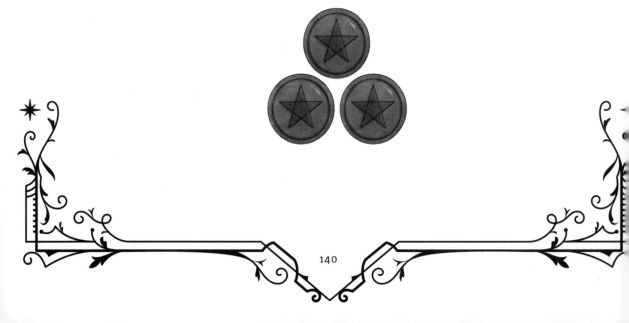

DEATH

13 – Death: Inevitable End and a New Beginning

The preceding card, The Hanged Man, symbolizes the death of the old ways. The Fool was not thinking about his own mortality. Death is that final letting go, the ultimate shift in The Fool's makeover. It represents transition, transformation, renewal, the death of old ways, and the death of the past, the end of relationships, even home or environment, that The Fool has accomplished so far – all of which indicate a new change that must come to be. Death is an inevitable change, a passage we all must go through. The Fool discovers how mysterious, secretive, healing and regenerating the end of the old ways can be.

Death is shown in the Tarot through a dramatic image. Death as a skeleton rides a white horse and is clad in black. Black is the colour of death because it absorbs all colour, just as Death absorbs all forms of life. White represents spiritual purity since it obliterates or blends all colours. Death is holding a black flag with an insignia of a five-petaled Tudor Rose, symbolizing a significant period of English history. A series of civil wars were fought between two rival Houses, Lancaster and York, which devastated the country, ripping it apart. The interwar ended when Henry VII, from the House of Lancaster, represented by a five-petaled red rose, married Elizabeth of York, whose emblem was a five-petaled white rose, ushering in a new era of stability.

Both were descendants of The House of Plantagenet, whose 300-year reign was the bloodiest and most devastating the British Isles ever experienced. Uniting the two warring rivals created a new dynasty,

The Welsh-French Tudor Dynasty, of which the last monarch was Queen Elizabeth I (known as Gloriana), who ruled 'gloriously' and peacefully for 60 years. The emblem of the new dynasty was the combination of the two roses: the Tudor Rose you see on Death's flag. Death represents this total transformation: death of the old structure and the emergence of a totally new system. The long conflict ended by uniting the rivals, thus transforming the old system into a new stable and successful era.

This example of symbolism shows how analyzing the deck you're working with can help you grasp the significance in its artistic rendering of the arcana. It stimulates yet another level of in-depth interpretation. The Rider-Waite-Smith-Colman deck was conceived and illustrated by British people only three centuries after the Tudor dynasty ended. The catastrophic era of their forefathers, The Plantagenets, and the War of the Roses would have been prominent in their consciousness.

The next thing we notice is that a skeleton is riding the horse! This is a metaphor for the body's hardest and most resistant part; flesh does not endure, but bone remains. It symbolizes the stripping away of material possessions. Death is symbolized by a white horse riding roughshod over a king (in the Rider-Waite-Smith deck) and stepping over his toppled crown, symbolizing the crushing of the last Plantagenet king. This imagery expresses that no earthly kingdom lasts. The horse rejects the Bishop's pleas for mercy, while the maiden is forced to turn her head away from the inevitable. It demonstrates that death is indiscriminate. It comes to everyone, regardless of how famous, wealthy, handsome, young or powerful they are.

The perennial sun rises in the background, a sign of hope and resurrection, between the two pillars symbolizing life's duality. The sun also symbolizes the start of a new cycle or a new dawn. This is another reference to the human evolutionary cycle, implying that death, like the process or cycle of self-evolution, is unavoidable. When this natural cycle of change is resisted, suffering is the result. Behind Death we see a boat effortlessly moving on a river, whose waters flow toward a new life, symbolized by the green scenery and reeds growing on the riverbank. This symbolizes a new life after death, and also that death is necessary to create and regenerate life. On the forebank of the river we see death and a ruined, arid land. On the other bank we see how the river of death also feeds and generates a new life.

In a reading, Death can signify the end of things in a variety of ways. Death, for example, may show in the spread of someone who is about to be married, as it represents the end of life as a single person, or in the spread of someone about to be divorced, representing the end of married life. The presence of the Death card could also represent leaving school, leaving a job or leaving a country, none of which indicate physical death. The Death card in the Tarot is associated with transition and change rather than literal death.

Under the effect of Death, feelings, emotions, thoughts and ideals undergo a transformation. It symbolizes the inevitable end of a cycle and the beginning of a new one. Willingness or reluctance to surrender to the impending transformation correlates to the degree of suffering experienced under the influence of the Death card. Death can indicate sadness or a welcome relief, depending on the seeker's circumstances. Nonetheless, Death needs to be recognized or acknowledged as the ending, mourned or honoured, just as the ancient Greeks honoured Death by paying the ferryman.

Getting married, for example, is a joyful milestone, but it also necessitates mourning the loss of freedom and youth that the single life usually delivers. Divorce, on the other hand, may reintroduce independence, but it must be mourned for the loss of integrated and collaborative life. Whenever circumstances change, it's important to recognize the need for change and to completely respect the process. Allow yourself time to examine, digest and integrate the changes brought on by the Death card. There is no right time assigned to the grieving or mourning process, so long as the river of life keeps moving you forward, even in small steps. For Death, in its essential meaning, is about decay.

Upright Meaning: Major changes lie ahead, and you may require some time to mourn the passing of what you are leaving behind. Loss of some kind, a relationship fails; a friendship ends; a job is lost. Transformation ahead; renewal and the start of a new life. As it heralds a fresh beginning, this card confirms the permanent end of the old ways. It teaches The Fool that the old ways are doomed and that he must change. He is transformed as he comes to terms with loss. According to its position in a spread, Death might represent a change of relationship or home.

Modern Interpretation: Imperative changes that are outside of your control (usually endings) affect new beginnings.

Reversed Meaning: Resisting changes; life very boring. Lethargy and inertia. Stagnation. Unable to adjust to new circumstances.

Exercise: As you consider the Death card, think about your own life. Have you ever been through the trauma of a metaphorical death? Was your life turned upside down as a result of it? Cast your mind back to when you were attempting to understand the hardship of accepting the end of your situation. What are you holding on to that you don't want to let go of? And what did you gain from it as soon as you accepted 'death'? In your Tarot journal, start writing your thoughts and insights as you explore answers to the above questions. *"I embrace endings and welcome new beginnings,"* is an affirmation that may help you emotionally and mentally accept the inevitability of change.

14 – Temperance: Harmony, Negotiations and Agreements
This card represents the transformed Fool, having confronted Death. He emerges with a sense of balance, elegance, integrity and moderation. As though some divine alchemical process has taken place, he now finds peace and harmony bridging the conflict

of accepting the renewal process of life. The Fool has learned to manage his thoughts (The Emperor, The Chariot) and feelings (Strength) and can now relate harmoniously to others. The message of this card is that the key to resolving any conflict is through forgiveness and making a compromise.

The image of the Temperance card is usually of an angelic figure pouring liquid from one cup into another. Temperance refers to a state of being moderate. The Temperance angel stands near a pool, one foot in the water and the other on the rocks, symbolizing continuity between past and future, conscious and unconscious, the subconscious and higher consciousness, as well as the spiritual and earthly worlds (remember the foot sticking out in the Justice card?). The angel represents the present, and heavenly intervention, which serves as a bridge between the spiritual and physical worlds. The angel's head is illuminated by a golden halo, and the circle with the red dot in the centre represents the eternity and continuation of the life-cycle; Spirit is the starting point that drives all material life.

A triangle within a square may be found on its chest, symbolizing the significance of reaching out to a higher mind, or Spirit, for inspirational guidance that drives a secure material life. The symbolism of the golden crown rising above the snow-covered mountains, which represent material or worldly triumphs, reinforces this concept by expressing that enduring achievements begin with seeking spiritual guidance or manifesting in partnership with Spirit. It encourages the maintenance of the balance between spirituality and earthly achievements, between the conscious and unconscious self, higher mind and subconscious mind, and balancing emotions. When the river of emotions flows freely, it nurtures the life flourishing on its banks, rather than flooding, which results in chaos.

Transferring the liquid of emotions between the two cups is a metaphor expressing the alchemical process that takes place as two people or two parties exchange their feelings honestly. When words are spoken from the heart, they are received by the heart – as the saying goes. So feelings are fluid, and need to flow or be expressed openly and in balance to achieve harmonious relationships. Speaking from the heart implies truth or spirit, rather than ego-centred self. In the same way that Justice (an air card) necessitates a balanced intellect, Temperance (a water or emotion card) necessitates a balanced heart. The alchemical process is depicted here by the two cups in the centre of the card, emphasizing that constant awareness of what needs to be balanced within The

Fool is required, and that feelings must be addressed and expressed.

Even water, if left still and stagnant, turns toxic. The image of the angel pouring water from one cup to another in a cautious and deliberate manner represents the necessity for continuous communication of truthful feelings between people (or parties) in a relationship and internally between the conscious and unconscious self. The Temperance card carries the unmistakable meaning of healthy and effective relationships, which are accomplished when the people involved are willing to compromise and cooperate. To maintain balance, fluidity and flexibility are required. The Temperance card's message is one of moderation. Nothing should be extreme.

Furthermore, since the angel is a heavenly figure, not an earthly one, Temperance implies heavenly intervention that 'magically' generates the ultimate result of keeping this balance; life will flow with ease and grace once balance is maintained, ensuring a serene and joyful life. When the Temperance card appears in a reading, it is time for a heart-to-heart dialogue, communicating sentiments rather than suppressing them. Truthful negotiations, by forgiving differences, will end conflict.

Upright Meaning: If this card appears in a spread with The Lovers card, it suggests a lovely relationship, rekindling an old flame or reaching an accord with others. It represents a balanced temperament, respite, moderation in behaviour, and the possibility of reaching a settlement through negotiation. Also, a cooperative collaboration on a project or business with others, a conducive working environment if a new job is started, and the ability to compromise and adapt in a relationship or when working with a team.

It represents a person who brings balance into a strife situation because they can see both sides of the argument clearly (a natural diplomat or a negotiator). It indicates that a conflicting matter can be successfully resolved, or fortunate changes. When Temperance appears in a spread, it is advising you to control events by accepting whatever fate throws at you.

Modern Interpretation: Mediator, motivator, conductor, someone who brings harmony and balance. Promotion at work.

Reversed Meaning: Things are out of balance. Quarrels and disagreements. Difficulty in getting on with others. Restless

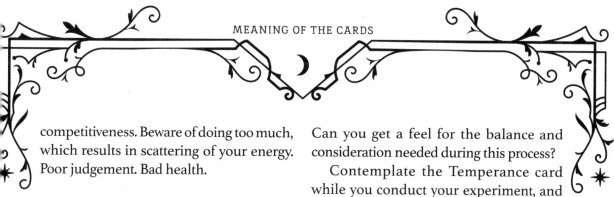

competitiveness. Beware of doing too much, which results in scattering of your energy. Poor judgement. Bad health.

Exercise: Try an 'alchemical' experiment with your hands to feel what it is like to mix opposites, and what results can be achieved by blending them. For example, take two opposites, such as salt and pepper, and blend them in equal measure. Or mix flour and water to achieve a consistent dough that can be kneaded and shaped. If you add too much water too quickly, what do you end up with? On the other hand, if you add too much flour, what do you get? What happens when any two ingredients are blended disproportionately?

Can you get a feel for the balance and consideration needed during this process?

Contemplate the Temperance card while you conduct your experiment, and as usual record your findings in your Tarot journal. Afterwards, continue writing in your journal, reflecting on your own life. How easy or difficult is it for you to express your true feelings, or keep your emotions in balance? How easy or difficult is it for you to form a sincere relationship without implanting your reservations or worries and unconscious feelings into it?

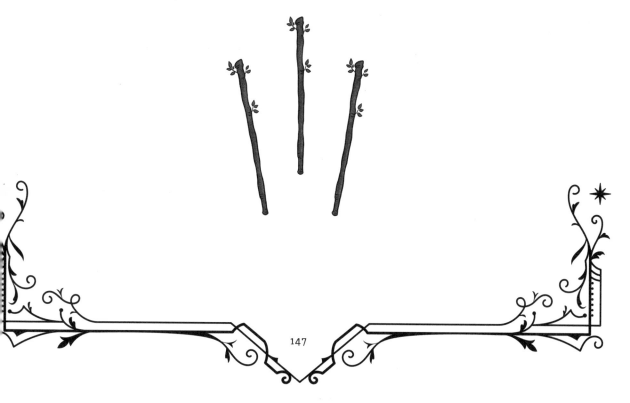

PHASE 3: FULFILMENT (CARDS 15–22)

The Fool went through recurring cycles of expansion and limitation in phase 2, prompting him to deeply explore himself and reconcile evolving components of his personality. He was also reminded that no matter how much he tries to control life, there will always be periods of suspension to prepare him for the next cycle of development and regeneration. To complete his metamorphosis, he must undergo comparable trials and lessons in phase 3, which are aimed to polish and reveal his true self as boundless consciousness in a human body.

He recognized that in order to advance to a greater level of awareness, he must continue to confront his duality and let go of old ways of living and conducting his life. The final stage entails addressing his dark shadow and releasing his human ego. 'Death' was the first in a series of dramatic stages of growth in which The Fool was stripped of all worldly pretensions in order to further clarify his individuality and how he connects with himself. After the repose of Temperance, The Fool is now ready to deal with The Devil within him – a formidable character from his unconscious realm.

THE DEVIL

15 – The Devil: Enslaved by the Ego

Despite The Fool's maturity thus far, he is still vulnerable to his personal demons – those of materialistic compulsions and addictions. The Devil represents the myriad shackles that prevent us from fully growing our spirit within a human form.

Ignorance, untamed passion, obsessions, consumerism, fanaticism, excessive wrath, petty attachments, poor impulse control and negative thinking are all examples of this bondage. Codependency, negative thoughts, self-imposed doubts and anxiety can all result from getting attached to desires of the ego – without wisdom of the spirit within.

The card's image is strikingly similar to The Lovers card, in which the couple stand before us naked. However, this time they are chained by the Devil in utter darkness. It symbolizes being enslaved to the untamed 'desires of the flesh'. Moreover, their imprisonment is voluntary – they chose to be in this relationship; however, they can only be freed if they let go of the chains they placed around their necks – their unconscious and unbalanced (extreme) desires of the ego. They must acknowledge their shadow side in order to be free. Otherwise, the untransformed aspects of their personality will keep them imprisoned.

The Devil is depicted in the Tarot as a crouching goat on a pedestal. Typically, a man and a woman are chained to the pedestal. The Devil is commonly represented as having bat wings and little horns on his head, highlighting his dark nature. However, his hands are human, and they are also free, implying that the pair, or the duality within a person, chooses to be imprisoned by The Devil. It depicts the dark side of our personality, the aspects of ourselves that we are least proud of, or reject, preferring to bury them deep within ourselves. The Tarot cards repeatedly allude to this dark aspect of our nature. You had the first glimpse of it in the form of The Chariot's untamed lions, and the beastly king, the lion, in the Strength card. While the imagery of both previously mentioned cards appears to be perfectly acceptable, even beautiful and majestic, the image of The Devil does not. It is repulsive, greedy and lustful. It is still in the dark since it has not yet been transformed.

The Devil card does not reflect evil in any way. It reflects the dark side of human beings – which is not evil, only in the dark. It forces The Fool to confront the murky, primeval side of himself that is inhibiting his complete transformation by releasing these aspects into the light. When facing the sun, the shadows fall behind. It symbolizes the possibility of releasing oneself from voluntary confinement to unconscious or repressed desires. In a spread, this card represents an imbalanced attachment to a relationship that is not serving our highest good, or being imprisoned by our concerns and extreme desires.

The Devil represents progress and liberation through opting to break free from such attachments. It is a positive card when it appears reversed in a spread, because the chains that bind The Lovers slip off! The arduous process of alchemical transformation is one of separation and reunion, purification and regeneration. Similarly, The Devil's temptations should be neither crushed nor permitted to entirely dominate the personality. Instead, they should be faced and worked through to become balanced. As The Fool accepts his shadow, he develops tolerance and compassion for himself and others. Acceptance replaces prejudice and blame; he realizes that all humans are made up of a mix of good and bad, light and shadow. This realization allows him to be human and embrace his human limitations and feelings. The Devil represents the promise that when barriers are removed, enormous growth and progress can be accomplished.

Upright Meaning: False dependencies on material gains or desires. Buying friendship or love. It represents hidden fears, limitations or restrictive circumstances. Often it indicates delays or difficulties in achieving one's goals. It also represents sexual attraction in the context of relationships – and not love. Moreover, the inability to break from a relationship that does not make you happy or being emotional blackmailed. The Devil symbolizes destructive, obsessive behaviour. A manipulative person who takes advantage, or an egocentric personality. The Devil stands for abuse of power, money, sex or personal charm depending on where it falls in a spread. It can indicate depression if restrictive circumstances have been going on for a while.

Modern Interpretation: Emotional or sexual addiction, abusive violent personality, sex-enslavement or trafficking.

Reversed Meaning: Obstacles or restrictions that have blocked your path are now removed. You can see your way forward. Emotional shortcomings are overcome, and inner truth is uncovered. The ability to see through shallow, materialistic types.

Exercise: The Devil card can encourage you to release self-imposed limitations that you are unaware of. As you place the card on the table, take a look at the image on it. What are your thoughts? Take note of any bothersome feelings or alarm bells that sound in your body. Pay attention to the places in your body where you experience constraints and ask yourself what they are about. Take a thorough look at your life:

- In what ways are you enslaved in your life?
- Are you tangled up in a web of unhealthy attachments?
- Are you acting out of greed and apprehension about monetary loss?
- Are you spending money to secure love and friendship?
- Are you staying in a relationship that you know is bad for you?
- Are you suffocated by material success?
- Are you fascinated with money or with sexual conquests?
- Do you let drugs, alcohol or other vices rule your life?

Turn the card around and look at the reversed image.

- What does it feel like to be free of your own shadow?
- Are you now ready to live a free and independent life?
- What constraints should you remove in order to achieve a sense of independence and liberation?

This may be the most difficult yet liberating exercise. Visit it again if you have found it difficult. But do attempt to write your thoughts and feelings in your Tarot journal. You will thank yourself later for bringing to light your subconscious fears.

THE TOWER

16 – The Tower: Sudden Destruction

After breaking free from the bonds of self-imposed limitations in his inner world, The Fool is struck by a tremendous bolt of lightning from The Tower to clear his external world. All that he has learned and gained thus far is destroyed in order to restore balance on a new level. The moral of this lesson is that one has outgrown rigid structures in their life, and sudden unexpected change is necessary to release any limitations and establish new structures. This can turn out to be a blessing in disguise. Flexibility and modification are key ingredients for a smooth-flowing life. Further transformation is taking place, where the inner and outer manifestation must be congruent – in harmony. If you like, the wisdom of this card is to help The Fool remain aware to modify the life he is creating, and in doing so fulfil his purpose. It unexpectedly disrupts an outgrown life cycle, heralding subsequent development without warning.

The Tower highlights the need to break free from oppressive relationships or patterns of life and set the framework for redesigning one's life by erecting new structures. It takes The Devil's teachings to a new level. The Tower is about external, physical and material losses or damage, and it completely annihilates the personality's ego. Any preconceived assumptions and attitudes he had about his previous world are demolished in order to make place for new ones. A new sense of freedom is arising to assist The Fool in developing a new identity – one of limitless possibilities.

The artwork on the card depicts a 'heavenly' lightning striking the highest part of a tower, causing the building to collapse and dislodging the crown (symbolizing the dominion of spiritual laws over man's). Two figures, a man and a woman signifying dualistic earthly life, fall to their deaths onto the rocks below. The sky is filled with 22 sparks of light, representing the Tarot's 22 Major Arcana cards. The Tower is constructed of bricks on a high rock and signifies man's effort to govern physical reality and reach 'heaven' by erecting tall constructions. The Tower card's symbology represents the destruction of The Fool's worldly illusions: false values and belief systems.

As a result of his encounters with Death and The Devil, he has acknowledged inner struggles, as well as the limitless possibilities he has at his disposal. The Devil has demonstrated the extent of his power, and Death has removed all sense of entitlement from him. The Tower will now destroy remaining outdated assumptions. Divine lightning (the fork of lightning) reaches the unconscious depths to dissipate dark energy and make way for fresh ideas. Change will be more painful if we allow ourselves to become rigid and inflexible. The message is to adjust to the current situation and move on with the flow of time.

Furthermore, The Tower is the only card in the deck that depicts a structure as its subject. The symbols on the other cards are cosmic bodies or figures, human or godlike. The structure represents society, and The Tower represents the totality of its laws and rules. The Fool must find out if his society's values relate to him. Change is the one constant in life, and this violent image represents that.

Upright Meaning: Exhilarating change turns your world upside down. Changes can be disruptive, even violent, but are necessary, promising a positive outcome. Breakup of relationships or lifestyles, financial losses may be incurred; the picture is about going through an unstable phase. It denotes receiving shocking news, sudden revelation, destruction of something corrupt. Depending on where it falls in a reading, it can also indicate sudden changes in health such as a stroke or heart attack, or sudden hospitalisation. Or loss of property, change of residence, loss of job, or separation of relationships.

Modern Interpretation: Sudden awakening, or realization that will change your life. Electricity, communication through the internet, receiving news by quick technology. Kundalini experience, where energy rises up the body to illuminate the mind.

Reversed Meaning: More disruptive and chaotic, need to accept upcoming changes. Not able to withstand pressure, can denote nervous breakdown. You are advised to take less on board. The process of change has already begun; not going with the flow will result in stagnation and more problems. If you are repressing feelings of grief, rage or disappointment, let them go and your life will soon improve.

Exercise: Did you ever experience a violent event, an argument, a sudden change that disrupted your life? Gaze upon the Tower card as you write down your thoughts in your Tarot journal.

What shocked you: the speed with which the event took place, or its aftermath? Cast your mind back to a memory that sticks out, to when the rug seemed to have been pulled from under your feet. How did you feel as you went through the event? How did your life change because of it? What has changed about you or your perspective? How did you participate in making it happen? In hindsight, was it a blessing? What would you do differently if something similar were to happen again? How has your previous experience prepared you?

17 – The Star:
Hope and Inspiration

The Fool sees The Star as a source of optimism and inspiration. It represents a new dawn after the dark tunnel of the inner world. He has learned that through flexibility, his personal resilience grew. Previous lessons taught him to let go of attachments, beliefs and environments that are not conducive to his growth. Continuous 'purification' and rebirthing lessons prepared The Fool to receive his true wishes. He is now ready for further growth, illumination and an easy-flowing life.

This is a cosmic card uniting 'heaven and Earth'. Kneeling beside a pool of water, naked, the lady of intuition and inspiration symbolizes the spiritual truth of thoughts and feelings. Her right foot is in the pool, signifying her connection to free-flowing feelings. Her left foot is planted on the ground, transmitting her healing intuitive abilities to the physical world. She pours life's waters from two cups, one in each hand (what card does this imagery remind you of?), implying that deeper purification of feelings is constantly required to be inspired onto the right path. The sun is represented by the golden cup, while the moon is represented by the silver cup, symbolizing the equilibrium maintained between yang and yin (activity and receptivity, respectively, logic and intuition). Seven silver stars shine above the naked maiden, symbolizing the seven cosmic bodies of classical astrology: Sun, Moon, Mercury, Venus, Mars, Jupiter and Saturn.

The sky above is dominated by a huge, bright star with eight points. The eight-pointed star signifies the balance of opposing forces (Justice. The Star also carries the vibration of the number 8, $17 = 1 + 7 = 8$) in the cosmos (above as below). The soil around the pool appears to be fertile. A lone tree stands atop a mountain behind The Star, symbolizing the goal to be achieved by The Fool's mystical quest: to unite Spirit and matter. The tree represents being well-rooted in earth to receive pure, exalted ideas and heavenly guidance (telepathy). The Star is linked to intuition, meditation, and nature's hidden aspects. The Star figure is inspired by the golden star in the heavens. She receives life energy from the golden star and transmits it to the Earth below, inspiring humankind.

Because The Star transmutes thoughts and emotions, it represents optimism, inspiration and excellent health by presenting a heavenly figure on Earth. When a positive mind-set is maintained, The Fool is connected to higher guidance, and 'inspired' to realize (make real) a well-balanced, fulfilling life as well as a healthy body on the material ground. This card exudes positivity and healing in every way. Although it is a night card, it is a bright and hopeful one symbolizing that no matter how dark and difficult times are, there is always hope for a new dawn and a brighter future. It's a message of hope, love and spiritual guidance, as well as happiness and fulfilment.

Upright Meaning: This card represents optimism and ascension to higher spiritual levels through emotional experiences. Hope, wisdom, adventure, travel, healing, a visionary, imagination, inspiration. This is a great time to reflect on what is important. There is hope for the future, and healing is possible. You are ready to both give and receive (heavenly) love.

Modern Interpretation: Professional sportspeople and performers who are focused and in control of their minds; people who are telepathic. Divine inspiration. Expansion of personalities and abilities. Telepathic communication (with different worlds).

Reversed Meaning: Pessimism and lack of judgement due to muddled feelings and thoughts (lack of inspiration), feeling a sense of failure, losing hope, depression, limited vision, and doubts. Mistrusting inner guidance, suffering a creative block, lack of motivation.

Modern interpretation: A person who can excel at sports: a healthy body in a well-balanced mind, positive mind-set that can

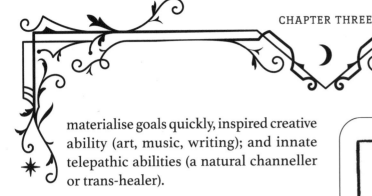

materialise goals quickly, inspired creative ability (art, music, writing); and innate telepathic abilities (a natural channeller or trans-healer).

Exercise: Take out the Temperance card and the Star card and place them side by side in front of you. Familiarise yourself with the imagery of each card, then write down any similarities and differences. Is The Star pouring water between the two cups in the same deliberate manner as Temperance does? Do you think this is significant, and what does it imply?

THE MOON

18 – The Moon: Hidden Wisdom

The Fool's quest for enlightenment is due to end. He is still travelling in the celestial realm of The Moon, representing yet another cycle of change and development. He realizes that there is still much to learn from the 'heavens'! He had a brief but wonderful respite with The Star after the dark series of cards in the underworld, only to realize that the next card, The Moon, is another sombre card. The Fool finds it difficult to preserve his emotions and see clearly while under the influence of the changing phases of the moon. Confusion, illusion, deception and a lack of clarity are all things that The Fool learns to deal with and overcome. His mind is not at ease, as hidden influences are at work. The Moon symbolizes subconscious memories. To be totally aware, The Fool must awaken his subconscious mind and trust his innate senses.

The night image appears to be identical to The Star at first glance, but closer inspection reveals that it is not as tranquil as it appears. For instance, there is not a human figure in sight – only The Moon's changing faces and the darkness that ebbs and flows, representing mood swings. In the foreground, a crayfish, representing innermost fears and anxieties pushing their way to the top of our awareness, is attempting to crawl out of the waters, only to be pushed back by the two animals on the shore: a dog and a wolf, who are howling at The Moon. The path between the two animals leads to the two pillars in the background, representing duality of the unconscious and conscious. Bringing unconscious memories to the light leads to a path of total awareness. It's like present-day childhood worries reappearing in adulthood, still causing fear and anxiety, despite the fact that rationally they may not be recognized.

The crayfish will remain under water until The Fool recognizes that it must be allowed to rise and leave the murky waters. This pool is not the healing waters of The Star, but the muddled waters of repressed memories and thoughts.

The Moon represents the ephemeral, vague, and ambiguous character of emotions. She is the goddess of dreams, fantasy, imagination and unconscious thoughts. By comparison, The High Priestess represents the unconscious wisdom revealed in a regulated manner; The Moon represents the unpredictable and uncontrollable surfacing of unconscious thoughts, memories and intuition. These attributes must be transformed into wisdom to be assimilated into The Fool's personality. This is why The Moon usually indicates an unpredictably fluctuating and changing phase in a reading. It denotes ambiguity, if not deception, and suggests that a solution to the problem might be found through the unconscious, namely dreams, rather than logic and reason.

The Moon is regarded as the mistress of the night, the womb where men go to rest, sleep and dream every night. It rules the unconscious – the realm of dreams, fancies and imagination. Ideas or revelations received through the unconscious are difficult to explain or put into words logically, compared to the Sun, where inspiration and drive are clear. The Moon reigns over subtly inspired creativity, where bits of information are revealed over a period of time, like the cycles of the Moon. If you like, a gestation period is necessary for the idea to grow. In this aspect, The Moon represents matters that are 'not yet revealed', secrets and pregnancies – all of which will come to fruition in time. Once the idea takes shape, it will be revealed under the light of the Sun, or given birth to.

As The Fool transforms, the unconscious must be paid attention to. Dreams are likely to change as he becomes more self-aware, because dreams are the language of the unconscious mind. Once the business of the day winds down, and The Fool prepares to enter the womb of the night, the unconscious begins to release what it needs to bring into the light of his awareness. At night, The Fool is not distracted by the demands of physical reality and can perceive the soft communication of the unconscious. This card is also about unifying the unconscious and unconscious, implying that we are

likely to suffer mood swings, or irksome anxiety if subconscious memories and beliefs are not worked with.

Upright Meaning: The Moon is related to the night and represents darkness, confusion and a lack of clarity. However, as Moon cycles change over time, the truth will be revealed through intuition or dreams. Psychic impressions, information from dreams. Unexpected change in a situation or feelings. Need for sleep. Rely on self. Mood swings. Emotional changes. Harnessed imagination producing creative output. This card indicates hidden issues, unspoken anxieties and guidance through dreams.

Reversed Meaning: Self-deception and self-destruction phase due to being misled by false intuition or illusion. Fear of unknown, hallucinations, not seeing problems in true light. Deception from friends. Negative illusions. Practical considerations take precedence over intuition or hunches at this time. Do not take any risks. Instead, work with the reality and the facts you have until the turmoil is over. Do not be concerned if you suspect someone is working behind your back. Their plans will be exposed soon. Could also indicate miscarriage or false pregnancy, depending on the other cards in the spread.

Exercise: At night, place The Moon card under your pillow as a message to your subconscious mind to release to your attention what you need to address. Write a statement in your own words, verbalising this request to your unconscious in your Tarot journal: "Please give me a dream that reveals what I need to address or resolve." Upon waking, write what you feel as well as any fragments you remember of your dream.

With practice, you will begin to remember more of your dreams, and be able to work with your unconscious in your sleep. Working with your dreams clarifies the language of your unconscious and reflects your conscious growth and awareness. Over time, you will notice how the themes of your dreams change, as you bring more of your fears and anxieties to the light. You can also ask your unconscious to help you find solutions to problems or ideas for creative projects. Date your dreams to observe how they evolve.

THE SUN

19 – The Sun:
Success, Prosperity and Joy

After emerging from underneath the light of The Moon, The Fool basks in the radiance of The Sun. The cobwebs of confusion and uncertainty dissolve as The Sun rises above The Fool. Instead, he experiences renewed energy and drive as well as clarity of thought. His ideas will come to fruition under The Sun, which promises a new cycle of renewal, success and happiness. The Fool returns to the faith and openness of a child; his confidence is renewed. Success and expansion have come because of his efforts in overcoming the challenges of this mindful transformational process so far.

The Sun has a longer cycle than the Moon, which was depicted in the preceding card. This represents long-term plans and ambitions that will require more time to be realized. It also represents the near future rather than the immediate future. However, we see The Fool in his child-like form, happily and effortlessly riding a white horse without holding the reins. This symbolizes the result of implementing the spiritual enlightenment he achieved in the material world and effortless success, as the sunflowers on the wall behind him grow toward The Sun. He is carrying a crimson banner, suggesting renewed zeal and optimism for the future. The rising sun in the blue sky sends her warmth up to the sunflowers on the wall, which represent not only renewed energy but also vitality, longevity, endless creative flow, sexual drive and vigour.

The message of the card appears to be that in the mystical journey for unity with spiritual understanding, innocence and purity are essential; efforts are rewarded by success and abundant creative energy.

Upright Meaning: This is one of the Tarot's most cheerful cards. In a reading, it represents joy, happiness and success in material gain, as well as good health. It also suggests that now is the time to explore your creativity and put into action any projects that desire to grow in the future. Now is the time for expansion and success. Happiness, vitality. Better finances, enjoying work and good health are indicated when The Sun appears in a reading.

Moreover, it indicates a person with great talent and skills that will be recognized. And also, the possibility of moving to a warm country, or significant meetings connected with overseas. Moreover, successful happy marriages or committed relationships, and the birth of a child are indicated. This is the start of a rewarding cycle in your life, and the best time to take advantage of opportunities presented to you. It is an invitation to live life to the fullest.

Reversed Meaning: The Sun reversed is never a bad card, but it has fewer positive qualities than when it appears upright in a reading. It implies that right now your future does not look as bright as it can be, or that you are not trying as hard as you can to achieve the success you desire. It can symbolize overconfidence, vanity and arrogance that blocks success, depending on the overall spread. Also, difficulties in partnerships, or worries about children can be implied – look for neighbouring cards.

Exercise: Allow yourself to connect with the attributes of The Sun card by gazing into it for a few minutes. Study the symbolism as you bring your focus to the four sunflowers growing effortlessly toward The Sun. What ideas, projects or goals do you desire to materialize in the coming 12 months, represented by the solar cycle? List your ideas and number them. Now look at your list, and ask yourself, "Will I be happy if I achieve number 1, but not number 2?" If your answer is yes, then number 1 on your list is your priority. Continue down the list until you are happy with your priorities. For example, would you be happy if you achieved number 3 but not number 2? Presenting your mind with this question helps you clarify your priorities.

Once you have identified the priority of your goals, list actions that you can take right now, no matter how small, that represent planting seeds to grow into the future. Next, draw a 12-month plan or table in your journal, and assign one goal to each quarter, giving yourself three months to achieve or implement actions for each goal in that quarter. Congratulations! You have now devised a plan of action to manifest your goals.

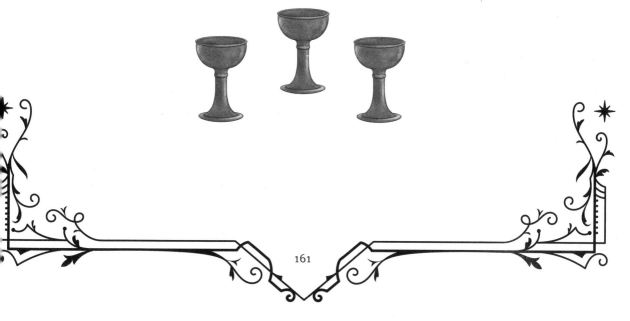

JUDGEMENT

of Judgement, which calls for spiritual rebirth and healing of his psyche, after being re-energized by the Sun's light. He goes through a complete transformation and is resurrected as his true self. He shall rise from the ashes like a phoenix. This card reflects The Fool's final evaluation regarding his development, wisdom and maturity.

The image of the Judgement card conjures up the most dreadful vision of judgement day. To the sound of the trumpet calling them to a better (way of) life, graves open and bodies emerge, raising their hands toward the angel above. This card is also known as The Resurrection or The Angel in different Tarot decks. The picture of the dead rising represents an expected new cycle beginning as the old one comes to an end. The hands of the naked resurrected are raised in joy at the next cycle to come, indicating some relief at shedding their worldly possessions and the limiting hang-ups of material personality – the final death of the past.

Extremes are evaluated. Excessive arrogance, like self-deprecation, must be brought into balance to ascend to the higher wisdom of living. The resurrected dead are undergoing spiritual rebirth. Judgement represents reaping what we have sown. The Fool must accept responsibility for the outcomes of the

20 – Judgement: Total Transformation

Every action we take in life has long-term ramifications. After being stripped of his ego (Death) and his possessions (Tower), The Fool is ready to be reborn to a new beginning, his true and larger purpose. He is now able to welcome the trumpet decisions he made along the Tarot journey. This is one of life's most important lessons: life is primarily shaped by the decisions we make, and we live with the consequences of our decisions.

Notice the snow-topped mountains on the horizon, indicating the ultimate spiritual goal of enlightenment. This is not a card of ending, for the child in the foreground faces the mountains in the background, signifying that he is looking forward to the future. Although the card looks ominous, Judgement in a reading marks the end of a karmic cycle, indicates a 'clean slate' and sends a message: "You have paid your dues; it's a time of rejoicing and renewal." Like the child in The Sun card, this child, the resurrected Fool, embraces the wisdom to come.

Upright Meaning: It denotes an inescapable positive shift, even though it appears to be unfavourable. Reward for past effort, re-evaluation, responsibility, outcome, resolution, acceptance. New lease of life, transformation, major decisions, changes, healing has taken place. Spiritual awakening. Death of old self. Death of previous lifestyle.

Reversed Meaning: Stagnation, refusal to accept changes. Delays in completion, success or achievement, overdue awakening – the old ways are no longer working for you!

Exercise: Judgement carries the number 20, which is the number 2 amplified. Find a quiet time when you can carefully consider the symbolism of this card. Cast your eyes around the image. What details do you react to most? Contemplate if you are ready to let go of something, to rise to better understanding, more wisdom and a renewed life. What false views or goals do you need to let go of? Are you willing to engage your true, trusting, child-like self and shed false beliefs you identify with? If anything is possible, what is the one thing you truly yearn for, before anything else in life? What do you need to let go of before you can live that goal? Judgement is the final purification stage, like the eye of the needle. To leap onto an elevated enlightened state of living, like The Fool, you must re-evaluate who and what you are, and the decisions you have made. What could be better in your life? How did your past decisions make things worse for you?

Take your time and try not to interrupt your writing. Keep writing until you feel your unconscious has released what remained deeply hidden until now. Do you feel a sense relief and renewal as you

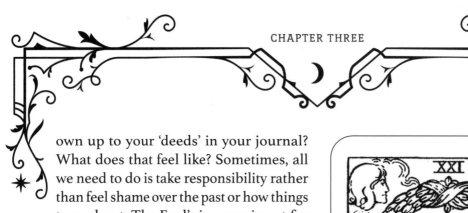

own up to your 'deeds' in your journal? What does that feel like? Sometimes, all we need to do is take responsibility rather than feel shame over the past or how things turned out. The Fool's journey is not for the light-hearted. However, all it takes is accepting responsibility for our decisions and understanding how we 'ended up here'. Wisdom is what truly empowers The Fool.

21 – The World: Total Integration

This is the final stage of The Fool's development into his full potential. The Fool floats like a foetus amidst the now-circling oval wreath in The World. This is the concluding card of The Fool's adventure. In contrast to his image as The Fool, card number zero, the small wreath over his hat at the beginning expanded to the large wreath he floats in, implying mystical existence. He succeeded in uniting his dualistic nature, having stripped himself of all false identities and ego personalities. The purple ribbon of spiritual wisdom covers his genitals, implying that his instinctive desire no longer controls him. Now he has a female appearance, similar to the figure in the Star card, representing his truthful (naked) non-dualistic nature, where male and female are united. Attaining equilibrium is symbolized by the two white wands the figure is holding and the four symbols at each corner of the image, where number 4 represents stability. He has successfully attained this state.

The four corner figures represent the four elements and four seasons. We have a complete circle in which all the minor cycles are linked to this long cycle of renewal. The four seasons also indicate that The Fool is aware of nature's changing cycles, and how other events are governed by cycles too. They represent the four aspects of his nature as a man, which he is now in command of: personality, instincts and desires, as well as his spiritual nature. The earthly head of a man in the clouds depicts winter and air elements, both symbolizing the personality. The bull in the bottom left-hand corner represents spring and the earth element,

denoting earthly desires and fertility. The lion represents summer and the element of fire, denoting primal instincts; and the eagle represents autumn and the element of water, signifying his spiritual nature.

In a reading, The World denotes the successful completion of a period of achievement and the beginning of a cycle of harmony and fulfilment. The Fool has totally blended with nature and the cosmos. He is one with all. The World symbolizes The Fool's past experiences, all of life's cycles, including beginnings and endings, losses and gains, separation and unification. He has bridged the gap between his spiritual and human self, transcending the duality of human nature. The end of these transformative cycles is announced by the trumpet of Judgement. The Fool has gained wisdom through understanding the various stages of the challenges he encountered. Actualisation of the self is now complete. Fulfilment and wholeness bring joy that exceeds that of The Sun. The World is his!

However, the cycles of life are not over. The World marks the beginning of a new cycle, presenting The Fool as a foetus who is about to be birthed – albeit on a different level. Prepare for cycles of growth, expansion and self-mastery, and all that comes with it. The next journey can be an enjoyable one now that The Fool has gained all the spiritual knowledge and wisdom.

Upright Meaning: In a reading, this card denotes the completion of a significant cycle or stage of life. Achievement and recognition are due. It signifies success, fame, harmonious living, fulfilment, receiving an award or the next cycle of expansion. It is time to celebrate and embrace recognition. It also announces a significant promotion or beneficial job change.

Modern Interpretation: Performing on stage, publishing, successful art exhibitions, expanded online presence, extensive travel, intelligent wisdom, further expansion of awareness and self-mastery.

Reversed Meaning: Like The Sun card, The World reversed is never a bad omen. However, it denotes stagnation, or refusal to accept acknowledgements or expansion, delays in completion, success or achievements at the moment.

Meditation: Do you have big dreams that you shy away from, believing they are too big to realize? If you are drawn to this card, it indicates that you have great creative potential, which you must 'give birth' to.

It may impact 'the world', although you do not believe so! Meditate on The World card, imbibing its vibrations of joy, success and fulfilment. Feel the relief that follows achieving a worthy accomplishment as you breathe out. Let go of any inhibitions about your talents and abilities, breathe in success and acknowledge your creative

work. Feel the creative buzzing in the palm of your hands. Enjoy watching the audience delighting at receiving your work, supporting you and sharing your success.

Make this image feel real; see it in high definition. Wave a purple sash in joy at the audience as you embrace your success and the fruits of your creative labour. You deserve it! Notice the smile on your face and the joy in your heart. How does that feel? Describe your feelings now in your Tarot journal. Before you end your writing session, ask yourself, if you were to start a creative project or business, what would it be? This is your gift to the world. Make it happen. Your judgement is the only thing holding you back.

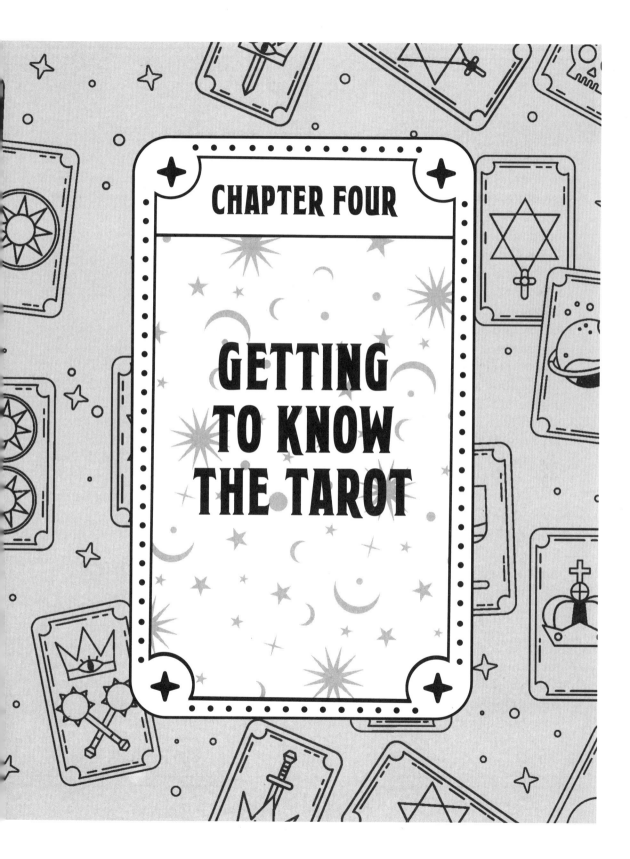

CHAPTER FOUR

GETTING TO KNOW THE TAROT

When getting to know your cards, it is valuable to contemplate the meanings of discrete components that create the overall picture on each card. Having shared the journey of The Fool so far, you might already be aware of the repeated themes, imagery and symbols in the Tarot. Mountains, for example, can represent major challenges, whereas rocks or hills can represent modest ones. Take a look at The Lovers card (number 6), for example. The first thing you see is a couple standing with a mountain in the background. The image suggests that cooperation, collaboration or a balance between the female and male aspects is required to conquer this obstacle and arrive at their goal. Your mind will link that interpretation with the numerological meaning of 6.

Animals frequently represent instincts, animal nature or desires. Consider the Strength and Devil cards, for example. Strength (number II, a master number) depicts a figure in command of a beast, in this case a lion, representing the wisdom of controlling lower instincts. Mind over matter is attained in this situation. What impulses or addictions are represented by the Devil card, depicting a beast with horns? This image demonstrates how habits and desires may enslave a person. Furthermore, water is also a universal symbol of feelings

and emotions. As you review the cards, group together all the pictures with water in them. Just notice how the water element is expressed on each card, as well as what overall picture and meaning are conveyed. Birds can represent ideas as well as spiritual goals. Can you spot Tarot cards that have symbols of birds? And the colours used in the Tarot, in addition to the specific symbols, have meaning.

Below are highlights of the most significant symbols and colours. You might find this helpful before you decide on a Tarot deck. Images, symbols and colours are important in Tarot cards. Images trigger the imagination and express what words cannot fully depict. Imagination sparks off intuition. As you interact with several decks or images, you will get to know which deck works best for you. More on that later in this chapter.

Tarot Themes

The Tarot symbolizes cycles of self-development that are transformative and alchemical in nature. They are designed to continuously 'recycle' and purify anything that holds us back from expressing our true infinite and creative nature. There are major dramatic cycles as well as minor ones, as change is continuous. To gain the necessary wisdom to create a fulfilling life, it is essential to fine-tune the human instrument, shedding any false desires or attachments that distract you from achieving what is possible. Fulfilment comes through maintaining balance and reconciling conflicts within the self, as well as harmonising with the exterior world.

The Tarot imparts a great deal of knowledge, expressed as images; that is why symbols are important. Nowadays, there are myriad themes in the Tarot decks. However, whichever deck you choose to work with, notice which symbols are featured and what they trigger in your mind as you study each card. In this book, the Rider-Waite-Smith deck is chosen for the abundance of symbols to help you develop your intuition. Historically, it is also the first fully illustrated deck of the Tarot.

COLOURS

Red: Earthly desires, creative drive, sensual and sexual cravings, instincts, power and authority are all represented by red. Red represents blood, life, desire and the planet Mars. It symbolizes vitality, strength, energy, sex, passion and a healthy body. It denotes the yang aspect of doing, accomplishing, building and producing. They have a strong presence in The Magician, The Emperor,

The Hierophant, and Justice. The majority of these figures symbolize the male side, which leads, controls, constructs, and has power or authority. It emphasizes the creative power that propels the universe and humans. It symbolizes material or worldly life. It is frequently balanced with the colour white, which represents how earthly achievements are attained harmoniously through spiritual inspiration or cooperation.

White: The second colour to consider is white, which represents spiritual understanding attained through self-awareness. It symbolizes illumination, daylight, joy, openness and enlightenment. The Magician card depicts man's actual essence.

A white garment is worn beneath his red robes. The Empress' garment is made out of red flowers on a white background, representing the material manifestation of creating with spirit. If she is hiding a pregnancy, the child she is about to bring into the world is a Spirit child. The inspiration for any business concept or creative effort is the same. The lush landscape surrounding her reflects the never-ending cycle of creation. The Hierophant wears a red robe with white marks over his chest, conveying spiritual insight to the mortal audience in front of him.

Tarot
Rider Waite
1910

Illustrated
Pamela Colman Smith

THE MAGICIAN

THE HIGH PRIESTESS

THE EMPRESS

THE FOOL

JUSTICE

THE HERMIT

THE WHEEL OF
FORTUNE

THE DEVIL

THE TOWER

THE STAR

*Figure 11 The
Major Arcana*

The Chariot's arms are white, suggesting acts and abilities inspired by Spirit. The flag on the angel's trumpet is red and white, symbolizing the resolution of Earth/Spirit conflict; Death is riding a white horse; Temperance's angel is dressed in white robes; and the egg-shaped wreath in the World card is ornamented with red ribbons, balanced by the white wands in the figure's hands – the greatest expression of the delight felt as a result of creative work. All cards with white are examples that convey heavenly involvement in the material world, emphasizing the importance of uniting Spirit and materialism, or transmuting opposites to create an ideal 'heavenly' outcome.

Yellow: Is the next dominating colour, representing intellectual wisdom or mind mastery. It appears as the bright background behind The Fool, The Magician, The Empress, The Lovers, The Chariot, and Strength. In The Tower, the bolt of lightning represents waking up or enlightening the intellect. Yellow is also the prominent colour of the major star in The Star card, The Moon, and The Sun, as well as the hair colour of the female characters and the Judgement card's angel (yellow hair symbolizing an illuminated head, or mind, through receiving spiritual thoughts). Heavenly planets can influence the mind, just as our thinking has the ability to influence what we create and the kind of connections we build. A well-balanced mind is necessary for living a fulfilling worldly existence.

Orange: This colour is not immediately obvious, but it is significant, continuously alluding to controlling man's sexual desires. The inside lining of The Fool's sleeves is orange at the start of his journey, maybe signifying the luxury or earthly links to materialism he will relinquish. The mountain behind The Lovers, their ultimate goal, is in orange; the beast that Strength is taming is orange; The Devil has orange skin; the dog howling at The Moon is in orange; sunflowers in The Sun card (and the Queen of Wands) are orange; and finally, the sash or banner The Sun card is waving is orange.

Orange is also the colour of sensuality and physical pleasures, or pleasures that necessitate the use of one's body! Spirituality or spiritual wisdom does not prevent sex; rather, it combines pleasure-seeking with wisdom. Perhaps the orange flashes in the angel's hair (of Judgement) indicate that corporeal life continues as The Fool is beckoned to a better life in the next cycle. Finally, The World card is grounded or stabilized in concerns of physical pleasure. The bull and lion are orange, as is the eagle's beak. It represents pride, ego, splendour, ambition, impulse, spontaneity and vitality.

Blue: In the Tarot, blue represents the colour of The Moon. It signifies the goddess inside, the feminine aspect of intuition, emotions, inner life and psychic ability. Moreover, perceiving inspirational wisdom through dreams, psychic abilities, the natural cycles of rest needed by man – night-time, where imagination and intuition peak and the mind receives hidden or secret knowledge from the heavens. There is a healing, soft quality to blue.

Purple: Purple is used mindfully in the Tarot. It is the traditional colour of royalty; it denotes nobility, pride, justice and the upper order of spiritual authorities. We notice it twice: once in the shawl of The Lovers' angel, embracing the couple with heavenly wisdom; and again, as the ribbon or sash spiralling around The World card's figure, signifying that spiritual wisdom is the goal of earthly endeavours.

Grey: Grey is usually the colour of storm clouds, mourning, bereavement, sadness or despair. In the Tarot, it reflects wisdom gained by experience, and reconciliation. It symbolizes spiritual wisdom manifested, as seen in the figure of The Hermit. It also indicates that spiritual metamorphosis is taking place in the body or skin colour of the Sun figure, as well as in the resurrected people in the Judgement card.

Grey is on the duality pillars behind The Empress, the chariot of The Chariot card, the background of The Hierophant and The Hanged Man, the thrones of The Emperor and Justice, the clouds beneath The Lovers' angel, and behind the bull and lion in The World.

Green: Green represents vegetation and a rich, bountiful existence. Hope, serenity, fertility, growth, safety, security, health, youth and abundant life force are all represented by it.

Black: Black is a striking colour that represents the card's important themes. It's like a stop sign that says, "Halt and pay attention!" It balances white (Spirit) and appears whenever the duality theme is represented, such as the pillars The High Priestess sits between, the two lions of The Chariot, and the Death card, where the steed is white but the Death figure is dressed in black, holding a black flag with a white outline of a rose. Black is also used to represent authority, as shown in the Knight of Pentacles, who is riding a black steed. It appears to be the end of a cycle and the start

of a new one. All of these are tiny nuances that, when observed, might spark your imagination and lead you to the correct interpretation.

Exercise: These are the eight prominent colours used in the Rider-Waite-Smith deck (in alphabetical order):

Black: Transformation, or the end of a cycle and beginning of a new one

Blue: Intuition, subconscious, psychic perception

Green: Growth

Grey: Spiritual experience or major turning point or transformation

Orange: Sensuality, pleasure, primal influences

Purple: Unification and balance of spirit and material

Red: Inspiration, drive, ideas, physical body

White: Inspirational guidance

Yellow: Intellect, mental activities, victory

Make a list of the various qualities these colours evoke in you. Then, using heavy paper or cardboard, cut out nine rectangles in a size convenient to you. Create your own colour deck by colouring each rectangle with one of the eight colours. Shuffle the cards and chose one, placing it face down on a surface at the start of the day and returning to it at the end. Turn it around and consider whether the colour meaning corresponds to how your day went. Have fun with this exercise; it will assist you in tuning in to the energy of Tarot colours. You may also modify this exercise to work with the colours of your favourite Tarot deck.

Moreover, whenever you are going through an uncertain phase, or starting a new phase or cycle and want to understand what is going on or the underlying influences, a 'colour' reading activates your intuition and provides insights you need to complete the picture. Shuffle your cards while you think about your day, select one card and place it face up. It may just give you the insight you seek!

NATURE & LANDSCAPES

Most Major Arcana cards represent a natural scene, emphasizing that the goal is to live a better life on Earth – it is a direct relationship to earthly existence, indicating the visible effect of man's actions.

Landscapes: Furthermore, the terrain frequently depicts a season, which provides further information. Consider the landscape of the figure, or the event taking place – as in the Minor cards – when looking at a Tarot card, whether major or minor. The landscape will frequently tell you whether it is the season of development and expansion (spring), joy and happiness (summer), deliberate strategy (fall), or tangible results (winter). They illustrate the seasonal cycles that govern nature and, as a result, govern man's actions.

Nature has a deeper meaning. On the one hand, it represents that there is always a proper time to act based on the 'seasonal' cycle. Furthermore, nature demonstrates the visible effect of our labour. In other words, we reap what we sow. The latter is the main key to transformation, owning up to one's actions in order to bring them back into harmony. What The Fool goes through in life is not by chance; it is a direct outcome of his thoughts, feelings and deeds. Moreover, the figures themselves in the Tarot are part of the element of earth. Health, or a well body, is essential to complete life's journey.

Moreover, consider the age of the figure in the card in relation to the landscape around it in each of the 78 Tarot cards. Note what age they are and how are they acting.

In the Five of Wands, although the figures are all holding Wands, the terrain is arid and not smooth, reflecting the trouble or conflict they are in. They are young and fighting – as youths do, when wisdom is lacking! You will find a correlation between all these elements in the illustration, particularly in the Minor Arcana, where we see the developmental stages of The Fool's four personality aspects as he grows: his body and ideas, emotions, thoughts and the results of his actions.

Water: Whereas the soil element (of landscapes) is solid (fixed) and depicts the direct results of actions, water is fluid and depicts emotions and sentiments. Water is depicted as flowing rivers or streams, lakes or seas. It can also be transmuted by pouring it between two cups, as in Temperance and The Star. It represents man's fluctuating emotions, which are likewise impacted by heavenly bodies, as in The Moon and The Star, providing a direct link between the elements of nature (the environment) and man. It is also present under The Empress' feet and hinted at by The High Priestess' flowing robes, connecting intuition and the feminine aspect of water. It is also beneath The Emperor's throne – a subtle indication that logic sits on a throne founded on feminine intuition, balancing logic and

intuition (however, not the Justice card, where pure reason is required).

It is also present as the river The Chariot must bridge before claiming triumph, as well as the barrier between Death and a new life. Water represents a fluid part of human nature that man must balance in order to progress to the next stage of his evolution. What is beneath the waters – the subconscious – is also significant. When you next work with Tarot cards, take note of whether the waters are stagnant or flowing. Are they clear or muddled? Is the sea choppy or calm? In a reading, all of these hint at a person's mental state. Emotions must be balanced by making the unconscious conscious. Water is often featured in the Swords suit as well, denoting how motions affect one's mental state. And the reverse is true, symbolizing aspects of how the mind and emotions dictate actions; all must be reconciled if man is to create heaven on Earth.

Mountains: In the Tarot, significant goals are symbolized by mountains, lesser ones by hills. They are often depicted in the background, as a goal to be attained by The Fool – the purpose of the passage or lesson he must overcome, if you like. Mountains can snow-topped, indicating the ultimate objective of growth; or nearby, denoting a goal that can be reached. For example, in the Two of Swords, the female figure sitting blindfolded, holding two swords, can't decide on a course of action because she is so afraid. The hill behind her indicates that all she needs to do is to *decide* and her stalemate would be over – the goal can be reached. Mountaintops covered with white snow may represent a long-term spiritual goal as well. It is these small details that make the Tarot an effective visual tool to trigger the imagination and intuition of the reader.

Gardens, forests and vegetation: Another motif in the Tarot is growing nature, which is especially evident in the Minor cards that depict the nature of each element. Nature sets the scene for each Tarot character. It explains the figure's impact, skills and abilities, or the lesson behind that stage of personal development. The Empress, for example, represents the capacity for, and the cycles of, creation represented by the four-season vegetation around her. Flowers and plants grow in the direction of the sun. The Tarot does not show punishment, but rather the outcomes of life as you awaken and grow (or choose not to!). Even The Hanged Man is shown undergoing a change while hanging upside down, but the wood from which he is suspended is flowering

with vegetation. His suspended state is beneficial to his own development.

Cards in the Major Arcana that lack flora, fruits or vegetation represent personal or spiritual growth. The absence of vegetation or nature allows the viewer to focus on the nature of the card itself, or the significance of this stage of development or transformation. The Hermit, Death and The Devil, The Tower and Judgement are all excellent illustrations of this. These cards do not show The Fool's accomplishments, but rather what he has to learn. He must take breaks from time to time to think on his life (The Hermit) before continuing. He must let go of false ideals and identities (Death and Judgement); he must let go of any addictions to material temptations (The Devil); and he must not be arrogant or take anything for granted (The Tower). The images are dark, stark or dramatic, emphasizing the significance of these pivotal times in one's own development.

Flowers: Three flowers only are depicted in the Rider-Waite-Colman deck: roses, lilies and sunflowers. Pomegranates and grapes (particularity in the Pentacles suit), as fruits, are also featured, symbolizing fertility and wealth, respectively (can you spot other fruits in the Minor cards? Note your observations in your Tarot journal).

Roses are often red, symbolizing passion, drive, initiation of inspired ideas and an abundance of creativity (the potential). White lilies depict a spiritual aspect to a situation, pure emotion, or the nature of the figure depicted in the card, symbolizing that creative ideas are inspired by Spirit. Often, they are small details on flower garlands, or in the foreground of the card's illustration, such as The Magician, where red roses and white lilies together symbolize the balance of thought and desire, or head and heart.

Consider The Two of Cups for instance. It is the male who is wearing a wreath of red roses on his head, symbolizing his passion, vigour, physical body and strength; all are masculine attributes he is offering his bride-to-be (his sleeves are white). Notice the presence of white lilies only in The Six of Cups, indicating happiness but also *pure* delight and innocence experienced when with childhood friends. The Fool, at the beginning of his journey, is holding a white rose, denoting the purity of his soul and intentions (notice the white dog, his best friend). In general, this red and white combination indicates that lilies are the creative thought and inspiration, and that the rose is manifestation. Together they represent unconditional love from Spirit, or unconditional love between two people that is beyond physical attraction.

Exercise: Set aside some time when you are not distracted and look at your Major cards first. Place them all in front of you and think about each one separately. Which ones have flowers, what are those flowers, and what do you think they indicate in relation to the theme of the card? Next, put each Minor Arcana suit in front of you, one at a time, keeping a record of the flowers (or fruits) you see pictured in each suit. Describe your thoughts on what they signify in relation to the suit.

OBJECTS

Objects that a figure holds, or is using, have a significance, adding depth to the meaning of the card. For example, crowns depict authority, having reached a degree of mastery, and the ability to govern and lead. Below are some of the notable objects in the Tarot.

Robes: Tarot figures' robes are fascinating! They wrap or envelop each figure in its prominent traits and attributes, completing their significance and what each card represents. To visually convey these features, much detail has gone into them. When viewing images of any Tarot deck, analyze what they are wearing not in terms of fashion, but rather the 'lifestyle' of the person in question. Their clothing would reflect what the figures had accomplished, who they are, and what aspects of human personality they represent.

Images activate imagination, and imagination opens intuition; therefore, visual interpretation of the Tarot is significant. The Queen of Swords, for example, is wearing a blue cloak with clouds, in contrast to her gown, which is a dismal grey colour (the mind is always in connection with Spirit and needs to be transformed or kept in check) with orange trim. Try it right now; what do you believe this imagery represents?

ACE OF SWORDS

Her crown and the sword in her hand, on the one hand, indicate that she is the Queen of Swords. Her cape, however, indicates that she rules over the domain of the mind, as represented by the shifting or floating clouds against the blue sky; and the orange trim indicates that, contrary to her stern facial expression, she does feel compassion, has feelings and enjoys pleasures or sensuality (in measure, however). There is a stream behind her throne, which adds an aspect of sentiment and intuition to this queen, but her decision is to be attentive, to rule fairly by reason, but to be ready to act whenever necessary.

Crown: The crown also represents the figure's 'crowning' skill or ability – the source of their capacity, skill, drive or sphere of sovereignty. A crown is worn on the 7th Chakra, The Crown, symbolizing the mind's sovereignty of matter. It is also the centre of receiving inspiration from Spirit. In the Tarot, there are at least 17 crowns, and no two crowns are the same! Notice how each crown is also decorated with other objects. For example, the crown on The Tower card signifies human rule or triumph over the Earth, as well as worldly achievement. The Tower is located on a high mountaintop, which serves as another emblem for the world's kingdoms. The lightning strikes the crown, a symbol of human glory or, indeed, arrogance, and it crashes back to Earth, along with

the people flung from the Tower by the bolt of lightning. What man establishes, believing it to be permanent, turns out to be actually transient.

That is a main wisdom of the Tarot: be mindful of how and what you create. Other crowns are presented as laurel wreaths, normally if the event depicted shows a triumph, in a Minor cycle, and over a great challenge. Usually, the authority of the figure depicted is less than that of a King or Queen – for example, the Six of Wands, or the female in The Lovers card, the Strength card, and the happily dancing maidens of the Three of Cups. Laurel wreaths or garlands as crowns tend to have a celebratory feel, rather than a Major achievement or authority (although, in the case of Strength, her crown is further enforced by the infinity sign over her head, indicating infinite possibilities of channelling spirt energy for beneficial use on Earth).

Crowns are decorated with flowers, reflecting the drive or vigour of the monarch, and their wealth and abundance if they are bejewelled (The Emperor, Justice). Sometimes they have hidden geometric shapes on them as well, like the crown of Justice (a square) or the illuminated crown of Temperance (a circle and a dot). Other times, crowns are seriously elaborate, denoting how powerful the figure is over his or her domain, such as in The High Priestess's moon crown, the intricate starry crown of The Empress, the towering, layered crown of The Hierophant reaching toward the sky, and The Chariot's crown, adorned with a big yellow star that combines logic and intuition.

However, two crowns are most intriguing in the Tarot: the one that sits atop the Ace of Swords, and the other on the head of the figure of The Four of Pentacles. Both are Minor cards, which are not Court Cards. The first symbolizes absolute mastery of mind over actions; the other symbolizes mastery of tangible manifestations of money – both achieved through balance.

Halo: Can you recall how many Tarot figures have a halo? The Hanged Man and Temperance are two figures with halos in the Major Arcana; both signify that an illuminated mind has been achieved. The first by pausing and (literally) seeing things from a different perspective, and the second implying that an illuminated mind (through inspiration, since the figure is an angel) can resolve any conflict. Its image in the Tarot is not confined to a heavenly figure with a halo, but rather to attaining wisdom and illumination (enlightenment). The only other Minor Arcana cards portraying a halo are the Seven of Cups and the Ten of Cups, where the cups are illuminated to attract attention, and announce something – a solution or a result.

In the first case, just the cup is lit to emphasize the correct decision. All the cups in the Ten of Cups are illuminated, making a magnificent rainbow, signifying that a wish will be granted – the impossible will become attainable. The Nine of Cups is another 'wish card', but the cups are not lit. They are arranged on a blue wall behind the figure, demonstrating the joy that comes from reaping the benefits of your intuitive and physical labour rather than inspirational intervention. A subtle picture of making the right decision through hard work and a balanced mind.

"Have faith, persevere, wishes will come true." So, when one achieves the results one hoped for, they appear to be 'heavenly' intervention.

Homes or castles: "An Englishman's home is his castle," as the saying goes. The Rider-Waite-Smith deck is the first Tarot deck designed and illustrated by the English (as opposed to The Mamluks, Italians or French of mediaeval times). Aside from the obvious, dwellings signify earthly accomplishments. A castle is the home of Minor card Kings and Queens who have mastered their element or personality aspect. As a result, the size and prominence of a castle are important. It represents the magnitude of one's achievements – the tangible result of the unification of dualities inside oneself.

IMAGE FORMATION

Foregrounds and backgrounds: The formation of images in The Rider-Waite-Smith-Colman deck has a significance too. Foregrounds tend to focus on the main message of the card, and backgrounds on the secondary influence or transformation that is taking place. The two cards that seem to be symmetrical on formation are The Wheel of Fortune and The World, where a central circular form is balanced by four smaller outer symbols in each corner. Balanced aspects (in the background) highlight the result of the central symbol in the foreground. On the next page there is a table highlighting possible interpretations of the Major cards' images.

Exercise: See if you can intuit comparable meanings for each of the Minor cards as an exercise in developing intuition. This would be quite beneficial to you when you get to Tarot readings. Symbols that stand out may differ from person to person. Choose the first thing that catches your eye in an image, and add keywords to your own table. It all depends on what you perceive first in a card.

DEVELOPMENTAL CYCLES

The four elemental suits of the Minor Arcana illustrate the evolving facets of The Fool's personality. They represent The Fool progressing from a Page to a King, who 'rules' through achieving his full potential and mastering his ego personality. The four Minor Arcana suits reflect the four stages of personality development as follows:

Wands: Wands represent The Fool taking initiatives to forge his own route in life, developing and implementing his own ideas and projects while listening to spiritual guidance. In other words, he is paying attention to, or becoming aware of, what inspires him. He is trusting himself, his own wisdom and potential, despite his lack of experience or skills. Without taking initiative, initiation of his true potential cannot begin.

Cups: Cups symbolize The Fool's emotional growth through forging alliances and partnerships. He falls in love, trusts others, and collaborates with them. He learns to distinguish between swinging emotions, which arise from attachments, upsetting his balance. But his true feelings, which are characterized by balance and harmony leading to growth, enable him to fulfil his passions and identify the right romantic and business partners in life. Having faith in his feelings involves keeping his heart open. Despite the possibility of disappointment, The Fool learns to reflect, confront his truth, and move in a new direction toward his goal. He persists in his search for the rightful, fruitful partnership, through which he can manifest his happiness and contentment. And when he trusts without being attached to false expectations, his wishes come true, as if by magic.

CARD	NUMBER	FOREGROUND SYMBOL	FOREGROUND KEYWORDS
THE FOOL	0	White dog	Innocence, intention
THE MAGICIAN	1	Red roses and white lilies	Creativity and drive
THE HIGH PRIESTESS	2	New moon, flowy robes	Psychic, moody, fluid state, uncertain
THE EMPRESS	3	Dried corn sheaf	Germination, potential, fertility
THE EMPEROR	4	Stone throne	Structure
THE HIEROPHANT	5	Two people	Advice
THE LOVERS	6	Two people	Two people, relationship
THE CHARIOT	7	Two lions	Balancing
JUSTICE	8	White foot	Justice on Earth
THE HERMIT	9	Snow	Height of spiritual wisdom
WHEEL OF FORTUNE	10	A symbol in each corner	Balance
STRENGTH	11	Lion	Primal desires
THE HANGED MAN	12	Illuminated head	Enlightenment
DEATH	13	Dead king, arid land	Death
TEMPERANCE	14	Water	Emotions
THE DEVIL	15	Chained couple	Imprisonment
THE TOWER	16	High rock/mountain	Big achievement
THE STAR	17	Water	Emotions
THE MOON	18	Crayfish crawling	Trying to get out
THE SUN	19	Child on a horse	Happy
JUDGEMENT	20	Dead rising from graves	Resurrections
THE WORLD	21	Symmetrical	A symbol in each corner

Figure 12 Foreground and background image formation of the Major Arcana

CARD *(continued)*	NUMBER	BACKGROUND SYMBOL	BACKGROUND KEYWORDS
THE FOOL	0	Snow-topped mountains	Objective, spiritual enlightenment
THE MAGICIAN	1	Red rose vine	Successful achievement
THE HIGH PRIESTESS	2	Pomegranate veil	Fertility, balanced intuition
THE EMPRESS	3	Growing forest	Success
THE EMPEROR	4	Stone throne	Structure
THE HIEROPHANT	5	Crown, two pillars	Higher wisdom
THE LOVERS	6	Angel	Balance
THE CHARIOT	7	Starry canopy & crown	Inspirational victory
JUSTICE	8	Purple veil	Truth to be revealed (consider all aspects)
THE HERMIT	9	Grey	Spiritual transformation
WHEEL OF FORTUNE	10	Circular object	Cycle
STRENGTH	11	Woman in white	Spiritual feminine influence
THE HANGED MAN	12	Tree trunk with leaves	Growth
DEATH	13	Water and life growing	Continuity
TEMPERANCE	14	Wings	Balance
THE DEVIL	15	Bat wings, reversed pentacle	Out of balance
THE TOWER	16	Bolt of lightning	Sudden
THE STAR	17	Stars	Inspiration
THE MOON	18	Moon faces	Change in progress
THE SUN	19	Sun	Joy
JUDGEMENT	20	Trumpet	Call
THE WORLD	21	Egg-shaped wreath	Cycle

Swords: The Fool discovers how emotions affect the mind and how his mentality affects how he feels. After taking initiative and learning to trust his genuine sentiments, he learns that balancing or regular adjustment of his thoughts is essential to arriving at the best decisions regarding his goals. He discovers that growth is a never-ending process, and that if he wants to attain tangible outcomes in life, he must acknowledge and overcome any unconscious worries or anxieties. His ultimate lesson is that if he does not decide, he risks becoming trapped by his fears and anxieties. His perception of a situation is sometimes far worse than the actuality of it. The upshot of developing a flexible intellect is a constructive decision-making process that yields positive, tangible results. In the next suit, he learns to own up and accept responsibility for his decisions.

Pentacles: As visible or manifested results, Pentacles reflect the completion of The Fool's individuation, and emotional and mental processes. Following his own course in life requires him to be accountable for achieving financial independence by expressing his potential creativity, ability and skills. The four suits, or aspects of personality, work together simultaneously. Each Minor Arcana suit has an impact on the others, illustrating the complexities of human maturity. If The Fool does not collaborate, or plan expansion, or have the right mind-set, no tangible results will be achieved. And if his efforts are not consistent, revised and flexible, no success will be achieved. The results symbolized by the Pentacles Minor Arcana are physically experienced in the material world. They are not inner feelings or thoughts that The Fool is undergoing, but present the consequences of current emotional and mental states. In other words, they manifest reality, where The Fool has to learn to be responsible for his own growth.

The table on page 188 summarises the essence of each of the developmental cycles as they are expressed in the Minor Arcana suits. When you first start interpreting Tarot readings or deciding which Tarot deck to choose (see the next section), you can refer to it for guidance.

Exercise: As you reflect on the table overleaf, arrange the cards of each Minor suit in front of you. Consider each phase separately, and keep your remarks in your Tarot journal:

- Assess your own development of each personality aspect.
- Which of the four aspects needs your focus currently?

- Which stage or aspect do you feel you need to develop further?
- Contemplate the keywords given to each step or card number below. Which step do you need to modify?
- What can you modify to bring more balance – and, consequently, fulfilment – into your life?

Choosing a Tarot Deck

How you relate to the cards has a big impact on the quality and accuracy of your Tarot readings. Choosing a Tarot deck, whether you're a novice or an experienced reader, can be tricky. Hundreds of Tarot decks exist, each with its own set of symbols, energies, traditions, mythology and artwork. The easiest way to choose a Tarot deck is to find one with which you have a personal and intuitive connection. If your best friend praises a deck but you break out in a sweat and go blank when you try to do a Tarot reading with it, it's not the deck for you.

Despite the fact that (most) Tarot decks are based on the same source, they differ greatly in terms of aesthetics, symbolism and overall impression, as well as the kind of readings they can help you generate. So, where do you start, and how do you pick the best one for you, one that represents you or your reading style? It all depends on whether you're a novice or a seasoned Tarot reader. If you're new to Tarot, you might want to start with the Rider-Waite deck, which is the most popular. It's easy to understand, the graphics are straightforward and informative, and it comes with a wealth of information. You can choose a deck with simple, minimalist imagery to make it easier to connect with the symbols (such as the Everyday Tarot deck). If you're more experienced, or looking for a new challenge, a deck like the Thoth Tarot deck, with its depth and intricacy, can be a good fit. You might also opt for Tarot decks that are more abstract. It's entirely up to you.

A rule of thumb is that the Tarot deck should be symbolically rich and include clearly illustrated visuals that, at the very least, allow you to recognize the card. It will be much easier to interpret readings if they are numbered and given titles, rather than depending solely on keyword memorization. So if you live near a new-age store or bookstore, pay a visit and look at the Tarot cards on display. What kind of energy does the deck give you? Do you have a personal connection with it?

CARD		KEYWORDS	WANDS	CUPS
Order of cycle			1	2
Season			Spring (planting seeds)	Summer (watering seeds)
Development process of personality aspects			Individuation (initiation of individual's path, project and ideas)	Nurturing (connection with true feelings)
Aspect		Phase or step	Connection to Spirit	Connection to heart
ACE		New beginnings	Inspiration	Intimacy
2	II	Establishing partnerships	Collaboration on ideas	Balance in relationships
3	III	Collaboration results	Planning next phase	Expansion
4	IV	Stability	Stable creative process	Unstable emotions
5	V	Uncertainty: attitude adjustment, acceptance of limitations	Adjust, refine process, new attitude	Adjust emotional attitude, new relationships
6	VI	Steadying influences	Receiving recognition	Nurtured through past relationships
7	VII	Wisdom, mastery, options	Mastering competitiveness	Mastering emotional choices
8	VIII	Feedback & organisation (results)	Organized plans, ideas, projects taking off in a new direction	Change of heart: moving in a new direction
9	IX	Wisdom gained from life experience: understanding leads to total fulfilment	Determination: keep your focus on your ideas	Emotional balance leads to fulfilment
10	X	Transformation through maintaining balance leads to fulfilment	Maintaining consistent effort leads to results (do not overload)	Steadying emotions leads to emotional fulfilment

Figure 13 Numerological interpretation of the Minor Arcana cycles

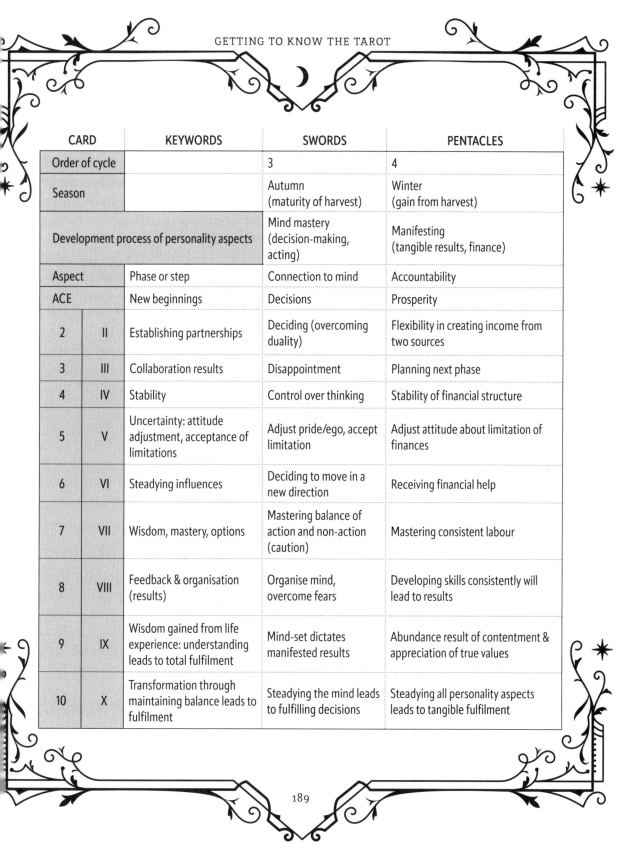

CARD		KEYWORDS	SWORDS	PENTACLES
Order of cycle			3	4
Season			Autumn (maturity of harvest)	Winter (gain from harvest)
Development process of personality aspects			Mind mastery (decision-making, acting)	Manifesting (tangible results, finance)
Aspect		Phase or step	Connection to mind	Accountability
ACE		New beginnings	Decisions	Prosperity
2	II	Establishing partnerships	Deciding (overcoming duality)	Flexibility in creating income from two sources
3	III	Collaboration results	Disappointment	Planning next phase
4	IV	Stability	Control over thinking	Stability of financial structure
5	V	Uncertainty: attitude adjustment, acceptance of limitations	Adjust pride/ego, accept limitation	Adjust attitude about limitation of finances
6	VI	Steadying influences	Deciding to move in a new direction	Receiving financial help
7	VII	Wisdom, mastery, options	Mastering balance of action and non-action (caution)	Mastering consistent labour
8	VIII	Feedback & organisation (results)	Organise mind, overcome fears	Developing skills consistently will lead to results
9	IX	Wisdom gained from life experience: understanding leads to total fulfilment	Mind-set dictates manifested results	Abundance result of contentment & appreciation of true values
10	X	Transformation through maintaining balance leads to fulfilment	Steadying the mind leads to fulfilling decisions	Steadying all personality aspects leads to tangible fulfilment

TAROT OR ORACLE CARDS?

Tarot decks are not the same as all divination cards or spiritual decks, better known as oracles. Although they are used in comparable ways, oracle cards and Tarot decks serve different functions. A Tarot deck typically has 78 cards (some artists decide to add their own signature card to the deck, so it may contain 79 or 80 in total). Oracle cards are distinct from other decks in that they lack a fixed format or hierarchy (no Major and Minor cards). They can represent anything the designer wants. So make sure to check the number of cards in the deck, as well as their arrangement and title, even though they might be sold as 'Tarot' decks. Before you decide to buy a specific deck, you should check the internet to see whether you can view the cards.

Oracle cards have their own meanings, and are designed to be used as spiritual guidance on a daily basis. They can be used in tandem with a Tarot card reading as additional perspective and visual stimulation to invoke guidance. For example, before starting a Tarot reading, you can select one card from an oracle deck to answer, "What is this session about?" or "What do I need to know about the issue I have in mind?" Some Tarot readers use oracle cards to conduct a brief spread before starting a session, to ask what their client's

main concern is, for instance. Using oracle cards in this way will help you tune into a Tarot reading, particularly when you're still learning the Tarot. Other Tarot readers mix the oracle cards and the Tarot in a reading; but once you get used to them, you will see that the Tarot is capable of providing insightful information on its own (it all depends on the complexity of the Tarot spread you use). They have distinctly different energies. Rather than combining them in a single reading, experiment using them independently to complement one another.

Furthermore, oracle cards, like the Tarot, can help you figure out what your dreams mean (see the Tarot Spreads section in Chapter Five). But first, perhaps the best place to start is to ask yourself whether you want to practise with traditional or classical Tarot, or modern Tarot.

CLASSICAL OR CONTEMPORARY?

Furthermore, you're likely to look for more information about readings with that deck on the internet. Ideally, the deck should correspond to the standard or traditional interpretation. While nothing can replace a physical Tarot deck, some offer applications (apps) that can be a terrific way to become acquainted with the deck without spending a lot of money. Before purchasing a physical deck, you can assess whether it is the perfect Tarot deck for you; see if you feel comfortable with it and form a relationship with it. It will be far more difficult for a newbie to intuit guidance from a deck that deviates significantly from the standard. If you choose, you will find it easier to use non-traditional cards later in your journey. Traditional decks are derived from different Tarot traditions, including Italian, French and, more recently, English, the most prominent of which is The Rider-Waite-Smith deck.

The majority of modern Tarot decks, featuring graphic designs, adhere to this tradition. Tarot de Marseille is a French tradition that predates Rider-Waite-Smith. The suits are depicted by simple illustrations; the Minor cards are just symbols of the four suits, with no scenery or figures. It may not have the same depth of imagery and 'storytelling' ability as, say, the Rider-Waite-Smith deck.

For example, the Thoth tradition incorporates spiritual and philosophical elements, such as astrology and Kabbalah, into the cards. It all depends on your interests. Before deciding, go through the decks you are considering one by one. Examine the Major and Minor Arcana cards to see whether the images speak to you:

- What was your initial reaction when you saw the images?
- Do you like the colours and patterns?
- Are you drawn to the artwork?
- Are there any additional decks that you think would be more appealing?
- Do you get a sense of what each card symbolizes when you look at them?

THEMES & ILLUSTRATION STYLE

Consider the deck's theme. Themes – whether planets, cats, dragons or fairies – are generally integrated into all 78 cards. If you keep being drawn to the same deck, trust your instincts and go for it. If you are familiar with the Rider-Waite-Smith theme, The Radiant Rider-Waite Tarot deck is a modified version of it. The artwork is very similar, slightly simpler, and has a brighter, more modern feel (hence the name).

Moreover, one of the first things you may notice is the artwork style and symbolism. This might be as basic as preferring clean, modern lines, or vividly coloured and contemporary graphics, detailed drawings, or even vintage-inspired Tarot cards. Some Tarot decks feature a few beautiful cards, but the remainder of the deck isn't as visually pleasing. So make sure you check all the cards in the deck.

SIZE MATTERS

Tarot decks are available in a number of sizes, including large cards that are more suited for group readings or parties, as well as pocket-size decks that you can carry in your handbag or take away with you. For in-person client readings or personal readings, regular-size Tarot cards may be ideal. Decks are typically 7cm by 12cm (2.75in x 4.75in); however, smaller and larger decks are available. This is especially important while handling and shuffling cards.

You or your clients may find it difficult to handle the cards if they are too big or too little. Before selecting a deck, handle the cards and try shuffling them. Furthermore, the majority of Tarot cards will be thick enough to last for many years. However, low-quality reproductions may be available, and the cardboard may shred or become damaged much more quickly. If you plan to use Tarot cards frequently, avoid the less expensive options. However, some bespoke sets have gilded edges, and while they look beautiful, they might get sticky in the palms of your hands with regular use.

THE INSTRUCTION BOOKLET

Most Tarot decks come with a book that describes the cards and their meanings. However, some decks include more information than others. So check the little white instruction booklet that comes with the deck to see whether the information it provides is sufficient for you to start with. On the one hand, several of the booklets included in mass-market decks are disappointing. They're sometimes recycled information, and they do not often relate to the artist's interpretation of the card's meaning. On the other hand, some Tarot decks are sold as a set with a thorough companion book that examines the cards in greater depth and provides important insights on the deck's personal meaning. You might feel entirely at ease discovering and interpreting the Tarot cards using your intuition and the connection you have with them. Experiment to find out what works best for you.

If you want to conquer learning Tarot, you've got to ditch your dependency on the little white book. Your best option is to keep building your Tarot journal, and learn from your intuitive feedback as you get used to your cards. In addition to the books that come with it, keep an eye out for workbooks specific to that deck. Facebook Groups are a great way to find help for studying specific decks. And by the way, there is no shame in keeping your journal next to you and referring to it when you start reading the Tarot professionally.

ONE TAROT DECK OR SEVERAL?

Be inquisitive! Examine several Tarot decks. And there's no reason to settle for just one if you are ready. As you develop skill as a reader, you will feel drawn to a range of Tarot cards. Some readers use different decks for different purposes: one for general and more comprehensive readings, and another for answering a client's questions. Moreover, some have their own personal deck for private use. In short, as a Tarot reader, you might end up with a collection of Tarot decks. This is something you can try later, when you're more comfortable with the Tarot.

Some decks will provide you with detailed insights over a longer period of time. Others provide shorter, more direct answers to your current questions. As you engage with the cards, you will realize that each Tarot deck has its unique 'voice', just as you do. If you are a professional Tarot reader, you might already have a range of decks, and may still be called to try a new Tarot deck. Experience will show you what is best for you and your clients.

SHOULD YOU BUY YOUR OWN TAROT DECK?

You may have heard that Tarot cards are solely given as a gift, and that you cannot purchase your own. Well, that is a myth! The Tarot is a visual tool that can help you better understand yourself and your life. The more grounded your attitude, the better reader you will be; therefore, resist the temptation to succumb to sensationalism. The only power your Tarot cards will have is the one you give them as the reader, interpreter and seeker of wisdom and knowledge. Although tradition and heritage connect us to our forebears, they don't have to confine us to blind sensationalism.

Over the past few years, Australia suffered a strange and shameful phenomenon. People were stealing Tarot decks from bookshops to fulfil the myth that you can't buy your first Tarot deck. The shops have resorted to displaying Tarot cards in a locked glass cabinet. If anything, this undermines both Tarot readers and the legitimacy of the Tarot as a self-development tool (which certainly does not teach or encourage stealing!).

So if you have always wanted to own a specific Tarot deck, do it without feeling guilty or superstitious. What matters most is your relationship to the cards. The Tarot is about self-empowerment. Wouldn't you rather buy the Tarot deck you feel connected with, than wait to be gifted one that may be unsuitable for you? Be as bold as The Fool, and do not be afraid to go out and seek, find and buy the right one for you (of course, there is nothing stopping you from hinting at a deck you have your eye on and would love to have for your birthday, or Christmas!).

CLEARING YOUR NEW TAROT DECK

It is such a thrill when you receive a new Tarot deck, especially if it's your first. You can't wait to rip open the box, take out your cards, and begin practicing straight away. Sure, rip it open and all that, but the first thing you should do is welcome the Tarot into your life by putting your energy into it. It could be referred to as your first act of bonding! Hopefully, you will use the Tarot for the rest of your life, and it will become your best friend. Remember that you will be building your own relationship with your chosen Tarot deck. The creator can express their purpose and offer their interpretations of the cards' meanings, but as you get to know your deck, you'll begin to form your own associations and develop your own interpretations. So don't feel obligated to take any instructions at face value.

Bonding with Your New Tarot Deck

Bonding with your Tarot is comparable to setting an intention for a crystal and programming it to do a specific function you have in mind. Everything has energy; therefore, whatever your cards are made of, and whoever manufactured them, all have left behind an energetic imprint on them, just as others, such as your friends or clients, would do when they use them. Tuning into energy and learning how to handle it is an important part of psychic training. The latter applies to both you and your cards. But a little later we will talk about you, the reader, and how to prepare for a Tarot reading.

Furthermore, Tarot cards are a self-discovery tool. This means you will need to form a bond with a fresh Tarot deck before you can trust it to reflect your inner wisdom and intuition. You will master the interpretation of its cards through this communication. Infusing your energy into your Tarot cards is another way of bonding or connecting with your new deck and getting better acquainted. You can do this by simply shuffling them often and putting them under your pillow at night. Keep in mind that if you sleep with something under your pillow, it will affect your sleep and dreams, so do not be surprised if your dreams are more mysterious, or have something to do with your deck. Even if you don't notice any different sleep patterns or dreams, sleeping with your Tarot deck close to you bonds you unconsciously and energetically to it. You can select a different card each night and place it on your bedside table (when it comes to the Devil card or The Hanged Man, it is probably best to place it reversed, expressing a positive interpretation).

Moreover, if you are into acting or the performing arts, an interesting way of bonding with the cards is to dress up or act out the figure in one of the Major cards that you are drawn to. That would really embody its significance! In any case, whatever method you feel comfortable with, the aim is to get used to your Tarot cards and to let them get used to your energy field as well. Their meanings will be revealed naturally as you become familiar with holding and shuffling them, and using them for guidance for yourself, your friends and family.

After working with your new Tarot deck for a while, or any specific Tarot deck you may add later on, you will become 'fluent' in handling the cards, laying them in a spread and finding your own rhythm when you hold a reading session. So be patient and take your time learning the cards. Another way to get acquainted is to start talking to your cards right away as you unwrap your deck and start looking through it!

Tell your cards what you are hoping to achieve with them. Let them know what kind of relationship you hope to establish, and where you wish to go on your Tarot journey. Infusing your new Tarot deck with these goals, objectives and intentions while you are cleansing and charging them is a great way to begin. You may do this by expressing your thoughts out loud, or simply focusing them on the cards while you handle them, shuffle them and explore their images. Remember that your Tarot deck is a wellspring of wisdom and inspiration that's waiting for you to be nurtured by it. So hold your cards in your hands for a few minutes, close to your heart if you wish, and repeat an intention aloud or in your mind, as if you were whispering into a newborn's ear.

Tell them why you bought them and what you would like them to assist you with. Next, thoroughly shuffle the cards multiple times, for a few minutes each time, until they are completely mixed and you can feel them becoming heavier and less slippery. Yes, your energy has a 'weight', which indicates that your new Tarot deck is now yours. Over the next few days, keep repeating this practice. You will know when they are 'yours'. Use them as much as you can at the beginning to reinforce the connection. Start by asking simple, direct questions every day, shuffling and selecting only one card to focus on properly. Select a card in the morning, at lunch or right before bedtime – whichever works best for you. Reflect on that card in relation to your question. Questions can be along the lines of any of the following examples:

Some useful questions are, "What do I need to know about today?"; "What element of my life do I need to focus on today?"; "How may I support myself today?"; "Which Tarot card do I need to consider today?"; or even just, "How will my day turn out?" Remember to note your observations in your Tarot journal and refer to your entry again to build up a glossary of interpretations for each card.

When you are done using the cards, separate the Major cards from the Minor cards and place the deck in a box or pouch with the Minor cards facing the Major cards. Also, make sure all the cards are the right way up before storing them. They are now ready to be used the next time you do a reading. You might wonder if there is a

ceremony or process to ensure that they are cleansed. Contrary to popular perception, this is not necessary, because energy begins to work as soon as you declare an intention! If you enjoy rituals, though, feel free to create your own.

CARING FOR YOUR TAROT DECK

Keep your friend in a safe dedicated place, and assign an area, desk or location in your home where you will normally do readings. Your home is your environment, so ask yourself where you would like your cards to live. Consider the setting in which your cards will be kept. Do you have little children, who have sticky fingers? Do you have pets? Do you have a lot of people passing by your home on a regular basis? If you don't have any of these issues, you might be able to leave your working cards out on a coffee table, desk or bookshelf. If you do, you'll probably need to find a secure location for your cards, whether it's your bedroom or a gorgeous box kept higher up, on a shelf, away from curious hands. There are a wide variety of ways to keep your cards organized, so get creative! The first thing to consider is whether this deck is for occasional personal use, or whether you will be working with it regularly or professionally. Do you have other decks that you use? Perhaps you are simply a collector and would use this new deck once in a while, or just for keepsake.

The most obvious way to store your Tarot deck is to keep it in the box it came in, especially if you are going to use it occasionally, or if it is a collectible deck; however, a nice box would be a good place to keep them. If you have a collection already, it would make sense to have a larger box. That way, you will know where they are when you need them. If you are going to use them frequently, a better place would be in a pouch. After using your cards frequently, they tend to get thicker, and may not fit easily back into the box they came in. Moreover, card boxes tend to show wear and tear right away, and sometimes break. A velvety or satiny drawstring pouch might be the most convenient place if you are going to use them often. And it is conveniently portable too, should you wish to take them with you.

You may find a few unique drawstring bags with stimulating Tarot themes on them that will allow you to focus your intention, as well as your mind, on the readings you are about to start. Alternatively, you might go for a bejewelled pouch, or one with embroidery work; whatever takes your fancy, so long as you shuffle them before and after each reading.

If you don't have much space where you live, wrap your cards in a cloth and store them in a drawer or basket, or on a tabletop or desk where you regularly sit. This is also useful if you intend to use them regularly. If you want to go all out, you might wrap your Tarot cards in a luxurious fabric like satin or silk. Another factor to consider is that some materials, such as silk, are supposed to deflect outside energies, preventing the cards from absorbing unwanted energy from their surroundings until they are used again. Regardless, how we treat our possessions reveals how we feel about ourselves. You may get a lot more enjoyment and pleasure if you give your Tarot cards some thought and attention. However, it is entirely up to you.

FULL MOON AND SUN BATHS

Since you are reading this book, you are probably sensitive to the cycles of The Moon, the ruler of dreams and psychic abilities. The full moon is one of the most potent times of the lunar cycle. So, make the most of its peak energy. Many psychic readers, too, find that the brilliant light of the moon during this phase has purifying and clarifying properties. Your deck will be cleansed of any lingering dull energy and charged by the moon's most intense light. Your dreaming abilities may be enhanced, too, when you go to sleep moon-bathing. Leave your cards (and wallet) on a windowsill where moonlight shines overnight. And try lying down on the floor, or a couch, even for a few minutes.

Full-moon timings according to location can be checked online (refer to timeanddate. com or the Full Moon app). First, check that all your cards are in order before you lay your deck out for a moon bath. Arrange the cards in ascending order, Major cards 0–21, and then Minor cards, Page to King, and then Ace to 10 starting with Wands, Cups, Swords and ending with Pentacles. Once you are satisfied with your deck's arrangement, place it where it can bask in the moon's bright and powerful light – for example, on a windowsill if you do not have access to the outdoors. Light from the moon or the sun through a window will work. You, as well as your cards (or crystals), can still absorb their energies.

Use the light from the sun or a full moon to recharge any time you feel you need to. Clearing your cards once a quarter is more than sufficient. Getting some sunlight, whenever you feel the need to, balances your energy and that of your cards, too. Allow your deck to soak up some sunshine on a sunny afternoon, for instance; but be careful not to leave it out for too long, or the print will fade. If you are sunbathing outdoors, remember to protect yourself, too.

MANIFESTING WITH TAROT

Tarot is a visual tool that invokes imagination and inspiration; it inspired French-American artist Niki de Saint Phalle (1930–2002) to create a sculpture park called Tarot Garden (*Il Giardino dei Tarocchi*) in Tuscany, Italy. Twenty-two extraordinary sculptures and numerous other works, including house-sized creations, represent her idea of the greater Mysteries of Tarot. The artist designed a wonderful Major Arcana Tarot deck, too (to see the garden, visit http:// ilgiardinodeitarocchi.it/en/). Some of the larger works in the garden may be walked through. During the development of the garden, the artist herself lived in the sphinx-like Empress for several years – embodying the spirit of the Tarot!

Artistic creativity can inspire you to bond with the Tarot and get to know the meanings its images symbolize. After all, The Fool's adventure taught him to express his potential, skills and talents. Let the Tarot help you do the same. Do you have a specific goal in mind? What aim do you want the Tarot imagery to help you manifest? Look over the Major Arcana and feel which cards call to you, keeping your intention in mind. Some cards will reveal themselves to you after a few moments. To depict a visual mantra of the goal you want to create, line up the cards that popped up. You can photograph the cards, shrink the image to a smaller size, laminate the printout and keep it in your wallet or under your pillow until it manifests. Placing your visual mantra somewhere visible and accessible to you, such as on your wall or on a shelf in your bedroom, also works. It's what our ancestors initially articulated and practiced as cave paintings, before they could talk.

Keep in mind, however, that in order to manifest any objective, you must first know exactly what you want, how committed you are to achieving it, and how strong your desire is to see it through. It's a good idea to scribble down a few sentences to clarify your purpose. There is no room for self-doubt or a lack of belief – it won't work. Your doubt and passion will cancel each other out energetically, putting you in a deadlock. Consider heating a liquid in a pan, for instance; if you continuously increase and decrease the flame, the liquid will not heat up or boil!

Here is a tip: the trick to manifesting is to first feel the relief, joy and gratitude that follows it happening. So, after visualizing and embodying the experience of attaining your goal, use your visual mantra as an affirmation. The next step is to act, no matter how small or big, to affirm your intention. The final step is to let go and let the energy accomplish what it needs

to do on your behalf. Do the work, then trust in the universe to help you. Do not let desperation or mistrust cloud your intention.

WHAT TO DO WITH YOUR OLD TAROT DECKS

There are many reasons why you may wish to dispose of your Tarot cards. For example, you may not have connected with them, or you may have used them extensively and are unable to draw any insights from them. Or you may simply have too many, and your shelf is becoming cluttered! Whatever your reason, there is no need to feel guilty, or make matters worse by believing myths about how to dispose of the cards. They are images that have been printed on paper or cardboard. The only magical power they have is the one you gave them by infusing your energy into them by using them. Tarot cards are a psychic or spiritual development tool that allows you to understand more about the world around you by using your intuition and energy. You, the Tarot reader, are the one who gives significance to your cards.

However, you may remove the 'magic' by clearing your energy from them first, restoring them to their original state as printed paper! You can do so by setting your intention. Thank them and let them know it is time to say goodbye. Place your deck under the waning moonlight for a few days or overnight in a bath of sea-salt water. Alternatively, if you're versed in using crystals, use a double-pointed crystal to clear their energy. Any infused energy would be removed. Safely dispose of the water and recycle the pulp any way you see fit. Burning your cards is not necessary and can be hazardous. That's all there is to it.

However difficult it may be to break away from an old friendship, think of it as an amicable separation. If this resonates with you, here are a few alternative suggestions:

- If your cards are in good condition, consider reselling them or giving them to a collector friend.
- Are there any images from this deck that you particularly like? Display your favourite cards, which have a unique meaning or significance to you, as visual mantras or affirmations. For example, you might associate a specific image with an aspect of yourself or a goal you want to pursue. Positive cards that symbolize your intentions can be intuitively selected and displayed in combination.
- Make a piece of art using your old Tarot deck. If the graphics on the cards represent someone you know, use them to make a greeting card for that person.

- Use your Tarot deck in creative art projects. For example, create a collage using a thematic selection, or add a few cards to a painting to provide a dynamic element and more depth, creating your own multimedia art! You can even create customized bookmarks.
- Giving a Tarot card to a special person in your life can be a small, thoughtful gesture that gives them courage and fortitude. A gift of encouragement may be exactly what they need. If a buddy is having a rough time, for example, shuffle before you select a card and ask, *"What can best support them at this moment?"* Let's say you draw The Chariot or Strength. Make a card or an email message with the image personalized (using Canva, for example), and send it with a message such as, "You're almost there – keep going!"
- If you happen to be mathematical and relate to numerology, you might make a card for a friend using the Tarot arcana that corresponds to their birth date. Alternatively, as an artistic endeavour, build a visual mantra that reflects that number by combining Major and arcana cards with the number that relates to their characteristics.
- Stick images you are drawn to in your Tarot journal and practice drawing an

outline, or your version of the arcana. This is a great way to embody the meaning of the card and get to know it better. You might even notice elements in the image that you missed at first.

Whenever you are ready to part ways with a Tarot deck, do not feel guilty or discouraged. Your relationship with your development tools, like you, evolves. Use this time to reflect on your experience with your deck and consider the ways it might be disposed of or repurposed. The worst that can happen is that your creative talents might be unleashed – and that is the gift of the Tarot (and our life).

Preparing Yourself for a Reading

INTENTIONAL TAROT MIND-SET

You can cleanse your cards in a variety of methods, including using essential oils, crystals, salt or sage – whatever works for you. However, rituals will help you concentrate on what *you* are about to do (which is communicate with the Tarot by conducting a reading), and will not harm the cards whatsoever! Moreover, it is better to avoid putting anything on the cards themselves, as this may make them sticky and difficult to shuffle. Also, unless you choose to do so, you do not have to keep them in the box they came in. Instead, you can store them in a designated drawer or a box you adore.

To get the best out of your Tarot journal, it helps to approach the Tarot with an empowered mind-set. And by the way, giving in to false beliefs or superstitions about clients or friends who should not touch the cards because they will 'contaminate' them with their energy will take your personal power away.

Always begin by setting your intention and requesting to connect with 'the highest source, for highest wisdom' to guide yourself, and/or your friends and clients. Furthermore, ask that the guidance be clear and beneficial, and that you feel protected on time-space levels as well as refreshed and revitalized afterward. Use language that makes sense to you so that your affirmation becomes an energetic template you use every time you consult the Tarot. That is all you need to get clear, accurate and insightful guidance. You might want to give thanks to your cards, silently, when you are done. Ask that they energetically clear as you shuffle them before and after every session. You will feel as if though a heavy weight has lifted, and the cards are fresh and 'new' once more. It is a simple and quick technique that works.

Each time you handle your cards as a Tarot reader, they will absorb your energy. Before turning the cards over to a friend or a client, you will be the first to handle and shuffle them, and the last to shuffle, clear and organize them before putting them away. Each time you perform this ceremony, your deck will be cleared by your intent. Your Tarot cards will help you develop your intuition and ignite your psychic powers in exchange for caring for them. So make sure you do your part by reading yourself. It is a good idea not to use your Tarot when you are tired or in a bad mood. Take time to relax and clear yourself, then try again another time. Otherwise, you will end up more confused and distort the clarity of any counsel you receive from your cards.

TAPPING INTO YOUR INTUITION

By practicing, you will improve your reading skills. You, like our hero, The Fool, are starting from scratch and embarking on a psychic adventure. So don't be fearful of embarrassing yourself! No one is judging you, so please don't judge yourself. It inhibits your imagination – the very thing Tarot helps enhance. It will help you become a better reader if you perform a ritual before starting a Tarot interpretation or reading. This is because it uses a grounding approach or procedure to train and improve your psychic capacity. As a result, creating a routine and sticking to it will calm your mind, enable you to take a step back and objectively perceive the insights the cards reveal.

Set aside some time when you are not going to be distracted and keep your Tarot journal close at hand. Take a few deep breaths and let go of the day's events as well as any expectations you may have placed on your abilities. You can also light a tea-light candle and focus your attention for a few moments on the flickering flame. Start this 'infinity exercise' by holding your pen or pencil steady and relaxed:

1. To begin with, draw an infinity figure at the back of your Tarot journal with your dominant hand.

2. Go over it as closely as you can to the original outline you drew, until you're comfortable with it and it flows without restraining your focus.

3. Now, using your weaker hand, trace over that outline, maintaining as much as possible the original infinity shape

Figure 14
Infinity
intuition
exercise

that you drew with your dominant hand. It may seem awkward at first, but that is to be expected, given that you may not be accustomed to using that hand. This simple 'coordination' exercise is training the brain, so be patient as one side of your brain learns to do what the other side normally does).

4. When you feel comfortable using your other hand, hold the pen with both hands and go over your infinity figure, staying close to the previously drawn outline. The objective here is NOT speed, but relaxed, mindful focus.

5. Repeat each step about 10 times, or until it flows smoothly.

The infinity exercise improves intuition and allows the hemispheres of the brain to work in unison.

MAKING A START

The easiest way to learn to use the Tarot is to do so as you get to know and trust the cards – especially before you learn any Tarot spreads, meanings or interpretations. This is because your initial intuitive reactions are important in determining what each card represents to you personally. It helps you build a connection with them, contributing to the knowledge you will gain later.

Be brave, and start investigating for yourself right now by doing readings for yourself, even if they are about mundane issues. It is a good chance to get your cards used to being shuffled by your hands and to put your own energy into them – especially if others will be handling your deck as well. Simply ask direct questions while you shuffle, and then choose one card from the entire deck. Place your chosen card in front of you and reflect on the image as an artistic expression.

You can follow the five steps below to help build your routine or approach:

1. Ask one question.

2. Always write down your observations in your Tarot journal, and date your entries.

3. Dating your entries allows you to reflect on significant milestones that shape your Tarot learning experience.

4. Describe the most obvious remarks first. This method grounds your intuition in logic. Once you have done that, your creativity will flow easily and you will be able to balance reasoning and intuition (as The Chariot), conquering the task at hand.

5. Establishing this technique helps you weave a story around any insights you receive when using several cards in a single spread. Over time, your readings will have context as well as relevance and accuracy.

Regarding Step 4, make your descriptions visual – doodle if you like – and poetic to stimulate your imagination. What colours and images on the card appeal to you? What symbolic meaning does that colour bring to mind? If the section on colours earlier in this chapter resonates with your sensibilities, refer back to it for more inspiration. Consider the number's vibrational meaning as well. What new insights does it provide? Begin by silently speaking the words to yourself, taking your time with this process.

Write each sentence mindfully, focusing on the words that signify something to you, and relate them to your life. If you have an image of a figure, for example, describe who he or she is, who they remind you of, what they are wearing, the expression on their face, and whether it brings back a memory? What sort of throne are they sitting on? Does it remind you of someone's attitude? Are there any natural factors such as breezes, clouds or vegetation in the image? Also, are there other objects in the image? If so, what is the purpose of those objects? And so on. Keep writing and describing what you see, and relating it to your experiences, impressions or memories. It is critical not to hurry this process.

Here are a few tips that can stimulate writing descriptions in your journal entry:

- Write longhand (do not type). Writing longhand allows brain waves to slow down and connect more deeply with the creative hemisphere of the brain.
- Do not stop writing. If you doubt

yourself, or hesitate, you will bring yourself out of this 'meditative' state; that might interrupt your imagination and obstruct your intuition from unfolding. If you run out of things to describe, write something like this: "I am looking at the image of the Tower... I am breathing deeply and I am relaxed, just gazing at this image. What I see is this... I do not know if the Tower is crumbling, but I can see that people are falling off..." etc.

- Do not take your pen off the paper. Doodle, write abstract words that come to mind, but keep your pen on the paper. It will build your confidence, teach you to trust your intuition, and train you to allow information to flow.

- You will know when to stop writing. Insights have a way of revealing themselves!

Your journal entries can look something like this:

Question: *"What am going to learn about myself today through you?"*

Card Selected: The Tower

Scene of a tower crumbling down.

Type: Major card.

Card number: 16 (1 + 6 = 7)

Factual description:
It is dark (night).
There is a bolt of lightning.
Crown knocked off.
People falling off a cliff.

My insights: *"Something happened all of a sudden, as quick as a bolt of lightning. It comes as a surprise in the middle of the night. There will be ramifications because the result of this is that the Tower is totally destroyed, and people are falling off. Change is (probably) permanent. I can relate to this because it reminds me of a time when I was taken completely by surprise. I feel that what I took for granted in the past was like that crown I wore on my head. Suddenly my crown was knocked off, and I was not prepared. My world was shaken, and it took me time to recover. What I believed to be true was suddenly and unexpectedly destroyed like this tower. Now I am looking at the number on the card. The card number is 7, because 16 breaks down to 1+6, which equals seven. Seven reminds me of the chariot image I read about In The Book of Tarot. Seven indicates a challenge to be conquered. I have a challenge to conquer. Maybe it is a belief I hold, since the crown is what I noticed most, and a crown is worn on my head. The belief I have currently in my head needs to be destroyed because it is*

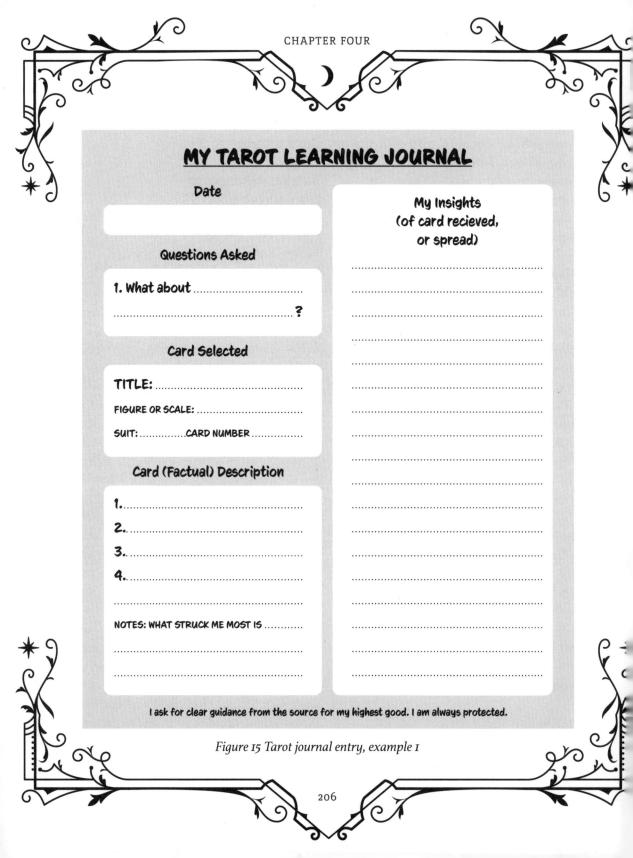

MY TAROT LEARNING JOURNAL

Date

Questions Asked

1. What about ....
   .... ?

Card Selected

TITLE: ....

FIGURE OR SCALE: ....

SUIT: ....CARD NUMBER ....

Card (Factual) Description

1. ....
2. ....
3. ....
4. ....
   ....

NOTES: WHAT STRUCK ME MOST IS ....
....
....

My Insights
(of card recieved,
or spread)

I ask for clear guidance from the source for my highest good. I am always protected.

Figure 15 Tarot journal entry, example 1

false, not true, and will be destroyed suddenly. If I am not aware of this, I might repeat an old memory. I am tired of repeating the past, so must therefore change something about my false belief or view of myself or my life. I feel uneasy, maybe because I need to let go and not repeat the past... The belief I have to change is ... And I need to build a new view regarding my view of ... There is no going back."

Your mind relaxes as you begin to describe the facts about the card's image and what first struck you about the card: whether it was an image, a figure, a symbol or a colour. Since what you're describing is logical and factual, your inhibitions or doubts will move out of the way. Soon enough, you will begin to connect with your imagination as you continue to write without pausing or thinking. And your intuition will flow freely with new insights relevant to your question. If you wish, you can shuffle again, asking the next (common-sense) question: *"What is holding me back?"* Draw a card randomly and start another entry in your Tarot journal to intuit what the card means to you in relation to the question you first asked.

By now, your creative juices are probably still flowing, and you're eager to find out what you can do to help you make that change, and unblock what you uncovered in Card 2. Shuffle your cards once more,

asking, *"What can support me in overcoming this challenge?"* Start another entry and see what insights you receive from your new deck. Next, look at the three cards you selected randomly, which are laid out in front of you. Start a new Tarot journal entry, and describe what you laid out, perhaps something like this:

Card 1 Question: *"What am I going to learn about myself today through you?"*

Card 2 Question: *"What is holding me back?"*

Card 3 Question: *"What can support me in overcoming this challenge?"*

Figure 14, on page 208, is an example of how your entry might look after you draw the first card. Congratulations! You have designed your first three-card spread and interpreted your first card reading! You will find more details on how to cast spreads in the next chapter.

Hopefully this section has inspired you to take a leap into the unknown and start your unique Tarot adventure. Remember the old saying 'practice makes perfect'? Keep it in the back of your mind. Experience is more valuable than information! Your Tarot experience helps you build a strong bond with the cards and enjoy a fluent and

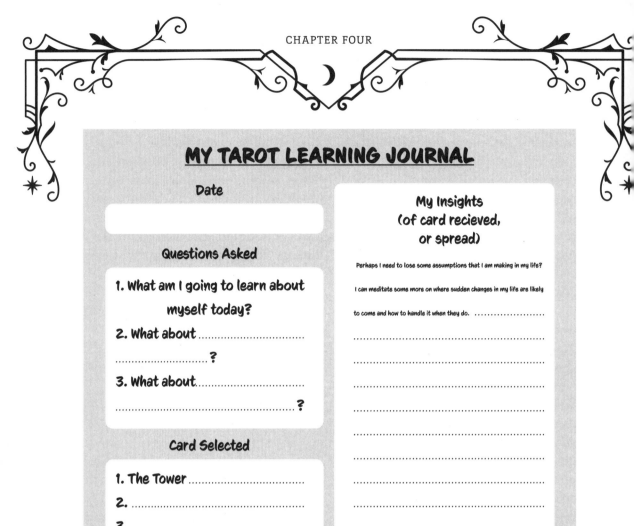

MY TAROT LEARNING JOURNAL

Date

Questions Asked

1. What am I going to learn about myself today?
2. What about ....
...........................?
3. What about...................................
...........................?

Card Selected

1. The Tower ....
2. ....
3. ....

Layout

THE TOWER
NUMBER: 1

NUMBER

NUMBER

My Insights
(of card recieved,
or spread)

Perhaps I need to lose some assumptions that I am making in my life?

I can meditate some more on where sudden changes in my life are likely

to come and how to handle it when they do. ....
....
....
....
....
....
....
....
....
....
....
....
....
....
....
....
....
....

I ask for clear guidance from the source for my highest good. I am always protected.

Figure 16 Tarot journal entry, example 2.

coherent conversation: you start to detect patterns and card combinations that speak to you personally, making your reading profoundly precise. When you first start Tarot readings, it is natural to refer to your Tarot journal or to this book. However, as your connection deepens, you will be referring less to other interpretations and more to your own Tarot glossary.

What a Tarot Reading Is

In the next chapter, several Tarot spreads will be explored to help you start reading the cards. Practice will let you know which ones to use and when. So, what exactly is a Tarot reading?

To put it simply, a Tarot reading consists of three components:

- You, the reader, and your psychic talent.
- The reader's understanding of each card's symbology and significance.
- The reader's ability to interpret the significance of a combination of three or more cards in a spread.

As you can see, you play an important role in what makes a great and enlightening reading. The more self-aware you are, and the more you work on improving and evolving as a person, the more meaningful your readings will be. Here are seven pointers to help you create clear guidance:

1. Establish a routine: create and stick to a routine before and after using the cards. Routine is the energetic structure that holds and supports the steady development of your intuition.

2. Adopt an 'inspire and empower' attitude (this is also a core value of the author). Whether in your psychic development or your Tarot readings, do not be spooked by, or look for, phenomena or drama. Go steadily and confidently. When reading for other people, try not to inject fear or doubt into their mind. Tarot is about empowerment, not woo-woo. So intend to stay authentic and ethical. You are a vessel for guidance.

3. Look after your own well-being. Psychic work can be draining and affect your health negatively. Centre yourself, and clear and recharge before and after a session. Drink plenty of water, eat healthily and get restful sleep. Human beings are walking batteries; water will help circulate, clear and maintain a steady energy flow.

4. Keep up your Tarot journal: your journal is the 'gatekeeper' of your learning and psychic journey.

5. Stop looking and start using what you've learned about the Tarot. Your learning journey has already begun; now plan to continue. Use the Tarot as much as you need to in order to fully understand your life's process and enhance your progress. When an answer is not clearly presented, especially one you do not want to confront, stop and check later, when you are more settled. When you start influencing the cards with your expectations, you lose your clarity and objectivity. And, of course, you miss out on learning the lesson behind your situation.

6. Hold your ego under control (like The Chariot) and stay true to yourself; the accuracy of a reading is dependent on your ability to keep an open mind and maintain your integrity with the Tarot. Before you start, take deep breaths, or meditate, and state your affirmation (as suggested earlier) before you start shuffling the cards.

7. Hold yourself accountable; it is empowering, as you learned from The Fool's journey. Whenever you're not sure how to interpret a reading, simply ask yourself,

"What does this card mean?" or *"What is it showing me?"* and your intuition will guide you. When you are reading for other people, simply say, *"I'm not sure what this indicates,"* without fear of losing credibility. You will jeopardize your integrity if you make up an interpretation or provide a bad one.

TAROT SPREADS

Tarot readings require laying out three or more cards or 'spreading' them according to a template or a designated layout where each position is preassigned a meaning. Insight into a straightforward issue or question is better suited to simpler spreads, such as a one-, two- or three-card spread. They are also ideal spreads to ease a novice into conducting a reading, and preparing for more complex spreads. The latter provides more extensive insights, spanning numerous layers and covering a longer period of time. Complex spreads also require multiple cards, and often combine Major and Minor cards. More complexity, more depth of insight!

A reading will provide more layers of interpretation and depth of information the more complicated a spread is. Take your time in getting to know the Major cards well, because they're the foundation of self-awareness and life direction. Minor cards are also important, but as you learned, they provide insights into everyday events and are best used to provide additional individualized insights, if you like, after having laid the Major cards. You will learn about and practice with a variety of practical spreads in the next chapter. Try your hand at using each spread, and determine which one to use, and for which type of reading. As with most readers, you will inevitably have two or three favourites. First, let's look at 'The Interview Spread' before we conclude this chapter on connecting with your new cards.

You do not have to be a seasoned Tarot reader to create your own spreads. In truth, it is an excellent technique to quickly grasp what the Tarot is. Even if you haven't memorized the specific meanings, you'll be able to understand the cards almost immediately. Practicing laying cards according to Tarot spreads gets you to the essence of Tarot learning. Furthermore, the spread you create is always appropriate for your needs. Creating your own spreads enhances your confidence and reminds you that you are learning Tarot in your own unique way.

Moreover, because there are so many spreads to choose from, it can be difficult to decide on the right one for you! You may even believe that if you don't have the proper spread, you won't be able to read the Tarot. This is not the case, as you will see in Chapter Five's demonstration of the one-card spread.

Tarot is about being creative and imaginative, and honing your intuition. When you design a spread, you engage in learning and construct your own path. After all, the Tarot is about The Fool developing his own identity and unique expression. You'll be doing the same thing. In other words, it will assist you in developing your own reading technique and forming a unique relationship with your deck.

The goal of creating a spread is to clear your mind, and to master asking the right questions to get good insights. A well-designed spread leads to a good reading. The Tarot cards require context in order to convey a 'narrative' through their visuals. In this manner, any insight provided will make sense.

Therefore, a spread is similar to a template in that it provides structure to insights. Moreover, it shapes the style of your readings by providing sequence or logic to intuitive insights. However, at first it may be helpful to follow a few established spreads to get a sense of how they work. But do not be afraid to make your own, as we'll do next by developing The Interview Spread to get to know your new Tarot deck.

Steps for Creating a Tarot Spread:

If you search Pinterest for 'Interview Tarot deck,' you will find hundreds of spreads. However, the first thing you must do is determine the goal of the spread.

1. What is the goal of making a spread? (In the Interview Spread, our goal is to 'meet' the new Tarot deck.)

2. Next, decide what you want to know. Write a brief paragraph and then divide it into a series of questions.

3. Keep your queries brief and to the point.

4. For each question, a card would be drawn. As a result, the number of questions may assist you in determining the number of cards in a spread.

5. Prepare your pen and Tarot journal to keep record of your discoveries.

THE INTERVIEW SPREAD

Purpose of interview: To find out if my Tarot card deck is a good match for me.

What I want to know: What is special about this particular deck, and what will I get out of it?

Can you recall a time when you had a job interview, or held one to recruit the right person for a position? The principle is the same. You are designing a spread around getting to know if a deck is a good match for you. You probably want to know what its features are, what its 'speciality' is, what its 'limitations' are, and whether you will 'benefit by collaborating' with it. Eventually, what you really want to determine is whether it is a 'good fit' for you and what you have in mind. Let's consider the keywords next:

1. Features: What is special about this deck?

2. Limitations: What are its limitations?

3. Benefits: What I will learn by working with it?

4. Outcome: Are we a good fit?

Methodology

- Now that you know you have four questions, including the outcome, you know that your spread will require you to draw four cards.
- The next step is to try several methods of laying out four cards. Experiment with a layout that feels natural: left to right, for example, or in a row, or having the

2. Limitations

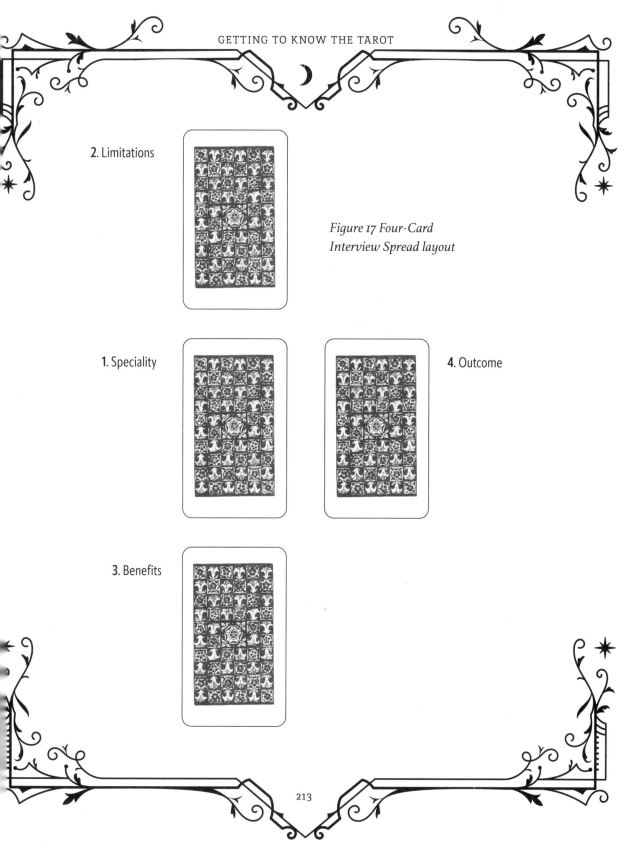

*Figure 17 Four-Card
Interview Spread layout*

1. Speciality

4. Outcome

3. Benefits

cards in a pile and drawing the first four. Alternatively, try the layout in figure 16 (page 213).

- Shuffle your cards to clear them (4–6 times will do).
- Start shuffling the Major cards only (to begin with) until you are satisfied that they are clear.
- Shuffle the cards again, asking the first question in your mind:
  "What is special about this deck?" Then put the cards down.
- Either cut the deck once from left to right, which is the most popular way, placing the bottom half over the top one; or we suggest keeping it simple by shuffling, repeating the question in your mind, and then randomly selecting the first card when you feel ready.
- According to the layout in figure 16, place the first card in position 1, face down.
- Repeat the process for each question, placing each one face down to avoid influencing your expectation and then put down the remaining cards (you will notice that none of the cards are reversed. Since this is an initial spread, there is no need to do so).

Let's say you got the following cards:

House 1: Speciality = The Emperor

House 2: Limitations = Wheel of Fortune

House 3: Benefits = Justice

House 4: Outcome = The Lovers

Before you read the next section on interpreting the Interview Spread, stop and take time to interpret the cards you got, journaling your insights (or do a fresh Interview Spread reading using your own Tarot deck).

Interpretation of Interview Spread sample reading:

House 1: The speciality of this deck is The Emperor, which signifies structure, authority and stability (a grounded intuition) – a good indication that this deck has the authority to do what is required. It also indicates that it is probably used in a structure; for instance, the reading or spread needs to be structured, or it allows for complexity.

It seems that it can grow and develop with its user. Additionally, it indicates the need for the user to look after the well-being of their body and health, and maintain a harmonious home environment as represented by the number 4.

2. Limitations
Wheel of Fortune

*Figure 18 Four-Card
Interview Spread example*

1. Speciality
The Emperor

4. Outcome
The Lovers

3. Benefits
Justice

House 2: The limitation of this deck is The Wheel of Fortune, which can indicate that it is quick to adapt, and can provide straightforward, direct answers as well as complex ones. It does not seem to be restricted by any limitation. So, it may be good to meditate on its cards, and use them as visual mantras as well.

House 3: The benefit of collaborating with this card is the Justice card, signifying that results could be achieved swiftly and fairly. The benefit to the reader of working with it is learning the lesson offered by Justice, operating in a balanced manner, and delivering balanced and fair answers to the enquirer.

House 4: The outcome of working with this card is signified by The Lovers, which is interesting! The Lovers represent a cooperative effort toward a harmonious result. This is a positive outcome card. The Lovers has the number 6 and represents service to humanity, implying that this could be a harmonious relationship, that the user and the deck are a good match, and that the user may be able to help others reach their life goals using this deck. This implies that the deck can assist the user in their professional practice. However, just like any other relationship, it has the potential to go either way! As a result, an additional card was naturally chosen to 'follow' the outcome card and define the course of this partnership. The Fool is the fifth additional card to this spread.

First additional 'follow-up' card: The Fool indicates that working with this deck will lead to an adventure. Despite the fact that the reader may not be familiar with the new deck, the extra 'follow-up' card is encouraging the user to trust the adventure and take a leap into the unknown, just like The Fool did! So, how will this 'risk' pan out? The need for still another 'follow-up' card was intuitively sensed, and the sixth card is Temperance.

Second additional 'follow-up' card: Temperance implies a harmonic, balanced conclusion in improving the user's intuition, confirming that the user and the deck are a good match. Also, as the halo on the Temperance figure shows, the user is expected to use this deck in a balanced, responsible manner because the outcome is 'illumination'. Because water signifies the unconscious, feelings and intuition, it is a fit for the reader's aim and can actually assist the reader in uncovering unconscious parts and bringing them to light.

This card resembles The Moon and The Star in that it features the water element, which is associated with unconscious qualities, such as dreams. This deck will aid the reader's personal self-development by balancing their unconscious side or psychic abilities with the logical structure provided by The Emperor, assuring that working with this deck will indeed be a great adventure!

Follow-up Cards

As you discovered in the Interview Spread above, the Tarot will sometimes give you an open-ended outcome card inviting you to investigate an issue further. The outcome could still go in either a positive or negative direction. This indicates that you do not yet have a final answer. A fluid outcome or result card depends on the nature of the card you draw, because certain Major (as well as Minor) cards have an open-ended interpretation, signifying a transition or the completion of a cycle and the beginning of a new one.

This is what makes the Tarot unique. It draws you in to investigate underlying currents and elements you are unaware of but should consider, particularly when a complex spread is used. The mystery deepens! Start practicing spreads and bring out the mystical sleuth within.

Exercise: Take a look at your Major cards first. Place them in numerical order, from 0 to 21, in front of you. Ask that your deck shows you which cards represent a transition, a change, or the beginning or completion of a cycle. Select the cards that you intuitively feel are open-ended as you gaze meditatively on them, from The Fool to The World.

Check to see how your selection corresponds with the table overleaf.

	CARD	FOLLOW	INTERPRETING UPRIGHT OUTCOME CARD
0	THE FOOL	YES	YES: FOLLOW to check quality of the outcome.
1	THE MAGICIAN	–	YES.
2	THE HIGH PRIESTESS	YES	Not known yet; all info is not in place. FOLLOW.
3	THE EMPRESS	–	YES.
4	THE EMPEROR	–	YES: but requires a lot of effort.
5	THE HIEROPHANT	–	YES: destined for.
6	THE LOVERS	YES	Important decision. FOLLOW.
7	THE CHARIOT	–	YES: brilliant!
8	JUSTICE	YES	YES: FOLLOW to see the quality of the outcome.
9	THE HERMIT	YES	Not now. FOLLOW.
10	WHEEL OF FORTUNE	YES	Quick changes: FOLLOW.
11	STRENGTH	–	YES.
12	THE HANGED MAN	YES	Delays. Suspended.
13	DEATH	YES	Won't happen but FOLLOW.
14	TEMPERANCE	–	YES.
15	THE DEVIL	YES	NO: But FOLLOW to see why.
16	THE TOWER	YES	No answer – everything is changing. FOLLOW.
17	THE STAR	–	YES.
18	THE MOON	YES	You are in doubt at the time of the reading: FOLLOW.
19	THE SUN	–	YES.
21	JUDGEMENT	YES	No decision is made at time of reading. Ask again another time. FOLLOW.
21	THE WORLD	–	YES. Expansion.

Figure 19 Table summarising follow-up of Major cards

	CARD	FOLLOW	INTERPRETING REVERSED OUTCOME CARD
0	THE FOOL	YES	NO: Bad risk. Serious mistake.
1	THE MAGICIAN	–	NO: Lack of information, of communication, or of inner abilities.
2	THE HIGH PRIESTESS	YES	NO.
3	THE EMPRESS	–	NO: Not really! Will not do well.
4	THE EMPEROR	–	NO: Too stressful.
5	THE HIEROPHANT	–	YES: Need unconventional approach.
6	THE LOVERS	YES	NO: Partnership will fail.
7	THE CHARIOT	–	NO: Don't force it. Let it go.
8	JUSTICE	YES	NO: Contract will be broken or will not happen.
9	THE HERMIT	YES	NO: Too confused.
10	WHEEL OF FORTUNE	YES	No decision yet.
11	STRENGTH	–	NO: No initiative, inner resources or good will.
12	THE HANGED MAN	YES	Delays: Follow.
13	DEATH	YES	NO: Final, you can't avoid it.
14	TEMPERANCE	–	NO: Matters are out of balance.
15	THE DEVIL	YES	NO: But follow.
16	THE TOWER	YES	NO. FOLLOW.
17	THE STAR	–	Will happen but may be delayed.
18	THE MOON	YES	You are not getting what you want: Follow.
19	THE SUN	–	YES: But can be a compromise. Follow.
21	JUDGEMENT	YES	NO: Judgement is against you.
21	THE WORLD	–	NO

CHAPTER FIVE

TAROT SPREADS

READING METHODOLOGY

The spread you use is determined by what you want to seek advice on. Start your reading session with a routine that you are familiar with. A brief invocation, a prayer, or just stating your goal sets the tone for the reading and creates a connection with the cards. Clear your mind and decide what you want your cards to guide you on.

Spend some time thinking about your questions. Writing down what you wish to enquire about is a fantastic way to get your concerns out of your head (see the section on The Interview Spread). Next, determine which relevant spread you will use to answer your question. Another approach is to consider whether your question is about a short- or long-term prospect.

- To begin, separate the two arcana and shuffle your Major cards in a single direction to clear their energy. Then, continue to shuffle while focusing on your question. There is, by the way, no right or wrong way to shuffle. Consider what you prefer. However, based on experience, it is usually advisable to shuffle the cards in a single direction, depending on whether you are right- or left-handed.
- The first time you shuffle, you want to clear the deck. As you shuffle, you might want to repeat the phrase "clear... clear." Then shuffle again, this time focusing on the question you're seeking guidance on.
- As you shuffle the cards, keep the question in mind and reverse a total of two cards from the Major Arcana anytime you feel like it. The purpose of reversing cards is to expose important concerns that require your attention. Your subconscious mind will guide you in drawing the appropriate cards. If you see any reversed cards in a spread, it indicates which part of your development needs your focus. They will frequently indicate 'the way out' of an unfavourable situation (refer to the table on reversed card meanings in Chapter One).
- As you become more acquainted with your deck, start combining Major and Minor cards in the spread of your choice. Typically, you would begin by arranging the main cards first, then repeat the process to select the Minor cards. The Minor cards are placed in the same order as the Major cards, according to the spread's sequence. This is known as 'covering' the Major card, which indicates that each Minor card covers, or complements, the meaning of the Major card it is associated with in that position.

- Draw the cards with your non-dominant hand, to stay connected to your intuition.
- Begin your readings by focusing on the Major cards first, which represent major events and cycles of transformation. Track the story that the Major cards are presenting. Consider reinterpreting that story by including the interpretation and significance of the Minor cards in their respective order. What additional insights do they inspire, and how are their meanings associated with each other?
- This helps you structure your reading by considering the big picture, or general outlook, first, before you move into smaller patterns and details. Additionally, it may offer a more accurate reading in the context of the spread. Place the deck face down in front of you whenever you are ready. With your dominant hand, fan the cards out in a line, and take a moment to release any attachments to an expected outcome. This will help you receive unbiased wisdom from your cards. Often, seekers try to feel cards to choose by rubbing their hands over the cards on the table. Unfortunately, this is yet another Tarot myth. Cards do not summon you. It is your energy field that interacts unconsciously with the image of a card.

So don't overthink this. Instead, keep breathing calmly and stay grounded and open to receiving the cards' counsel.

Moreover, when you get used to shuffling, you might find that you do not need to fan the cards out by laying them down. You can randomly draw the required cards as you hold them in your hand, and place each in its respective order before you draw the next one.

The steps to undertake when starting a reading session are outlined below:
- Determine what you need help with.
- Figure out whether it is a short- or long-term issue.
- Phrase your questions mindfully.
- Choose a spread.
- Separate Major cards from Minor cards.
- Shuffle the cards in one direction to clear them.
- Concentrate on a single question.
- Reverse two Major cards only.
- Put the deck down.
- Select cards at random (don't overthink it!).
- Place the selected cards according to your chosen spread, one card at a time.
- Repeat, using the procedure above if you intend to use the Minor cards in the same spread.

PHRASING YOUR QUESTION

You can consult the Tarot cards for insight on any level, from the ordinary to the spiritual. The Major and Minor cards both address developmental cycles and difficulties we confront in life. The mystical has infiltrated the mundane. People frequently seek spiritual advice while they are struggling in their prosaic, earthly lives. So when reading for others, don't underestimate your enquiry or the seeker's question. Furthermore, as one learns the spiritual 'rules' or processes that lead to a harmonious life, one's day-to-day living improves. Any seemingly insignificant question could open a door to further 'enlightenment' or self-awareness. This is why taking time to clarify the question is important. Use simple and succinct sentences.

Describing Your Situation

If you are not sure what you want to know, or how to phrase your question, describe it to yourself in writing. Maintain a straightforward approach! Begin by describing your background story, for example. What circumstances led to your wanting to consult the Tarot? What are you concerned about? Write a brief description in your Tarot journal to get your intuition working. For example, "Today is a big day for me; how will (describe) go?" Or "It is my birthday today, and I want to know what my new year will be about." Choosing the one-card spread will unquestionably reveal the theme, and you can then ask more questions to further explore what the cards will indicate (see examples of Tarot spreads below).

If you are still not sure how to phrase your question to the Tarot, describe what you want by writing a few lines or a paragraph as if you are speaking to a friend. Read your conversation out loud, then start modifying the wording until you get clearer. You do not need to do this every time, but it is a good way to train yourself, at the start, to clarify your intention. The quality of the advice you receive will depend on what you ask, because you will be the one interpreting the spread! Remember that, as a rule of thumb, vague questions will create vague interpretations and confusion, not clarity – which is the purpose of the Tarot.

Interpreting Tarot Spreads

Whether you are opting for a simple short-term spread or a more complex long-term one, the end card, also known as the result or outcome card, occasionally requires an additional card to follow it. The follow-up card clarifies the outcome of the spread. For example, if your result card is The Fool, it indicates that you are about to take a leap, start in a new direction or take an unknown risk. You have no idea how this new path will pan out. Is the leap you are about to make a risky or a worthwhile one? In such a case, you would draw an additional card to evaluate whether you received a decisive answer. Another example of an open-ended outcome card is the Wheel of Fortune. It symbolizes speedy and unforeseen changes in your situation. Therefore, you follow it with an additional card (after you shuffle once again) to determine the nature of the changes to come.

Moreover, when a Tarot card appears reversed in a reading, it has a somewhat different meaning than the upright one. In general, if you focus on the card's imagery, or use the 'walk into the picture' technique described earlier, you will be able to deduce its inverted meaning (and of course you have the table summarising those meanings). A reversed card emerges in a spread to draw your attention to underlying currents or elements around your issue of concern which you are not aware of at the time of the reading. Even though the follow-up can be used with any Tarot spread when required, drawing four or more cards will

confuse the outcome! Stop, and return to asking about that issue at a later time.

What is also interesting is that the seeker's desire for a specific outcome can occasionally be so intense that it influences the cards they draw. In that instance, take the cards into your own hands, shuffle them to clear them, and then draw the appropriate number of cards on the seeker's behalf. If you work online, you are probably already doing this. It makes no difference to the reading obtained as long as you (as the reader) are centred and maintain your connection to the 'highest source' of guidance.

This strategy provides structure to the reading while also facilitating the interpretation of more complex spreads and developing your intuition. Insights without context are like a boat with no rudder or oars – not very helpful! Moreover, the purpose of a Tarot reading is to provide insights as well as enhance your own understanding. So you need to capture the essence of the Tarot cards' advice, whether for yourself or someone else. In other words, you need to be able to integrate all the information by starting with the details and gradually weaving a 'Tarot tapestry' stitch by stitch. Let's do that next.

Keep in mind that when Minor cards are used to supplement Major cards in the same spread, it is recommended that you reverse two Major cards and five Minor cards when you shuffle each; two to five cards, respectively, appear to be the optimal number. More or less than that will not provide clear insight. However, as always, see what works best for you.

Additionally, you can select all the cards of the spread and place them according to the spread's template, either all at once or by shuffling again before choosing the next. It doesn't make a difference. If you are a beginner, however, shuffling and repeating each question in your head before you select the card for the next position may help focus your mind and memorize what the card positions, or houses, stand for.

THE ONE-CARD SPREAD

Let's keep things effortless, shall we? Whenever you're unsure how to formulate a question, imagine or pretend that your deck is conversing with you, asking, "What is 'your story' leading to your query?" For example, you may write, *"This is a big day for me because ... and I'd like to know how it will turn out. Is it as important as I believe it to be, or a passing opportunity that I should miss?"* Or if you are starting a new project or business, *"This is the official start of my new home-made business, and I'm curious about how the first three years will pan out."*

To get your mind unstuck, you can just shuffle your cards, asking, *"What about the issue I have in mind?"* before selecting one card to get your thoughts unstuck. The first card you draw will set the ball rolling. Your mind will prompt you to ask further questions as you consider its meaning. This one-card method will assist you in phrasing any subsequent queries and determining the best spread to use. Let's give it a go using Major cards only; shuffle and reverse two cards.

Examples of how to phrase questions for a one-card spread:
- What do I need to know about the issue I have in mind?
- (meeting, project, job offer, property, person)
- What does my heart tell me about ...?
- What is holding me back from ...?
- What are my strengths?
- What is my weakness?
- Why am I experiencing this obstacle now?
- What will help me overcome this situation?
- What is my relationship with ... about?
- How will ... develop?
- What can I learn from this experience?
- What is the dream I had last night about?
- What is the best way to handle this issue?

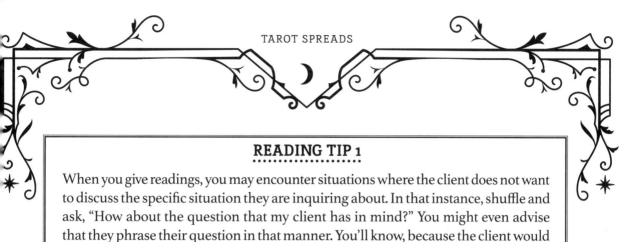

READING TIP 1

When you give readings, you may encounter situations where the client does not want to discuss the specific situation they are inquiring about. In that instance, shuffle and ask, "How about the question that my client has in mind?" You might even advise that they phrase their question in that manner. You'll know, because the client would probably ask, "Do I have to tell you what I want to know?" Sometimes you may be unclear how to phrase a query. In that instance, consider your circumstance for a moment before phrasing the question in the same manner.

- What do I need to focus my energies on this year?
- What do I need to develop to attract the right soulmate for this lifetime?
- What do I need to work on to help this goal manifest?
- What about my physical health?
- What about the physical health of ...?

Sample reading 1: Dan is in his mid-sixties, lost his beloved wife about five years ago, and is wondering if he will meet someone.

Question: *"What about Dan having a meaningful, fulfilling relationship with the right partner?"*

Card: Temperance

Interpretation: Temperance represents emotional healing, symbolized by the angel figure pouring the water between two cups. It relates to healing Dan's grief over his deceased wife, and indicates that he will experience a nurturing, stable and harmonious relationship again. He delighted with the outcome of his reading!

Sample Reading 2: Susan, who is a therapist, became acquainted with a healer whom she worked with from time to time. He proposed that they work together; however, she was confused at this sudden opportunity and wondered what it was about. She had many questions in mind, so we decided to ask:

Question: *"What about the issue I have in mind?"*

Card: The Hierophant

Interpretation: This card represents spiritual matters, as well as someone who speaks their truth and is spiritually aware. It denotes someone who wants to serve others and most likely operates ethically, as The Hierophant represents accessible greater wisdom. It might be describing Susan or the healer, but it is a positive omen in any scenario. Susan, on the other hand, wanted to delve more into the guidance provided by this card. She decided to shuffle and draw another card.

Second question: *"Why is this healer interested in collaborating? What are his intentions?"*

Card: The Hermit

Interpretation: The Hermit denotes more study, more knowledge and a selfless individual who 'lights' the way for others. The Hermit can also signify a recluse, someone who works alone, withdraws into his own spiritual world and presumably avoids the trappings of materialism. It refers to the male healer who wanted to collaborate with Susan. It also provided an answer to her inquiry and symbolized the healer's motivation. He wants to teach Susan, or share healing information with her; as The Hermit, he has no ulterior

motive other than to serve people. Despite being happy with this answer, she wanted to dig more, and drew another card.

Third Question: *"How will this collaboration develop?"*

Card: Justice

Interpretation: Justice denotes formal legalisation of the collaboration. They might both sign an agreement, showing that this collaboration will be a fair and just one. Susan was delighted at this prospect and became eager to know more. She asked to draw another card.

Fourth Question: *"What type of formal collaboration will this be?"*

Card: The Magician

Interpretation: The Magician represents the possibility of starting or bringing a project or partnership. It also implies that information will be transferred, as shown by the white 'communication' rod The Magician is holding toward Spirit, and the finger of his other hand pointing downwards, bringing the information down. It also reflects Susan's inner abilities and potential as a person who has everything she needs within her; this is symbolized by the 'four elements' objects on the table in front of The Magician. The exchange of knowledge might be progressive, as symbolized by the infinity symbol over The Magician's head and the Snake biting its tail around his waist. While meditating on the 'belt,' an image of a snake shedding its skin flashed clairvoyantly.

Perhaps the collaboration will take place over stages, progressing from one level to the next. It demonstrates the growing nature of the collaboration. In any event, because The Magician also represents two-way communication, Susan and the healer may soon communicate, most likely via text messages or emails (information travels quickly between the two hands of The Magician). The outcome of the spread is that a collaboration will be beneficial, and that Susan is quite capable of assessing her situation as it unfolds. She can take this collaboration as far as she sees fit if it continues to suit her goals. In any case, she has everything to gain by working with this healer.

Reading Summary: Several queries were spontaneously prompted without any planning. A four-card spread proved to be the most effective reading strategy. It is an example of how to clarify an issue as well as how to construct a spread. Furthermore, it demonstrates how Major cards on their own can provide straight and unambiguous counsel. You can modify and apply the one-card strategy to create subsequent spreads (refer to the Interview Spread in the preceding chapter).

READING TIP 2

Identifying what you want to know determines the number of questions to be asked and thus the number of cards required. Keeping each question short and basic helps clarify the process even further. Asking open-ended, double-barrelled questions creates uncertainty, so stick to one straightforward query across a small number of steps to gain clear guidance.

READING TIP 3

After you have thought about each card in a spread, think also about the cards next to it, and the one that precedes it. This will assist you in beginning to weave a story. Then, repeat with the Minor cards. Consider each card individually, then look at the previous and following cards to discover how the story unfolds. Finally, as if you were gazing at a painting, look at the elements first, then step back to look at the big picture. Can you identify a theme to the painting?

Sample Reading 3: In this sample reading, we will begin with the Major cards in the spread and progress to the Minor cards. It will give you an idea of how they can provide more information, adding details to a reading. Consider separating the Major and Minor cards. Shuffle the Major cards first, reversing just two cards, and then draw a card. Repeat the procedure with the Minor card, reverse five cards while shuffling, and 'cover' the Major card with the Minor card you draw.

John's 60th birthday is approaching. This is a big milestone. He was reflecting on his life and wanted some insights on what is coming up for him. What does he have to look forward to, and what would be the main focus?

Question: *"What is the significance of John's 60th birthday?"*

Card 1: The Sun

Interpretation: Woo-hoo! This is one of the best Tarot cards to receive for such a question. The Sun denotes a new cycle of renewal and growth. The Sun is card number 19, nearing the end of The Fool's journey, signifying that he has undergone a cycle of transformation and perhaps some rough times. However, The Sun now heralds a joyous life. Whatever he has been struggling with, or working hard on, is nearing its conclusion. On a personal level, he is beginning to feel more comfortable in his skin. He is not holding back, as he may have been in the past. Instead, he is looking forward to this new cycle marked by his upcoming 60th birthday.

This is symbolized by the naked child riding the grey horse of spiritual transformation. Moreover, the orange banner waved by the Sun child denotes renewed vigour; John could very well meet someone or travel abroad. The difficult emotional period he may have gone through (indicated by the preceding card to The Sun, The Moon) helped him clear all the cobwebs and face unconscious fears. He is now heading toward The Sun, and as ready as a transformed Fool can be for a new adventure, symbolized by the red feather on his head – which the Fool was wearing at the beginning of the journey. John will not be retiring from life. There's a wonderful adventure waiting for him.

To demonstrate how the Minor cards can support the Major reading, we are going to assume that John wanted to know the main character or theme of this new cycle. If you were conducting this reading, you would shuffle the Minor cards, (reversing five cards for the sake of adding complexity and more information). Then you would select one card.

Minor Card: Queen of Cups

Interpretation: The Minor card John selected was a water element, the Queen of Cups. This adds more information, enforcing that his 'bad cycle' was about healing his unconscious feelings. Perhaps he suffered a loss or the end of a relationship in the past, or he had fears about entering a new relationship in the future. In any case, this card symbolizes that he has overcome past challenges. As a man receiving this card, it denotes that his duality is well balanced and that he is in touch with his feminine side and his intuition. It is a calm image of authority.

The cup that the Queen of Cups is offering John is a rather large one, denoting significant happiness, joy and harmony in the next cycle. It could be describing a romantic partner too; in this case, she would be nurturing and supportive. The kind of relationship they would share would be a harmonious and well-balanced one. The Queen is sitting on a throne away from the shore, suggesting that he might meet this woman abroad, or that they might move abroad.

THE THREE-CARD SPREAD

This is a traditional and well-loved Tarot spread. The template of the three-card spread is quite versatile and can be adapted to any level of enquiry, from the mundane to the profound. It is also ideal to obtain quick answers to long-term issues such as, "How will my marriage turn out?"

Moreover, you can create your own three-card spreads that correspond to what you wish to know. See the previous example of creating the Interview Spread.

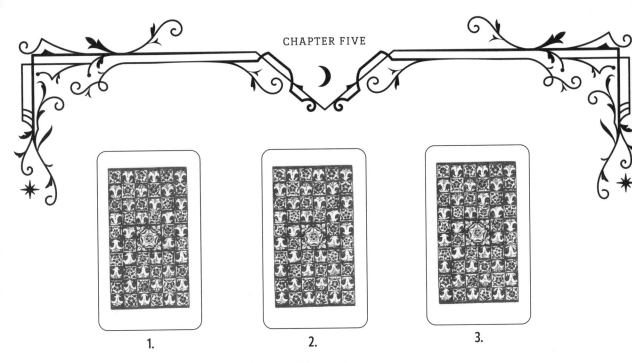

1. 2. 3.

Figure 20 The 3-Card Spread layout

Figure 19 shows some variations of the three-card spread, which you can adapt to suit your goal. For example, you can create a three-card template for personal growth, career growth, a fulfilling relationship or interpreting your dreams.

Additionally, you can combine the Minor cards with this spread for additional information, as in the sample reading below. What you need to decide first is what each of the three 'houses' or position stands for. Figure 19 is a template you can vary to create your own three-card spread:

Sample Reading 1: Liam is a young man who has recently graduated from university. But his excitement about starting his career and independence was short-lived. The start of the Covid-19 pandemic and lockdown made it extremely difficult for him to find suitable work or launch his career in the field of film production. Currently, he has an 'OK' job that he found after lockdown restrictions had been lifted. However, he remains concerned about what will happen to the career he is passionate about.

Question: *"What about Liam's career in film production?"*

Card 1: Underlying issue – The Devil
The Devil is about becoming enslaved to attitudes or habits that are no longer benefitting us. In truth, their sole purpose is to divert our attention from our goals and

3-CARD SPREAD TEMPLATE

CARD 1	CARD 2	CARD 3
Past	Present	Future
Body	Mind	Spirit
Subconscious	Conscious	Higher wisdom
Underlying issue	Factors to be considered	Outcome
Issue	What is blocking me?	Outcome
Strengths	Weaknesses	Outcome
Nature of issue	Benefit	Outcome
Nature of issue	Risks involved	Outcome
Where I am	Where I need to be	Outcome (best version)

Figure 21 The 3-Card Spread, sample reading 1

from expressing our potential and what we genuinely seek. This card represents Liam's unconscious pessimistic attitude, which was most likely impacted by lockdown. Perhaps he still feels imprisoned by the 'underworld' and the confining negativity and despair. His mental state has not changed, despite the fact that his life has returned to 'normal' in recent months. The Devil depicts unconscious patterns that need to be cleared to ease his way forward. The following card hints at how he can achieve that.

Card 2: Factors to be considered – Strength

Inner fortitude and perseverance are the qualities of Strength. It suggests that Liam has what it takes to overcome those 'beastly' stifling conditions around him, no matter how daunting they appear. He has a tremendous reservoir of strength, charisma and skills within him to conquer his issue and make his way to his goal. All he has to do to activate this inner strength is believe in himself and enable himself to display these characteristics. It is time for him to perceive himself as an adult with the right to pursue the future he desires. Furthermore, he appears to have innate creative potential, as shown by the infinity symbol above Strength. Liam may lack

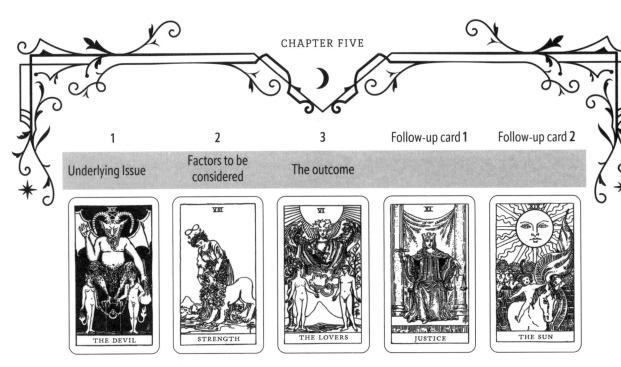

1	2	3	Follow-up card 1	Follow-up card 2
Underlying Issue	Factors to be considered	The outcome		

Figure 22 Liam's reading

experience, but he has what it takes to succeed in a field that he is passionate about. He'll never run out of creative ideas! This intrinsic ability, however, signifies confidence, which he must allow himself to reveal and express, especially when meeting with possible employers, as the following card suggests.

Card 3: Outcome – The Lovers

The Lovers is about collaboration and relationships with others, and it portends an upcoming interview, which could be the opportunity Liam seeks. It appears that he will find the ideal employer, with whom he will get along and enjoy a pleasant work atmosphere in which he will be nurtured and supported to develop. The Lovers

signify a choice between two options. Should he take this new opportunity when it arises, or stay in his current position? A follow-up is required.

Follow-up Card 1: Justice

This card represents a legal agreement. The future is looking brighter for Liam! The interview indicated by The Lovers card may result in an agreement and an employment contract. Is this contract a sensible and positive one for Liam? To determine the outcome, an additional follow-up card is required.

Follow-up Card 2: The Sun

The Sun affirms Liam's success and happiness as a result of signing this contract. The sunflowers imply that this could happen before the conclusion of the current summer. As the flag the 'Sun child' is flying symbolizes, Liam is reminded to exhibit his passion and fervour in his job. The next job will help Liam forge his career and reputation in the field, as The Sun signifies. Moreover, The Sun also indicates the conclusion of a transformative cycle (giving up a negative mind-set) and preparation for the next one, in which Liam will be totally fulfilled!

Reading Summary: Looking at all the cards together, it appears that Liam is undergoing a transformation; he must believe in himself and abandon the cautious, pessimistic attitude that he may unconsciously assume to be realistic. He must allow his actual creative spirit to shine through, and freely express his confidence and passion. He must persevere in his search for the right job, because the appropriate opportunity is on its way! A contract will be signed, and Liam will enjoy working in that conducive environment. Success is guaranteed.

Sample Reading 2: In the following reading, Major and Minor cards were used. Andrea had a crush on Thomas, who had been sending her confusing signals

for approximately two years. For a few months, neither of them defined or acknowledged their relationship. When she confronted Thomas, he went berserk. She felt exhausted and preoccupied by this so-called romance, and she could not really figure it out in her mind. What was the purpose of it?

Card 1: The nature of the issue – Death

Death inspires a variety of interpretations on a number of different levels when it comes to the question of relationships. It depicts the point of no return, the end of the old and the beginning of the new. It might apply to both Andrea and her friend. However, since she is the one inquiring, let's start with her. Death suggests that her life is undergoing a metamorphosis that could not have been avoided. The fact that the card is upright indicates that she did not resist this tough adjustment (the reader did not ask for more details). Death suggests that there was a sacrifice, that the previous 'king' was crushed by Death's horse. As a result, this relationship is unlike any she has had before – she is treading uncharted ground. Was the relationship 'dead' and over before it even started?

Card 2: The benefit of the relationship – The Hermit

The Hermit represents solitude. Perhaps it is inviting Andrea to withdraw and reflect on what she is going through, or implying that she needs to be alone to reflect and understand. It also implies that more information will be revealed along the way. Perhaps her aloneness gave this issue more significance; nonetheless she wanted to find out more. The connection with Thomas also initiated a spiritual lesson, or learning phase, according to The Hermit. The Hermit is card number 9, denoting the end or completion of a process (of adjustment), right before starting a new one on a higher level (nine moves into 10, which represents fulfilment). On another

level, while being in a relationship, she feels alone, as The Hermit suggests. She may be unknowingly retreating from life (because of whatever circumstance Death brought about). She is advised to investigate whether she was unconsciously avoiding romance by distracting herself with one that does not appear to be promising (no 'love' cards appeared so far).

Card Three: The Outcome – The Hanged Man

This card denotes another type of transition or change, where Andrea really needs to see the matter from an entirely different perspective. The progression of the three cards indicates that this crush instigated the completion of a personal development

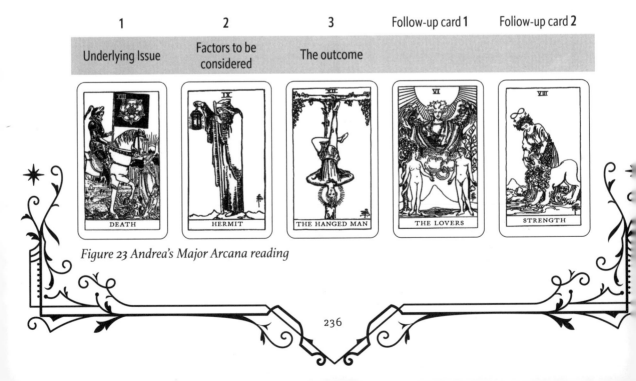

Figure 23 Andrea's Major Arcana reading

she was undergoing prior to meeting him. The final step in this cycle is to step back and see things differently. The issue does not seem to be about their relationship together, but about her finding out what kind of relationship she was after.

Was she after a fulfilling one? Or was any relationship better than no relationship? Considering the three cards together, perhaps it was The Hermit who did not wish to come out of his solitude either. In any case, as she 'hangs upside down' like The Hanged Man, she will see the light and change her perspective, as the halo around The Hanged Man indicates. To see how her transformation will unfold, two additional follow-up cards were required.

First Additional Follow-up Card – The Lovers

Andrea's life appears to be building up to a decision, possibly between two people. What she seeks is a balanced, supportive relationship that will help her achieve her goals (represented by the mountain in the distance, behind the couple). Her current relationship with Thomas lacks the emotional security that comes from being with the correct person in a balanced relationship. A further follow-up card is necessary to find out what the decision is.

Second Additional Follow-up Card – Strength

Strength is about training primal instincts to evolve to a higher level of awareness, one where Andrea will be connected with herself and her true feelings. She will be able to appreciate her own charm, beauty and strength. Her newfound self-worth will end this state of confusion and distraction over a non-working relationship that distracted her for too long. The new level of mastery she will attain will bring about self-healing and regeneration (since efforts are ill-spent nurturing the wrong relationship). She will have the fortitude to overcome the situation until she meets her equal.

If, on the other hand, The Hermit represents Thomas, he may be going through a period of self-growth in which he chooses not to be with anyone. The pressure of having to decide is what most likely freaked him out. He wasn't ready to leave his seclusion. Intuitively, he appears to want to travel light, like a hermit, at this moment, rather than share life's journey with a companion.

To add an additional layer of information, the cards were shuffled and three Minor arcana cards were chosen, one for each of the first three cards, in respective order 1 to 3.

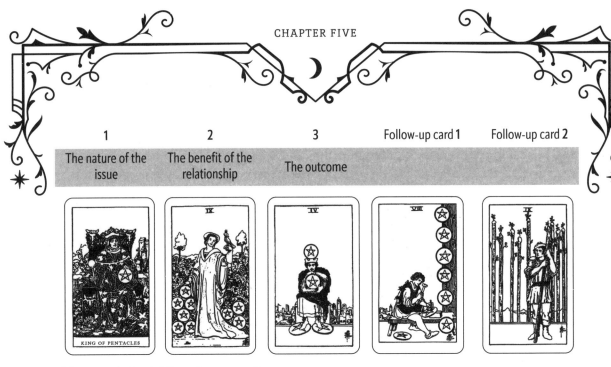

1	2	3	Follow-up card 1	Follow-up card 2
The nature of the issue	The benefit of the relationship	The outcome		

Figure 24 Andrea's Minor Arcana reading

Minor Card 1: The nature of the issue – King of Pentacles

The King of Pentacles represents a kind and loving person who is well balanced and stable, and understands the spiritual wisdom behind creating an abundant material life without any attachments or hang-ups. He is man who is comfortable and knows where he belongs. He is also at the end of his growth cycle (pentacles); in other words, he is accomplished. This does not seem to correspond to Thomas, the person Andrea is crushing over. Since the Minor card falls underneath the Death card, it relates to the previous man Andrea was in relationship with, which ended.

Minor Card 2: The Benefit – Nine of Pentacles

Andrea is represented by the figure of the Nine of Pentacles enjoying her bountiful surroundings. Because it falls under The Hermit card, it explains why Andrea is advised to 'withdraw' from this relationship. Her career ambitions and aspirations are about to be realized (number 9), and she has to focus on her career. This is a very positive card that also represents why the relationship was not meant to work. Andrea was most likely disregarding herself, her profession and other joyful areas of her life. She has clearly achieved something substantial, as evidenced by the accomplished woman represented in the Nine of Pentacles. Her interest in Thomas pushed her out of her loneliness and made her focus on herself, her appearance (a very well-dressed figure in exquisite clothes) and her career.

Minor Card 3: The Outcome – Four of Pentacles

The Four of Pentacles, the outcome card, is about creating financial stability. It is advising Andrea that what she needs to view differently today is that her priority is her business which should be developed now. Furthermore, in response to her query about relationships (consider the cards before and after this one), the ideal partner would be one who supports and encourages Andrea to pursue her career goals ('The Lovers). Her emotional stability will aid in the establishment of her financial security. She is also advised to organize her finances (number 4) in order to achieve financial security by reinvesting some of her profits back into her business and saving some for the future (notice how the figure in the Four of Pentacles is holding the pentacle like the wheel of fortune; money needs to circulate or keep flowing). The financial wheel will keep turning if you save and reinvest.

Minor Follow-Up Card 1: Eight of Pentacles

This card shows that Andrea possesses (or has the potential to acquire) abilities that can strengthen, enhance and improve her business income. When these two cards are read in sequence, they signal that Andrea can attain financial success and expand her business by investing in mastering a skill directly related to it. Six Pentacles are displayed on the wooden beam in front of her, indicating that she already possesses the right skills, which she can expand on. All she has to do now is keep applying those skills in her business (the cards are indicating how her business can grow). The second Minor card implies that she already manages her own business rather than being employed. This is depicted by the figure of the lady who has already achieved a certain level of financial success in the Nine of Pentacles.

Because the first Minor follow-up card is below The Lovers card, the partner she meets may be prepared to support her in improving her business and directing her skills. The four Pentacle cards form the spread so far, and 'cover' the Major cards; this indicates that Andrea's attention should be on her finances, rather than her love life, at this time in her life. That was something she wasn't really aware of. The developmental cycle, if you will, is about finance and money, which Andrea should think about before entering into a romantic relationship. This is what the Hanged Man card is alluding to. If you like, this is the 'season' for growing finances (before love).

Minor Follow-up Card 2: Nine of Wands

The message of the Nine of Wands is fortitude and perseverance. Drawing this card is fortunate, because it covers the Strength card in the spread, and thus reinforces it. The card is showing Andrea that she has the fortitude to go through the current phase, and that if she sticks with her business and steadily grows it, she will be able to overcome any difficulties that appear insurmountable at the moment. The eight wands behind the figure represent Andrea's struggles.

The figure holding one wand only denotes that Andrea feels ill-equipped to meet those challenges. Moreover, the facial expression on the figure enforces how worried she must feel. The eight wands behind the figure in the card also indicate that she has already been through a lot, which gave her the experience she needed to deal with life struggles. However, the worst is over since the eight wands are already behind the figure, not facing him. Andrea is at a good point in her life. She now has the experience, strength and skills needed to continue with her journey.

Reading Summary: Andrea had a difficult time in both her business and her love life. There is a sense that she is beginning a new life, and at a definite cut-off with her previous life. She wants to know why she has such strong feelings for Thomas, despite the fact that their relationship hasn't truly grown over the last two years. What is the point of this life experience? Her cards indicated that in order to understand what she is going through, she needed to change her perspective and recognize what she was unaware of. Her romantic interest in Thomas assisted her in refocusing on herself, coming out of her withdrawal after suffering a loss and recognizing that she was not feeling fulfilled.

What she was looking for was emotional stability to propel her development, which she was not receiving from Thomas. Thomas could be going through something similar, and the way he is coping is by refusing to engage in relationships. He may be alleviating his load by not taking on the responsibility of supporting anyone else. Instead, the cards encouraged her to concentrate on growing her business, which is what will bring her fulfilment at this point in life. She has already invested in and accomplished a lot with it.

Despite her prior difficulties, she is now well-equipped to thrive in her life. Her efforts must be focused on honing her talents in order to expand her business. Fulfilling her ambitions is what will bring her out of her isolation. She will then be prepared to share and enjoy a fulfilling, caring relationship with a supportive and loving partner.

THE 6-CARD PYRAMID SPREAD

Arranging the cards in the shape of a pyramid helps you recognize how the Tarot story (refer to Reading Tip earlier) is building up to its purpose. It is a versatile spread that you redesign to fit the purpose of your reading, as you will see below. Moreover, this spread energetically and visually directs your attention toward a specific personal goal, which makes it ideal for designing visual mantras in which to manifest them.

Because the questions are thoughtfully phrased, this spread is appropriate when you are aware of your current situation but are unsure how it is impacting your future life. It gives you a bird's-eye view of your situation from the soul's perspective, allowing you to see how the present is shaping the future your consciousness is driving you toward.

Cards 1, 2, and 3, in the bottom tier of the pyramid spread, reflect where you are now, in terms of your life's journey.

The second layer denotes what can help you, and the action you must take, which is aimed at achieving your purpose – what you truly yearn for. And the top layer, like the cherry on top of a cake, depicts the culmination of pursuing your soul's plan.

List of questions that helped design the six-card Pyramid Spread template:

1. What am I yearning for (reason for the problem)?

2. What is blocking me (block experienced)?

3. What is distracting me (unconscious block)?

4. What will help me overcome this issue (support and change of attitude required)?

5. What do I need to do (physical action)?

6. Will I succeed in realizing it (ability to achieve goal)?

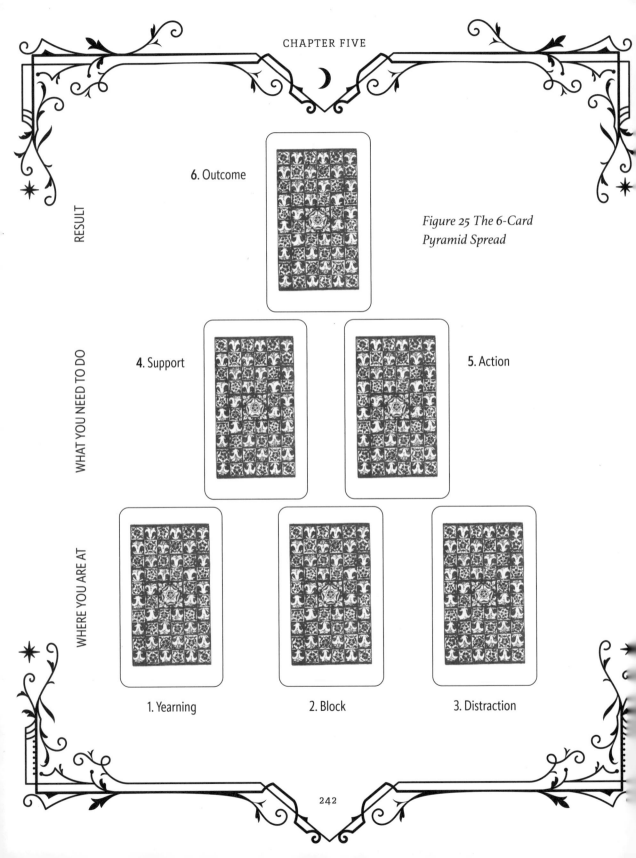

6. Outcome

RESULT

Figure 25 The 6-Card Pyramid Spread

WHAT YOU NEED TO DO

4. Support

5. Action

WHERE YOU ARE AT

1. Yearning

2. Block

3. Distraction

When and How to Use This Spread

When we are not in sync with our soul's purpose, we often feel confused. Or, to put it another way, when we are unaware of what we genuinely desire and yearn for in life, our false view of life, or beliefs, can distort our perspective, leading us to navigate life blindly and without inspiration (or higher guidance).

As a result, it causes confusion among the heart, head and ego – the purpose behind The Fool's transformation. The Tarot's alchemy is a personal one: balancing the various aspects of the personality with our essence as spiritual consciousness. This spread can be used as a visual mantra to address both the conscious and unconscious self, affirming the path to the goal.

1. The first step is answering question one. It reveals the background or our genuine desire, with which we are not connected – the cause of the anguish, if you will. What does our consciousness desire? Once it is determined, the next stage is to determine what is 'technically' impeding us.

2. Question 2 focuses on how we are experiencing that obstacle physically or consciously, or what we are specifically resisting, or what we are unable to accept about our current situation. What is the 'big picture' – the overarching strategy that we are not aware of?

3. Question 3 focuses on the subconscious, specifically on what we do to divert ourselves. We frequently do not want to perform what life requires of us. This is due to the fact that it is often easier to do what we can do rather than what we *need* to do. Question 3 uncovers how the person you are reading for, for example, avoids the challenge. What are they worried about, or what are they investing in instead of moving forward? What particular detail is preoccupying them? It is like focusing on one tree and failing to notice the forest they are walking through (they can't see the wood for the trees, as the saying goes). To put it another way: how do people unknowingly obstruct themselves?

4. Question 4 investigates what can help the person overcome the block they are facing, both consciously and unconsciously (the reason for the reading). What steps must be taken to redirect their attention and efforts toward their desire?

5. Finally, the plan's outcome: How adept is the person at achieving their objective? What transpires if they follow the counsel given to them through the Tarot reading?

Sample Reading 1: Nick is at a major turning point. He is about to make a big decision that will require him to relocate to a different country and change occupations. He has lately undergone a job transition, and this would be his second. Additionally, he lost both parents and a brother in the past few years. Despite the fact that he is excited, and is unmarried with no attachments, he is feeling apprehension and is unsure why. He is curious about what is going on in his life, and what the best course of action is.

Question: *"What about the new job offer Nick received?"*

Card 1: True desire – The Fool

The Fool affirms that Nick is yearning for a new beginning – leaving the past behind. Accepting this offer feels risky to him because there is a great deal of uncertainty in changing country, job and career. However, if he remains open-minded, like The Fool, and connects with his trusting innocence, his inner resources will help him adapt to this new situation. The card denotes that what he truly yearns for is a new beginning, leaving the past behind, in order to find himself and create the life he wishes. This also alludes to the trepidation he is feeling – fear of the unknown. However, as the following card affirms, it is exactly what he must do!

Card 2: Current block – Death

Death confirms that this is the end of his current cycle; a leaf has been turned over. Now is the right time to start a new life. Moreover, Death comes to all – he cannot escape from this call to start anew. Both cards point to a fresh new beginning, symbolizing leaving the past behind, turning over a new leaf and starting a new life. In other words, he is meant to go through this change. The opportunity offered to him seems to be well-timed. It is the door that – if he chooses to go through it – will deliver him to what his heart desires.

Card 3: Current distraction – Justice

Nick is distracted by the legalities of the situation. For example, resigning from one job and signing a legal contract for another. Or simply being concerned about the logistics of relocating from one country to another, with everything that it entails. He also has to cancel his rent contract, notify the landlord, and so on – and all of this appears to be preoccupying his mind, preventing him from focusing on the amazing opportunities that this offer brings.

Card 4: Support needed – The Emperor

The Emperor is all about structure, process, method, consistent effort and discipline.

What Nick needs right now is to discipline his thoughts and develop a list of what he has to do. He also needs to organize his schedule so that he can put this list into action. Being practical will help him deal with this transition. The Emperor is all about strategizing for long-term success. This entails devising a realistic process or plan to achieve long-term goals – as well as acting consistently. The Emperor is more concerned with doing than with thinking.

Nick is therefore advised to take practical measures toward this move. This applies to his life in general, because the next card depicts an absolutely fabulous outcome! He needs to discipline his mind by focusing on action rather than fretting about things. If he adopts this attitude, he will create a permanent legacy: his accomplishments will be worthwhile. Moving toward his goals in small, regular stages can help him achieve what he desires.

Card 5: Action advised – The Empress
The Empress is about nurturing and abundant living. The Empress is a planner. She plans her seasonal garden and is in touch with her intuition. She knows when to take the right action in order to achieve the right results. She also rules through her intuition and rules over her 'fertility' cycle. She is attuned to nature and to the cycles of planets and stars. She is aware of the right timing to fertilize her intentions and give birth to new beginnings (symbolized by her planetary necklace, denoting the number of planets, and her starry crown, representing the 12 signs of the zodiac and the 12 months of the year). The Empress confirms that it is the right time to make this move and receive the success and abundance that is on the way. In a sense, she completes what The Emperor stands for. Plans, without taking the right action at the right time, do not yield results!

Card 6: Result – The Star
The Star is a symbol of healing, optimism and inspiration. She confirms that Nick's ambitions will be realized. The card also represents the healing of anxieties or past struggles. The Star promotes emotional and mental equilibrium, heart and mind connection, and connection to one's spiritual essence – in other words, soulful direction in life. It also suggests that Nick may have innate 'mind' capabilities, namely telepathy. However, if his mind is preoccupied with worrying over details, he will lose out on receiving the guidance that he has naturally connected with. The ultimate result is peace of mind, as well as hope that inspires and promises success.

RESULT

6. Outcome

THE STAR

Figure 26 Nick's Pyramid Spread reading

WHAT YOU NEED TO DO

4. Support

THE EMPEROR

5. Action

THE EMPRESS

WHERE YOU ARE AT

THE FOOL

DEATH

JUSTICE

1. Yearning

2. Block

3. Distraction

Sample reading 2: Neil has a difficult relationship with his siblings. Now that his mother has passed, he wonders if he should cut off all contact, or try harder with them.

Question: *"What about Neil's relationship with his siblings?"*

Card 1: Yearning, or the core of the issue
Major Card: The Moon
Minor Card: Ace of Cups

Card 2: Block/Resistance
Major Card: The World
Minor Card: Ace of Wands

Card 3: Distraction/Unconscious block
Major Card: The Chariot
Minor Card: King of Pentacles

Card 4: Support/Attitude required
Major Card: The Hanged Man
Minor Card: Seven of Swords

Card 5: Recommended Action
Major Card: The High Priestess
Minor Card: Nine of Cups

Card 6: Outcome
Major Card: The Lovers
Minor Card: Nine of Cups

Follow-up Card
Major Card: The Emperor
Minor Card: Knight of Swords

Interpretation: Neil appears to be emotionally vulnerable to his siblings' poor behaviour due to his sensitive nature (The Moon and The High Priestess). This issue is impeding his personal development and intuition. It is preventing him from reaching his own goals (The Chariot). What he needs to realize is that he must first balance himself in order to be unaffected by what they do or say. In other words, he needs to connect with his nature and transcend how he identifies with himself as a sibling of theirs (The World). Furthermore, the issue is impeding the growth and success of his business or career, which is about to take off (The World followed by The Chariot). A new business partner or investor may appear in his life shortly (King of Pentacles), who may assist him in accomplishing this. Neil must be mindful of opportunities coming his way, rather than being sidetracked by family matters.

Major Cards 1, 2, 3, 5 and 6 are 'duality' cards that call for self-unification. Neil yearns to be emotionally happy and fulfilled. However, his family's situation is impeding his self-mastery and blocking the new cycle of expansion that he is about to embark on (The World). Once that is accomplished, his siblings' conduct will no longer throw him off guard. Furthermore, he appears to be reacting emotionally to their behaviour rather than responding objectively to it (Queen of Swords). He needs to decide how to respond, and to what measure, as and when things happen (both number 5 cards).

Furthermore, the 'duality' cards are about understanding the opposing side's point of view and accepting their inherent nature. In other words, there is a sense that he is not accepting his siblings for who they are. Therefore, he is not coping with the reality of the situation by seeing them for what they are. If you will, their behaviour has nothing to do with him personally, but rather is an extension of their level of awareness and how they deal with their circumstances. Looking at the situation from this angle is what can support him in creating a different reality (The Hanged Man).

As The World card depicts, Neil's current struggles are actually ushering in the final stage of his own transformation: overcoming his limitations. When combined with the Ace of Wands, it signifies the beginning of this cycle of personal growth, of which Neil is unaware. The battle is inside himself (The Chariot) – wanting them to behave differently than he believes they should, in order for him to be happy (Ace of Cups). The Chariot indicates the need to master his intellect and reason over desires of the ego.

The Moon, with The High Priestess, represents emotional turmoil and (dis) illusion. As a result, the situation is fluid, not straightforward. Taking a stance will exacerbate the conflict (Seven of Swords). Instead, prudence and diplomacy are required on his part, as well as cautious behaviour or attitude. Another attack from a brother is possible, as indicated by the Knight of Swords follow-up card. Neil will be able to cope with the realities of the situation more rationally if he sees them for who they truly are. Siblings are humans, and people sometimes behave strangely!

The advised course of action is for him to use his intuition as and when incidents arise – but also to be assertive in his attitude. This is a tricky balance to maintain. In other words, they are not going to change or improve overnight. Therefore, he ought to adapt his response to each situation as it arises. Furthermore, an intuitive woman is offering him sound practical advice that he must consider. This is represented by the two women in position number five – recommended action. Given that the final card is The Lovers, this may be his partner or wife.

So far, the cards do not indicate a decisive, affirmative cut-off action between Neil and his siblings. What seems to be required is measured involvement: agree to disagree without confrontation. He does not need to clarify how he feels about them either. The Moon and The High Priestess are also about the unknown; information will be revealed in the fullness of time. They suggest discretion when dealing with his siblings.

Reading Summary: Overall, the outcome of the reading is The Lovers card denoting balance and harmony in his marital life and personal life (The Lovers combined with Nine of Cups). A particular personal wish is about to be realized, making both partners happy. Adopting this strategy or perspective will bring Neil harmony and happiness (Nine of Cups). However, he will need to maintain this attitude toward his siblings for a fairly long time (The Emperor) before he could see any changes.

THE 7-CARD CHAKRA SPREAD

This spread is based on the human energy field, or aura. The aura is composed of seven primary layers that vibrate externally from your physical body, one layer on top of the other. Each layer is connected to the next by an energy hub, or wheel, known as a chakra, derived from the ancient Sanskrit language. They form your aura, or energy field. Understanding the chakra energy system helps you improve your interpretation of the 7-card Chakra Spread.

Chakras and Personal Growth

We live in a multidimensional reality, and the chakra system is an ancient metaphysical concept that depicts the interdependence of numerous components of our multidimensional structure: bodies, emotions, actions, ideas and thoughts.

Chakras are energy vortices that spin inside us as a result of the interconnectedness of consciousness and the physical body. They become sites of activity for the reception, assimilation and transfer of life energy as a result of this combination. Chakras are a sphere of energy radiating from the spinal column's core nerve ganglia. Chakras, in addition to nerve ganglia, correspond to the endocrine glands and many biological

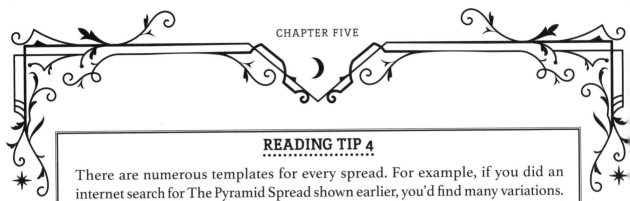

READING TIP 4

There are numerous templates for every spread. For example, if you did an internet search for The Pyramid Spread shown earlier, you'd find many variations. However, remember to keep any spread simple! It needs to fit your purpose and help you read the cards. Therefore, think of your objective and design your spread template mindfully by considering how you phrase your questions to the cards – it is a two-way communication. By practicing laying the cards in a particular spread, you will uncover what fits your reading style, trigger your imagination and, more precisely, find out how your brain connects images, information, symbols, colours and numbers in a spread to arrive at a meaningful interpretation.

activities such as breathing, digestion and reproduction.

They represent the energies of earth, which is solid, heavy, and dense; water, which flows; fire, which radiates and transforms; air, which is gentle; sound, which communicates; light, which reveals; and thoughts, which store knowledge. These energies are a metaphor for each chakra's expression. Other correspondences have been assigned to the chakras, colours, music, gemstones and archetypes, which might help us understand the core nature of each chakra.

Moreover, the chakra system is a metaphor that explains and ultimately assists in grasping how we operate as consciousness (or energy) in a physical body, and our self-development process,

as each chakra is associated by location to the functions of glands in our body. You might have started noticing how this relates to The Fool's adventure into self-awakening. In this section, we are going to design a Chakra Spread.

Psychological correspondence of Chakras

Chakras 1–7 correspond to survival, sex, power, love, communication, imagination and spirituality, in that order. The chakra system's association with personal development is conveyed through the seven essential rights each chakra represents. Because the aura connects the physical body to its surroundings (and the universe), the conditioning environment, such as family, culture or society, encroaches on the chakras, distorting their optimal functional state, which results in psychological consequences or struggles (blockages).

When this 'distortion' is not resolved via self-awareness and development, each chakra may overcompensate by either becoming excessive or shutting down, causing its function to become inadequate. It is comparable to the process The Fool went through during the three phases of awakening (refer to the beginning of Chapter Three). The Fool faces struggles on several levels to transform a distortion in balance, until he eventually awakens by understanding the wisdom hidden behind life's difficulties and emerges in his optimal form as The World.

Psychological Rights of Chakras

The psychological rights of chakras are a way of interpreting how the chakras, or centres of energy in the body, influence the mind and human behaviour. The list below explains how the flow of energy gets interrupted or blocked for each centre. A 'right' symbolizes the natural state of energy flow, or balance.

1. The right to have: When we are denied the basic essentials of survival, such as food, clothing, a healthy atmosphere and physical touch, we will doubt that right throughout our lives in connection to many things, including money, possessions, love and time to oneself.

2. The right to feel in a culture where emotional expressiveness is frowned upon.

3. The right to act that is restrained by abusive authority.

4. The right to love and be loved: When a child does not receive constant love, when love is subjected to conditions, a judgemental attitude, the dominance of one culture over another, and when we are emotionally wounded.

5. The right to speak and hear the truth: When we are denied the right to express ourselves, told to preserve secrets, and told to maintain familial lies. When we are judged for what we say and when our trust is betrayed.

6. The right to see (the truth): When we are informed that what we see is not real, when what we see is ugly, frightening or inconsistent, and when things are hidden from us, such as a parent drinking, it distorts the function of this chakra.

CHAKRA	PSYCHOLOGICAL INTERPRETATION	PSYCHOLOGICAL RIGHT	COLOUR
Chakra 1	Survival	The right to have	Red
Chakra 2	Sex	The right to feel	Orange
Chakra 3	Power	The right to act	Yellow
Chakra 4	Love	The right to love and be loved	Green
Chakra 5	Communication	The right to speak and hear the truth	Blue
Chakra 6	Imagination	The right to see	Indigo
Chakra 7	Spirituality	The right to know	Violet

Figure 27 Psychological interpretation of chakras

7. The right to know: The right to the truth.

To summarize, think of the aura as a 'psychic' memory drive containing your programming about how you manage various aspects of your life, which plugs into the hardware of your physical body. The drive's 'operating system' comprises your 'thoughts and awareness'. Self-awareness is the work that is done to remedy the system's flaws and debug it. Furthermore, when a distorted pattern is allowed to continue unnoticed, or when the individual is unaware of what they need to work on and balance, their distorted energy begins to influence the physical body, bringing dis-ease and, eventually, physical illness. Furthermore, when one energy centre, or chakra, is blocked or inadequate, it affects the centres above and below it, impairing their performance.

Figure 25 summarises the sort of information stored or received by each chakra as well as the colour of each chakra. It may inspire you to design your own 7-card Chakra Spread to balance and heal yourself as a clear channel for receiving psychic revelations. As with any design, you can modify it to fit the purpose of your spread and any areas of your self-development, healing or personal growth you want to learn about. This will be demonstrated in the sample readings below.

Locations of Chakras

Chakra 1 is placed at the base of the spine and is associated with the adrenal glands, kidneys and sex organs. Their roles are associated with the development of internal organs, bones, muscles, blood and the bladder. If the energy in this chakra is low, it might emerge as a lack of vitality and general weakness, particularly in the legs. It represents the past, childhood programming, beliefs and experiences of perceiving the physical world, and your personal will to manifest basic needs into the physical world (such as security of home finances, and material needs).

Chakra 2 is characterized by its orange colour. It is situated in the front of the pubic area, and the back location is around the kidneys. It is associated with the reproductive system and the small and large intestines. This chakra's qualities include vitality and life energy. Chakra 2 represents the start of individuating, forming one's own relationships and making one's own decisions; the unique personality emerging, including unique expression of the creative soul.

Chakra 3 is yellow and is placed around the solar plexus, in the front of the body, and in the rear around the adrenal glands. When this centre gets blocked or weak, it has an impact on the digestive organs. A person may, for example, have doubt, fears, anxiety and low self-esteem. Psychologically, it represents one's personal will in manifesting goals in the physical world, and how much a person can be overshadowed or influenced by other people's views (rather than believing in their own power or uniqueness).

Chakra 4: The Heart Centre unifies and balances our personality and spiritual aspects. It vibrates green, and is positioned at the heart, front and back. It represents one's ability to receive and give unconditional love to all sentient beings. It is also the cauldron that balances personality with spirit, transmuting all blocks and imbalances when it is functioning at optimum level, or energy flowing into it and out of it is not impeded. It is also the centre for connecting to the astral dimension, out-of-body experiences and the universe.

Chakra 5 is located in the front and back

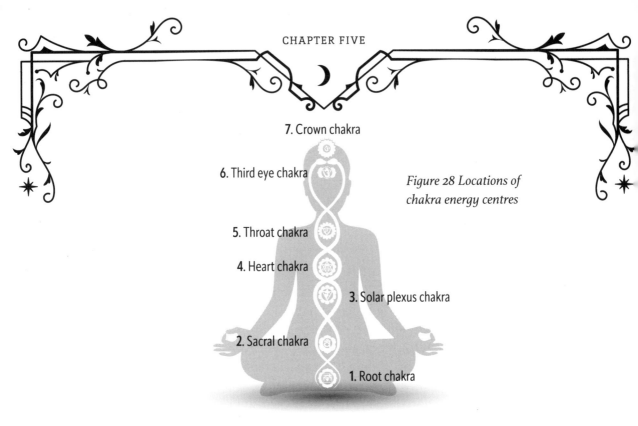

7. Crown chakra

6. Third eye chakra

Figure 28 Locations of chakra energy centres

5. Throat chakra

4. Heart chakra

3. Solar plexus chakra

2. Sacral chakra

1. Root chakra

of the throat. It is linked with psychic communication, hearing, speaking, smelling and tasting. It represents one's ability to trust their intuition and follow it, as well as their ability to perceive truthful insights.

Chakra 6 vibrates around the pituitary gland's front and back. It is known as the third eye and is in charge of the other major chakras. It represents your 'vision' of the world, how truthfully you perceive your life's experiences, and your personal will to express and manifest your dreams and visions into the world.

Chakra 7 is the final major chakra, often known as The Crown. It is placed right above the crown of the skull and is linked to spiritual connection, growth, channelling and receiving inspiration, and alignment with your soul's path.

Energy Currents

Any field energy, whether from a human, animal, plant or object, contains information, or 'data'. When two energy fields are connected (for example, you and your Tarot deck, or you and the person you are reading for), information is exchanged.

There is a two-way communication flow between them. Moreover, within an energy field, energy flows according to a direction or current. Each direction has a purpose or an interpretation, as follows:

Liberation Current

The flow of energy in the human aura runs up the spine, from the first chakra's 'dense' energy to the 7th chakra's lighter spiritual energy. This direction of flow is known as the liberating channel because this is how our awareness rises to let go, or liberate, and transmute negative accumulated energy as we deal and interact with life. When the liberation channel is clear, your aura is receptive to spiritual or intuitive insights, which travel down the manifestation channel and materialise in physical reality. A poorly developed liberation channel can lead to a sense of boredom, tyranny, sadness, being stuck, difficulty getting off the ground and lack of enthusiasm.

Manifestation Current

Thoughts enter consciousness and work their way down through the chakras, becoming more specific and denser with each level. An idea becomes a mental image, then words are said, an action is performed, and a result is achieved. This is how we get ideas, inspiration and guidance. If you like, when a thought pops into your mind and your aura channel is clear, as energy travels downward you start to envision the idea, or dream about it, then talk about it, communicating to others. Your heart gets impassioned by it, so you mobilise your self-will and initiative to make it happen, perhaps by seeking partners or others to collaborate with until it becomes a tangible reality.

In a similar way, as we reflect on experiences, we gain knowledge and wisdom from them. Wisdom heals, or liberates blockages in our aura, which allows this energy to flow up the channel from one chakra to the next. In other words, matter's stored energy is released. When both channels are open and clear, you would easily evolve, arriving at the enlightened or transformed state of The Fool! This is the reason that you are advised to look after your well-being and personal development and, in turn, your perspective and understanding of life.

Perception and Expression Currents

The combination of the first two currents creates a third and fourth current. The front of the body is how we perceive the world around us, and is referred to as Perception Current (the front of the chakra). The back channel is how we express ourselves in that environment and is referred to as the

YOUR HUMAN ENERGY FIELD

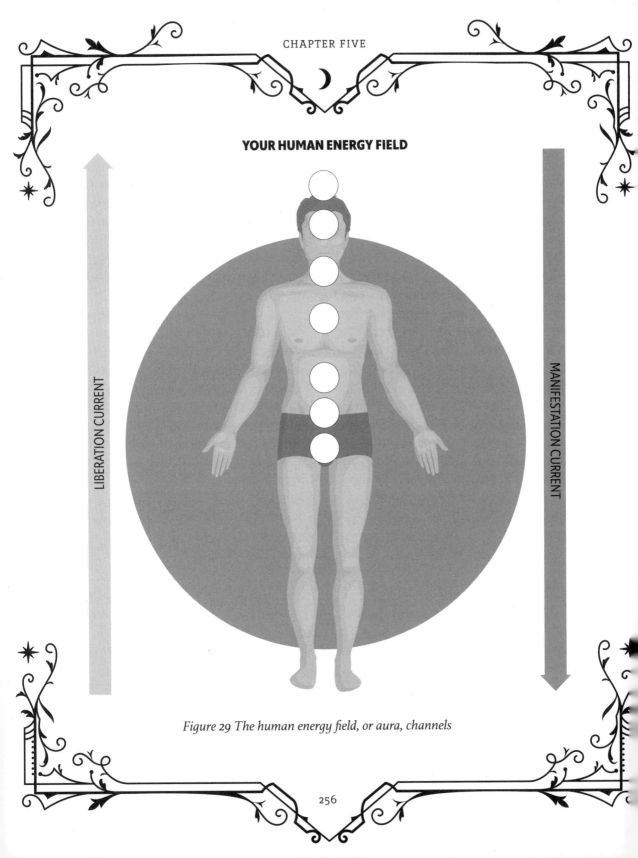

Figure 29 The human energy field, or aura, channels

Expression Current (the back of the chakra).

Think of a flute with small holes in it. The overall sound of the flute is determined by the number of holes that are covered or open. In a sense, how the chakras are functioning is responsible for one's whole sense of self. A chakra that is blocked or distorted can neither receive nor express our potential. The objective is the same as The Fool's: to consciously manage and master challenges – in other words, to deliberately manage the opening and closing of each chakra.

For example, a person with well-developed psychic skills may deceive their customers and make them reliant on psychic readings on a regular basis if their third chakra (self-will) is not fully developed. In contrast, a well-developed individual would act from a position of integrity, and a genuine desire to guide and truly serve their customers through the psychic insights they receive. In other words, a person's spiritual abilities may be well developed, but if their personality is not, they will be out of alignment. How they express themselves in the material world will not be for the 'highest good' or the purest of intentions.

YOUR PSYCHIC DEVELOPMENT

Your aura is a live energy field that interacts with your environment as well as your life events. If you have a lot of anxiety, for example, and do not deal with it, it will affect your mental health and how you process psychic insights. Furthermore, if you have physical aches and pains, or suffer from ill health, you are less likely to have enough energy to open the upper chakras, through which guidance is received.

Therefore, developing your psychic clarity requires a holistic approach to your overall well-being. Your aura, as a channel for intuition, is inextricably linked to your self-awareness. It reflects your personal progress as well as your physical, emotional and mental well-being. A balanced way of life fosters the development of psychic clarity, or clairvoyance (see Figure 28).

Figure 28 reflects the essence of a healthy aura. Chakras 1–3 reflect the formation of the personality and the past; chakra 4 begins to merge the dualism of the personality into higher consciousness of its spiritual essence and present attitude of how the person connects with and trusts the process of life (true feelings); and finally, Chakras 5–7 represent higher awareness, wisdom, and a deeper connection to inspiration and one's sense of purpose and awareness of their true essence as consciousness in a physical body.

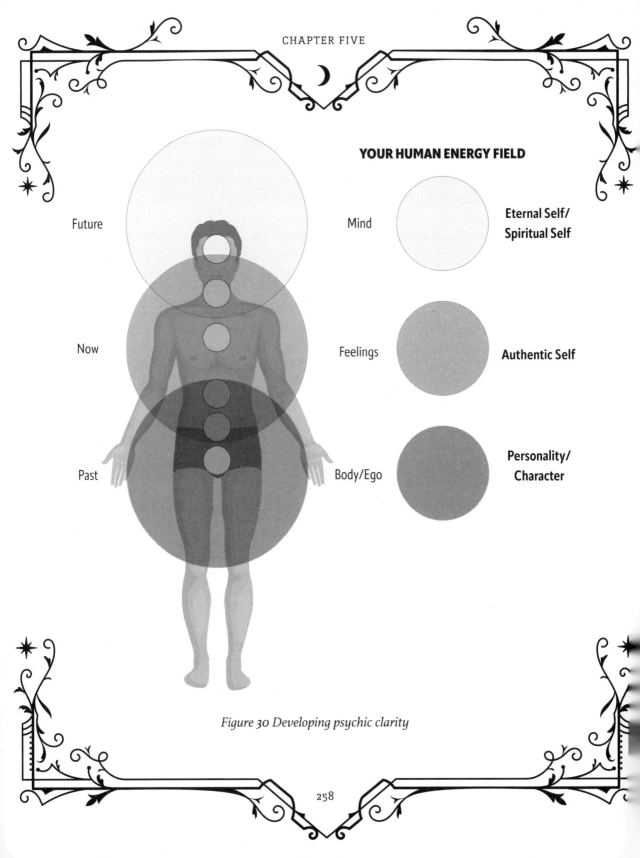

YOUR HUMAN ENERGY FIELD

Future

Now

Past

Mind

Feelings

Body/Ego

**Eternal Self/
Spiritual Self**

Authentic Self

**Personality/
Character**

Figure 30 Developing psychic clarity

As a psychic Tarot reader, the more conscious you are of past patterns that hold you back and face yourself in the now through love and compassion, the clearer your (spiritual) insights will be. When any issue, lesson or block, if you will, is not addressed and worked through, it will affect or influence other aspects in yourself, impeding a total transformation into The World, your true nature. This spread is ideal for checking your personal growth and what you need to address and transform along your Tarot path.

Just to remind you: whenever you feel off-kilter, whether physically, emotionally or mentally, it is not a good idea to undertake a psychic reading until you have cleared, recharged and balanced yourself. A Tarot reader is a psychic channel for guidance. If the aura is not clear, any guidance you receive will also not be clear.

Exercise – Aura Cleansing Meditation

Try this colour meditation to purify your aura every night.

As you lie down to rest, take a few deep breaths and envision yourself swimming in a clear pool of red water. Recognize how you feel as you swim in the red water with all your senses engaged. Next, imagine or pretend that the water changes colour as you swim around in your imaginary pool, from blue to orange, then yellow, and so on.

While swimming in each colour, keep an eye out for any distinctions you observe. Try to perceive the colour's quality: is it heavy or light, stimulating or soothing? Is the weather hot, warm or cool? Which part of your body is affected by each colour's sensation? What emotions does it elicit in you?

Such inquiries might help you judge the quality and type of information provided by each colour. This is more than simply a mental exercise in tuning in to energy fields; it will sharpen your perception as you explore the 'bandwidth' of information contained in colour. Swimming in colour images also aids in the cleansing of each chakra, the restoration of aura balance, and the promotion of relaxation and deep sleep. As usual, please note your observations in your Tarot journal.

The 7-card Chakra Spread template

Let's start with a basic version of the spread, asking a 'What about...?' question for a general overview. This spread is perfect for enquiring about your personal path. Or, if you are a professional therapist, healer or counsellor, it can give you insights into the developmental path of your clients. Furthermore, when interpreting the spread, consider position I to be the past, building

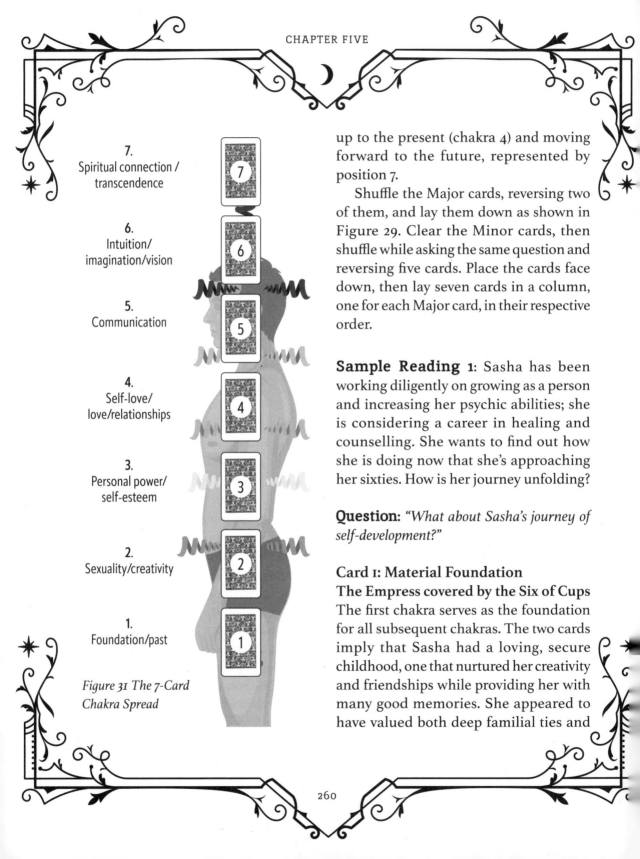

7.
Spiritual connection /
transcendence

6.
Intuition/
imagination/vision

5.
Communication

4.
Self-love/
love/relationships

3.
Personal power/
self-esteem

2.
Sexuality/creativity

1.
Foundation/past

Figure 31 The 7-Card Chakra Spread

up to the present (chakra 4) and moving forward to the future, represented by position 7.

Shuffle the Major cards, reversing two of them, and lay them down as shown in Figure 29. Clear the Minor cards, then shuffle while asking the same question and reversing five cards. Place the cards face down, then lay seven cards in a column, one for each Major card, in their respective order.

Sample Reading 1: Sasha has been working diligently on growing as a person and increasing her psychic abilities; she is considering a career in healing and counselling. She wants to find out how she is doing now that she's approaching her sixties. How is her journey unfolding?

Question: *"What about Sasha's journey of self-development?"*

Card 1: Material Foundation
The Empress covered by the Six of Cups
The first chakra serves as the foundation for all subsequent chakras. The two cards imply that Sasha had a loving, secure childhood, one that nurtured her creativity and friendships while providing her with many good memories. She appeared to have valued both deep familial ties and

long-lasting childhood friendships. She is not afraid to go after what she wants, as seen by the stability represented by both cards in the first position of the spread.

She was most likely an energetic child, full of vigour, imagination and creativity (The Empress), with dreams of a prosperous future. Because both cards represent family and friends, or relationships with other people, and are 'happy' cards, they imply that Sasha loves spending time with people she cares about and having excellent relationships with people in her life.

Card 2: Sexuality/Creativity
The Tower, covered by the Six of Swords

The second position represents distancing oneself from the 'crowd' in order to forge one's identity and make one's own choices. We typically experience this when we have intimate relationships with others, comparable to The Fool meeting The Lovers. The two cards together indicate that an intimate relationship arose or was abruptly interrupted (The Tower), signifying a desire to move away from what was familiar or break away from the past.

If you like, the relationship, or split, set her life on a new path, leaving difficulties in her wake. This could also imply that Sasha underwent a transition. This experience resulted in a complete shift in her outlook on life. In any case, it denoted leaving anything she had established behind and starting over in a new country, as symbolized by the 'travel' card of the Six of Swords, and also considering the next set of cards.

Card 3: Personal Power
The World reversed, and the Five of Pentacles reversed

The World and the Five of Pentacles are both reversed. This indicates that the event represented by the preceding cards in position 2 affected Sasha's life and self-confidence. However, they also suggest remarkable fortitude and drive to re-establish her life in this new country. She must have faced financial difficulties, yet she did not give up. Instead, she appeared to have worked hard and put forth constant effort. The World reversed suggests that she experienced a period of stagnation in her money flow. This can also refer to working for herself as opposed to having a salaried job that provides a consistent income, possibly even starting a new career in healing (considering the next card – Strength).

Card 4: Self-Love/Love/Relationships
Strength, covered by the Three of Cups, reversed

The fourth position of the spread is centred on the heart chakra, indicating the ability to receive and give unconditional love. It demonstrates that Sasha's experience with adversity and starting anew did not diminish her ability to be true to herself, or to open her heart to life and receiving love. It also represents a pleasant time in her life, perhaps when she was in a love relationship or when she gained satisfaction from embarking on a new professional path.

Furthermore, it demonstrates how she learned to tame 'beastly' situations to her advantage, or that the adversity she endured taught her what is valuable in life, such as pleasurable interactions with people. Both cards also imply that Sasha received emotional support from friends and loved ones, possibly including a partner. Strength reassures her that she is on the right track, expressing her essence as a healer or therapist. Furthermore, she may have experienced the premature loss of a happy friendship or partnership. The reversed Three of Cups denotes sadness over the loss of a happy situation.

Card 5: Communication
The Sun, covered by the Seven of Pentacles
Chakra 5 represents the right to speak and hear the truth. It also relates to psychic abilities like mediumship and channelling (communication). Sasha's heart is connected with 'the truth' she speaks or communicates

with. It seems that her development is aligned with her purpose, and that she handles her career with integrity. However, she might be suffering from a lack of excitement about her work, and worrying about cash flow.

The Seven of Pentacles indicates that her 'harvest' is right there in front of her, and if she refocuses on what she needs to do, finances will balance themselves. Her attitude needs to change, as she is already blessed, but perhaps needs to feel grateful for what she has accomplished in spite of past setbacks. This confirms preceding cards; Sasha seems well on her way to better and happier times.

Card 6: Intuition/Imagination
The Hermit, covered by the Queen of Pentacles
The two cards together suggest a person who earns money through being a 'guide' or a mentor to others. Together they represent a balance between spirituality and material life, symbolizing Sasha's vision or expression in life. The Hermit represents what Sasha does by guiding others on their journey. It could also be a valuable mentor who has assisted her on her journey.

In any event, it denotes spiritual knowledge or wisdom, and also that her learning has led to her enjoying or having financial independence through her work. Despite personal hardships and a lack of financial security in the past, her journey has led her to a fulfilling career as a therapist. Furthermore, while the journey may have been lonely, she has grown wiser as a result of her life experiences.

Card 7: Spiritual Connection/ Transcendence
The Fool covered by the Queen of Swords
The Fool represents yet another beginning of a new cycle, implying that the next cycle will be different (looking at the follow-up cards) from the difficulties and heartache Sasha faced in the past. Sasha's development continues to a new level. But what will help her is her capacity to regulate her mind, think for herself and take decisive action, as the Queen of Swords represents. Sasha's emotional reaction appears to be under control in the next cycle.

The wisdom she gleaned from past occurrences is what allowed her to keep an open heart without bitterness toward life. And it will help her master her mind and what thoughts enter her 7th Chakra, if you will. The Queen of Swords has mental mastery and represents a decision to be made. Sasha can train herself to master her mind by choosing which thoughts to entertain. This will keep her on track and

promote a continuous, clear flow of energy in her body and life in general. What fresh beginning does The Fool card proclaim in the 7th position of the 7th Chakra? An additional follow-up card is required to determine that.

Follow-up Cards: Temperance covered by the Nine of Pentacles
Temperance suggests that the next cycle's theme will be balance, harmony and emotional healing. Sasha can now begin to enjoy a new cycle of ease, joy and financial prosperity, as symbolized by the Nine of Pentacles. This outcome is the result of her ongoing awareness and working through the hurdles she faced. It does undoubtedly mark the beginning of a joyful cycle. Temperance can also represent meeting a new partner or collaborating with the appropriate partner.

The new relationship will develop gradually, eventually bringing the two partners together (in comparison to The Tower, which indicates being suddenly struck by love, for example). At first it may appear to be a 'special' friendship, as Temperance also represents a smooth, natural coming together of two people, or two parties, in what could turn out to be a supportive and loving relationship – a match made in heaven (symbolized by the alchemical purifying of emotions the Temperance angels depict). Sasha has a lot to be excited about in the future!

Reading Summary: Sasha's past (chakra 1) provided a strong supportive environment. Yet disappointment in her earlier relationship (chakra 2) dented her confidence and affected her self-trust in rebuilding her life. However, it did not stop her from welcoming life into her heart. It may have propelled her to seek a new career as a therapist or healer. Moreover, it may have helped her recognize what to look for in the right romantic partner (chakra 4). She needed to continue applying her skills, despite setbacks (chakra 5), to achieve financial stability. Moreover, through her continued learning, she was met with supportive mentors who guided her further on this new path, which eventually helped her establish financial independence through her psychic skills (chakra 6). Her dedication aligned her with her soul's purpose (chakra 7), and she needs to maintain mastery over her mind from now on as she enters a new cycle of ease and joy, which could lead to a loving, supporting relationship.

Sample Reading 2: Dan is a 33-year-old yoga therapist who recently started his own business. Despite the fact that he has achieved significant financial success and continues to work on himself, he longs for a loving, fulfilling relationship. He wants to find out what is preventing him from having a meaningful relationship and what needs to be addressed. You can vary the 7-Card Chakra Spread to gain more insights as follows:

Begin by drawing one Major card for each of the seven positions in this reading. Then, on the left, form a column by drawing seven Minor cards from 1 to 7. Next, form another column on the right by drawing additional seven Minor cards, placing them in order from 1 to 7.

The Left Column (LC) will represent how he perceives life. And the Right Column (RC) will represent how he expresses his will to materialise his goal, or the rights of each chakra. By varying the spread in this manner, Dan may be able to determine the precise issues he is called to investigate.

Cards 1 to 3 represent the foundation of personality development in terms of the right to have, the right to feel and the right to act; energy flows through the chakra in a healthy, balanced manner without any obstruction caused by distorting our perceptions of these rights through negative experiences.

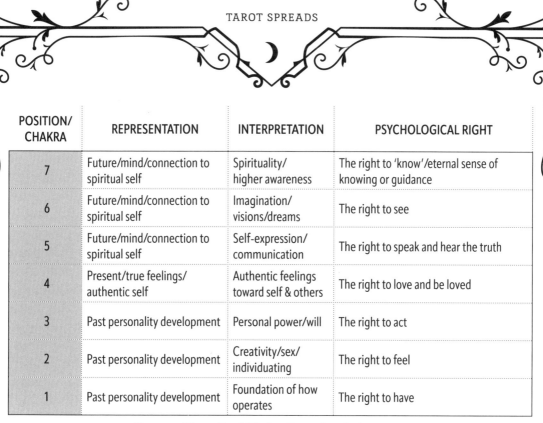

POSITION/ CHAKRA	REPRESENTATION	INTERPRETATION	PSYCHOLOGICAL RIGHT
7	Future/mind/connection to spiritual self	Spirituality/ higher awareness	The right to 'know'/eternal sense of knowing or guidance
6	Future/mind/connection to spiritual self	Imagination/ visions/dreams	The right to see
5	Future/mind/connection to spiritual self	Self-expression/ communication	The right to speak and hear the truth
4	Present/true feelings/ authentic self	Authentic feelings toward self & others	The right to love and be loved
3	Past personality development	Personal power/will	The right to act
2	Past personality development	Creativity/sex/ individuating	The right to feel
1	Past personality development	Foundation of how operates	The right to have

Figure 32 The 7-Card Chakra Spread variation

Cards in position 4 reflect the growth of one's personality 'in the now', or up to the present; how a person perceives and acts in the world, as well as how well they are in touch with their true feelings and connect with others as a result.

Cards 5 to 7 reflect the person's relationship to their 'higher self', or wiser aspect of themselves. Essentially, they reveal how far their spiritual development has progressed or how much of their consciousness influences their personality. In other words,

they represent alignment with the mission of one's soul or purpose.

Take note of how the question is worded for Dan's reading.

Question: *"What inner work does Dan need to do to align with his soul's purpose and meet his true partner in this lifetime?"*

Answer:

Personality foundation

Position 1: Material Foundation – The Right to Have
The Star – Optimism and ascension to higher spiritual levels through emotional experiences.
LC: Two of Pentacles – Creating income from two sources.
RC: Two of Swords – Making a decision.

Position 2: Sexuality/Creativity – The Right to Feel
The Emperor reversed – Immature behaviour.
LC: Eight of Wands – Sudden movement, or air travel.
RC: Ace of Wands reversed – strong creative potential and initiative.

Position 3: Personal Power – The Right to Act
Temperance – Balance, emotional healing, harmony.
LC: Knight or Pentacles reversed – Too focused on money.
RC: Six of Pentacles reversed – Stingy behaviour, or material loss.

Interpretation: The Star and Temperance (card 1 and card 3 of the past, which represent the foundation of personality) show that Dan had a positive healing foundation that promoted his creative initiatives, a balanced personality development, and that he enjoyed a balanced, loving home environment. The Emperor reversed, on the other hand, reveals some distortion in his capacity to retain his balance, most likely because of the family's frequent travel or moving countries, which could have significantly affected his sense of security and continuity. Furthermore, as a child, he may have had a broken relationship in his early adolescence that warped his perceptions of what ideal loving relationships should be like. Perhaps it had something to do with the fact that his father's (The Emperor's) card was reversed.

Some unfavourable influences may have hampered his development in terms of making the proper decisions (reversed Ace of Swords), or his capacity to keep control over his anxieties. The Minor cards indicate a distortion in how he perceived material life, and how he expressed himself in his world. The reversed Knight of Pentacles indicates immature behaviour, perhaps financially, and the reversed Six of Pentacles indicates that he mistrusted people, or that he was deceived by their behaviour. In any case, they lead to him forming a less than healthy attitude toward finance. However, in the end, that phase ended positively by bringing the necessary emotional healing (Temperance).

Authentic self

Position 4: Self-Love/Love/Relationships – The Right to Love and Be Loved
Judgement – Start of total transformation.
LC: Five of Cups reversed – Short-lived phase of unhappiness.
RC: Ace of Swords reversed – Troublemaker, deceitful.

The Judgement card underlines how difficult it was for Dan to mature into an adult and establish his own perspective on life. Some kind of event changed the life he knew. This forced him to start creating a new life for himself, although he might have been unprepared to face these sudden circumstances. He could have become a troubled adolescent as a result of the trauma he witnessed. The perception channel represented by the reversed Five of Cups, on the other hand, indicates that this was a brief phase. The 4th chakra is still probably undergoing transformation, which can explain the delay he faces in meeting the right person.

Dan still needs a period to adjust and leave the past behind.

Spiritual awareness/sense of knowing

Position 5: Communication: The Right to See and Hear the Truth
The Magician – Fluid reasoning process forming.
LC: Ten of Swords reversed – Backstabbing or legal disputes.
RC: King of Swords reversed – Represents a manipulative person.

Dan's top three chakras suggest that he has psychic potential or, to put it another way, that he is building a strong connection with his greater purpose. He appears to be eager to develop his self-awareness and balance his perspective on life. The Magician represents his ability to initiate his own advancement, as well as the spiritual insight required to express them in the material world. It also represents his ability to achieve his personal goals and his openness to receiving direction and insight.

Furthermore, he is starting to create a sound reasoning process. However, he continues to be disappointed by others, which means he fails to recognize them for what they are and places unrealistic expectations on the outcomes of interactions he establishes with others. Because of the number of disappointments he faced in his relationships with people, he may have expressed himself as a selfish or manipulative person, which led to him mistrust the process of life. The cards in the sixth position reinforce this.

Position 6: Intuition & Imagination – The Right to See

Wheel of Fortune – A cycle of quick changes.
LC: Five of Wands reversed – Backstabbing or legal disputes.
RC: Ten of Cups reversed – Feeling let down.

Dan can learn and open up his psychic centres quickly, as The Wheel of Fortune suggests a cycle of quick development where he has begun to see the truth of his own patterns. He is adapting to the world he perceives just as quickly. However, he continues to feel let down and disillusioned by his relationships with other people. Because of his mistrust in other people, it blocked and delayed meeting the right person. The 4th chakra still needed balancing, if you like. However, this quick cycle of transformation is also helping to meet the challenges he needs to work quickly as well. It implies that if he maintains a balanced perspective on life and does not emotionally overreact, he may meet the appropriate person soon.

Position 7: Spiritual Connection & Transcendence – The Right to Know

The World – Authentic self has emerged.
LC: Ace of Cups – Start of a new relationship.
RC: Ace of Pentacles reversed – Indicates a difficulty with the tangible world.

The World is the culmination of Dan's personal evolution. More specifically, it denotes the direction of his personal development, which is total fulfilment! As the Ace of Cups suggests, he will meet the appropriate person for him. And he will most likely be focused on the happiness and joyful emotional balance that this connection will offer. However, he must be careful not to get overly focused on money, which has previously resulted in immature or disruptive behaviour.

The Ace reversed represents the difficulty one has in achieving his aspirations in the practical world, and it revealed that Dan was preoccupied with finances to secure his survival in the aftermath of the devastating life experiences he underwent. It explained his survival attitude by securing financial independence, in a sense above anything else. Instead, his cards indicate that he should work on achieving a more practical, balanced approach by reasoning and choosing the right people to collaborate or fall in love with.

Reading Summary: Dan's childhood environment was favourable to his personal development. A significant event changed his life, and he became distrustful. Because of his repeated disappointments in relationships, he may have acted in a manipulative manner to accomplish what he desired and secure his financial standing. As a result, it appears that he lost touch with his true feelings and what he longed for. He persisted, however, and was determined to sort himself and his life out. Dan is nearing the end of his transformation, as represented by The World, in which he will discover the ideal partner and become less concerned with money! The delay was necessary for him to feel safer in himself, and for his heart to trust the process of life rather than taking disappointments personally.

Exercise: Compare the results of the above sample reading enquiring about Dan using both the seven-card and three-card spreads. Which three-card spread variation would you use, and what would you assign to each of the three-card positions? How does your reading compare using both spreads for the same enquiry? What conclusions do you draw? Keep a Tarot journal to record your insights.

YES-OR-NO SPREAD

When to use this spread: Whenever you need a simple yes or no answer, use this spread. Because the answer truly hangs in the balance, the Justice card is placed in the background as a reminder that the outcome is critical, a just and fair one that will have consequences. When the outcome card is inconclusive, draw a follow-up card as explained earlier in Chapter Four under *What a Tarot Reading is* (page 209); and please see Figure 18 (pages 218-9) for the interpretation of the outcome cards, and which ones you need to follow.

When your enquiry is about legal matters, however, you can use the Judgement card as a background instead of the Justice card.

In this spread, you can use only the Major cards. There's no need to cover with Minor cards, as the former will provide decisive answers. As discussed earlier, questions you phrase need to be clear, so double-barrelled questions will give a confused reading. Instead, just ask *"What about this issue?"* or *"Will I succeed in …?"* and not *"Will I buy this house, or not?"*

Sample Reading 1: *"What about John's physical health after surgery?"*

Background

Background

The YES-and-No Spread

1

THE TOWER

Outcome

Outcome

JUSTICE

3

JUSTICE

THE MOON

STRENGTH

2

THE WORLD

*Figure 33 Yes-or-No spread
sample reading*

Turning Point

Turning Point

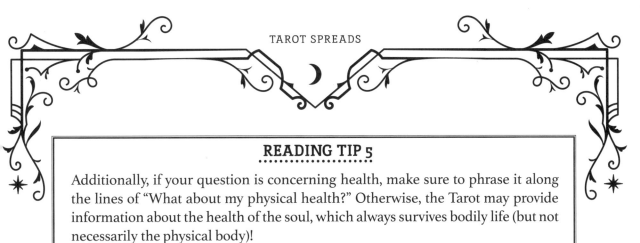

READING TIP 5

Additionally, if your question is concerning health, make sure to phrase it along the lines of "What about my physical health?" Otherwise, the Tarot may provide information about the health of the soul, which always survives bodily life (but not necessarily the physical body)!

Furthermore, if you want to know if something will happen in a specific time frame, incorporate it into the query: "What about hearing back regarding my job interview within three weeks?" This will give you an idea of how long it will take. Please refrain from asking the same question many times. Allow yourself to let go of your need to know (attachment) and inquire again in a few days. You will obtain a more accurate reading.

Cards 1: Background – The Tower

Card 2: Turning Point – The World

Card 3: Outcome – The Moon

Follow-up card: Strength

Interpretation: The Tower shows that John's illness abruptly changed for the worse. The World card, on the other hand, suggests that he will have a positive turnaround. Finally, Strength denotes recovery and the body rallying. The spread indicates that John will regain his health.

Sample Reading 2: *"What about Charlotte's relationship with Mark?"*

Card 1: Background – The Star

Card 2: Turning Point – Death

Card 3: Outcome – The Lovers

Follow-up card 1: Judgement

Follow-up card 2: The Magician

Interpretation: The relationship's background is The Star, which indicates that this relationship will provide healing and emotional balance to both lovers. Death and Judgement, on the other hand, are significant transformation cards. They indicate that both parties will go through major transformations because of this partnership, which is not to imply that this relationship is undesirable because the cards are stacked against it. In fact, the opposite is true: In order for this relationship to work, both Charlotte and Mark will have to confront whatever issues they did not address individually in the past. If you will, the relationship serves as a vital catalyst propelling further personal development. It urges or calls them both to confront and resolve their own issues.

The Lovers card implies that this connection will allow both of them achieve balance and harmony as a result of realizing that neither of them can continue in any relationship unless they endure the 'Death' of previous attitudes or preconceptions about what a partnership is. The follow-up Judgement card represents more transformation, or purification. Both will go through this process in order to entirely remove any hurdles that are preventing them from having a healthy, positive relationship.

Finally, The Magician verifies that this relationship will be successful if both parties communicate openly and honestly with each other. Being clear about their needs and working through their individual issues will reap dividends. It will be a rewarding, balanced and supportive, as well as stimulating, partnership.

Sample Reading 3: Tamara and Neil are in their mid-thirties. They live in a small flat in London with their son, who is four years old. Both would like to try for another child, which would require moving to a larger, more appropriate home. They put their current home on the market, and want to know when the move will be possible.

Question: *"What about Tamara and Neil moving to a larger home within the next three months?" or "What about the sale of Tamara and Neil's current home within the next three months?"*

Card 1: Background – Temperance

Card 2: Turning Point – The Lovers

Card 3: Outcome – The Hierophant

Interpretation: Temperance indicates that the timing is favourable for this decision to happen. There will be an agreement or understanding that Tamara and Neil have made the correct decision to sell and relocate. The Lovers represent a choice between two options. This can refer to a decision between two buyers for their current home, or a choice between two homes for them to purchase. It is a beneficial card, because it signals that a sale will take place and that alternatives are open. The Hierophant, the outcome card, is a resounding yes! So it appears that a house move is feasible within the next three months.

THE 12-HOUSE ASTROLOGICAL SPREAD

In the 12-house astrological spread, 12 Major cards, then 12 Minor cards, are arranged over two rows of six cards each, according to the respective order of the 12 astrological houses, as outlined in Figure 32 below.

Methodology:

Begin by centring yourself and shuffling the cards to clear them. Separate the two arcana, and shuffle the Major cards first, reversing a total of two cards any time you feel like it. When you feel you have shuffled enough and you are ready, put the cards down. Draw 12 cards randomly, without thinking too much or feeling the cards, and lay them out according to the figure overleaf in their respective order.

Repeat the same process with the Minor cards, reversing a total of five cards, placing the cards in their respective order. In the top row, cover each Major card with a Minor card by placing the Minor card above the Major one. Do the opposite for the bottom row, where you would place the Minor card

below the Major card in houses 7 through 12, respectively, as Figure 34 demonstrates:

As you noticed, the 12 cards are divided into two rows of six cards each. You would interpret each card in connection to the astrological house it falls in and is associated with, as well as in relation to the cards that precede and follow it, and then in relationship to the Minor card that covers it, noting its placement in the top or bottom row.

You may be familiar with the 12-house Astrological Spread, which is laid out in a circle. Many Tarot readers follow that circular layout with a 13th card to sum up the reading. However, when the 12 cards are laid out over two rows, they provide additional levels of interpretation. House combinations will be spotted more easily when relevant, and you might find out that you get a far more in-depth reading. Furthermore, you can designate the top row to represent short-term changes and the bottom row to represent long-term changes. Sample readings are demonstrated below.

When to Use the 12-house Astrological Spread

This spread is ideal for:

- Long-term, prospective or general life overview; anytime you need to take a step

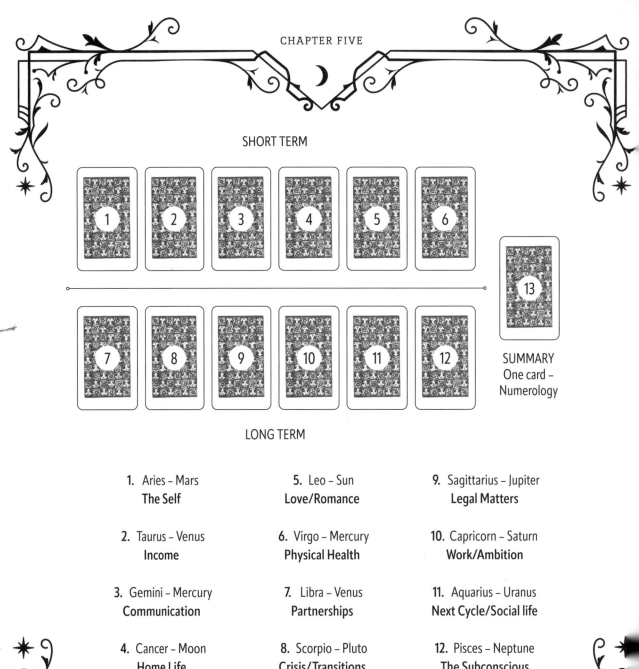

SHORT TERM

LONG TERM

SUMMARY
One card –
Numerology

1. Aries – Mars
   The Self

2. Taurus – Venus
   Income

3. Gemini – Mercury
   Communication

4. Cancer – Moon
   Home Life

5. Leo – Sun
   Love/Romance

6. Virgo – Mercury
   Physical Health

7. Libra – Venus
   Partnerships

8. Scorpio – Pluto
   Crisis/Transitions

9. Sagittarius – Jupiter
   Legal Matters

10. Capricorn – Saturn
    Work/Ambition

11. Aquarius – Uranus
    Next Cycle/Social life

12. Pisces – Neptune
    The Subconscious

Figure 34 The 12-House Astrological Spread

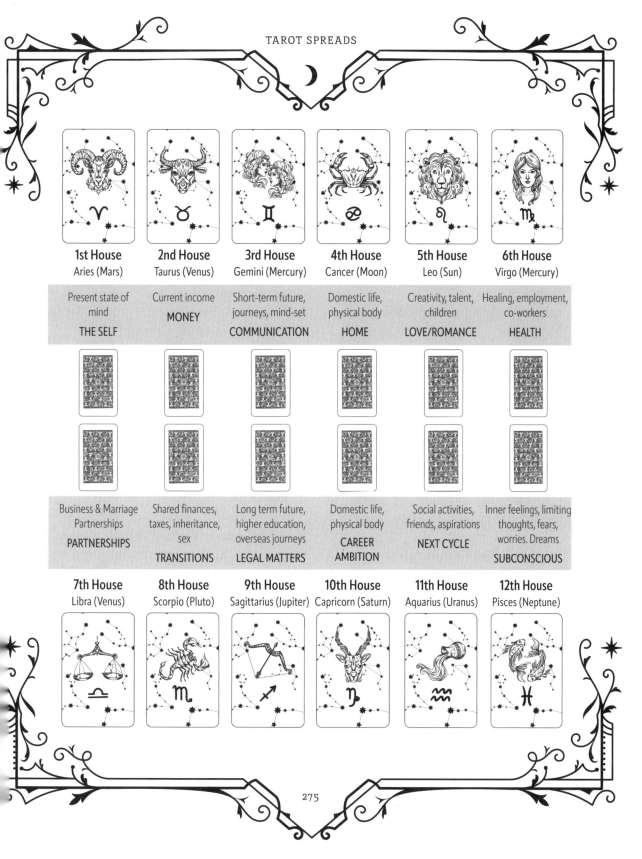

1st House	2nd House	3rd House	4th House	5th House	6th House
Aries (Mars)	Taurus (Venus)	Gemini (Mercury)	Cancer (Moon)	Leo (Sun)	Virgo (Mercury)

Present state of mind	Current income	Short-term future, journeys, mind-set	Domestic life, physical body	Creativity, talent, children	Healing, employment, co-workers
THE SELF	**MONEY**	**COMMUNICATION**	**HOME**	**LOVE/ROMANCE**	**HEALTH**

Business & Marriage Partnerships	Shared finances, taxes, inheritance, sex	Long term future, higher education, overseas journeys	Domestic life, physical body	Social activities, friends, aspirations	Inner feelings, limiting thoughts, fears, worries. Dreams
PARTNERSHIPS	**TRANSITIONS**	**LEGAL MATTERS**	**CAREER AMBITION**	**NEXT CYCLE**	**SUBCONSCIOUS**

7th House	8th House	9th House	10th House	11th House	12th House
Libra (Venus)	Scorpio (Pluto)	Sagittarius (Jupiter)	Capricorn (Saturn)	Aquarius (Uranus)	Pisces (Neptune)

back and view things clearly. Think of it as a strategic reading at the beginning of a new year, a birthday or any time you transition into a new cycle.

- Anyone who has not had a Tarot reading before and seeks in-depth guidance on their life's journey.

Meaning of the 12 Astrological Houses

The 1st House: The Self
The enquirer's personality and temperament at the time of the reading, the current cycle or influences they are under at the moment.

The 2nd House: Finance
A person's capacity to generate material wealth and possessions, as well as how they earn it and their attitude toward money.

The 3rd House: Communication/Mental State
Mental state at the time of the reading, the ability to express themselves, communication skills with others, writing talent, imagination, the intellect and short-distance journeys.

The 4th House: Home
Represents both actual home (property) or home life, influences at home or home life, as well as the physical body (as in 'the abode of the soul'). Property transactions, for example, buying, selling or losing a home.

The 5th House: Partnerships/Creative Talents/Children
Represents romantic affairs (of the enquirer), marriages, forming business partnerships, creative abilities and talents as well as pregnancies and children.

The 6th House: Daily Life/Environment
Represents routine in the office, working habits, relationship to co-workers, healing potential of physical health, imprisonment, recovery, daily habits and attitudes, for example, toward diet, food as well as service to the community.

The 7th House: Partnerships/Unions
Represents ongoing partnerships, both romantic and business (the other party).

The 8th House: Transformation, Crisis, Legal Matters
Represents shared finances or partners (romantic or busines), sexual relationships, windfall (for example, bonuses), return on investments (not income), or winning the lottery, crisis, tax troubles, beginnings and

endings, transformation of partnerships (divorce or breakup), physical death (should be interpreted with caution in combination with other houses. Look for additional cards which must indicate major transformation in Houses 1, 4, and 6).

The 9th House: Long-Term Future
Represents law, legal matters such as contracts or lawsuits, higher education (such as master's or doctorate degrees), long-distance travel or moving countries, people coming into the enquirer's life from countries that would be 'foreign' to the enquirer; one's life philosophy or outlook; and long-term future or outlook.

The 10th House: Work/Career
Represents ambition, career development, success in career, current conditions around a job.

The 11th House: Social Contacts, Personal Ambitions
Represents how the personality of the enquirer is perceived by their environment or other people around the enquirer, and also represents one's expression in the world – their aspirations and ambitions. For example, receiving acknowledgement or accolades, successful ambitious goals, fame,

supportive contacts and acquaintances, the completion of the current cycle, and an indication about conditions around the next cycle.

The 12th House: The Next Cycle
Also, the subconscious, constraints, hidden adversaries, discharge from hospitals or confinement and imprisonment, the start of a new cycle.

House combinations
The 12-house Astrological Spread is ideal for the Tarot to tell you a story that unfolds according to the layout's respective order. Because the cards are arranged in the sequence of the 12 houses, each card's interpretation adds another layer as you proceed along the houses. As the story unfolds, each card interpretation adds onto the next. Furthermore, it is an inspiring approach to organically structure your reading as you follow the story unfolding.

After you've laid the cards, think about house combinations. Lovers in the 5th House, for example, indicate the possibility of a romance. Next, examine the cards in the 7th House of partnerships, followed by the cards in the 9th House of legal matters (and the future), to determine if this relationship will lead to marriage, for example.

If health is a concern, or if the person you

HOUSE COMBINATIONS

SHORT TERM

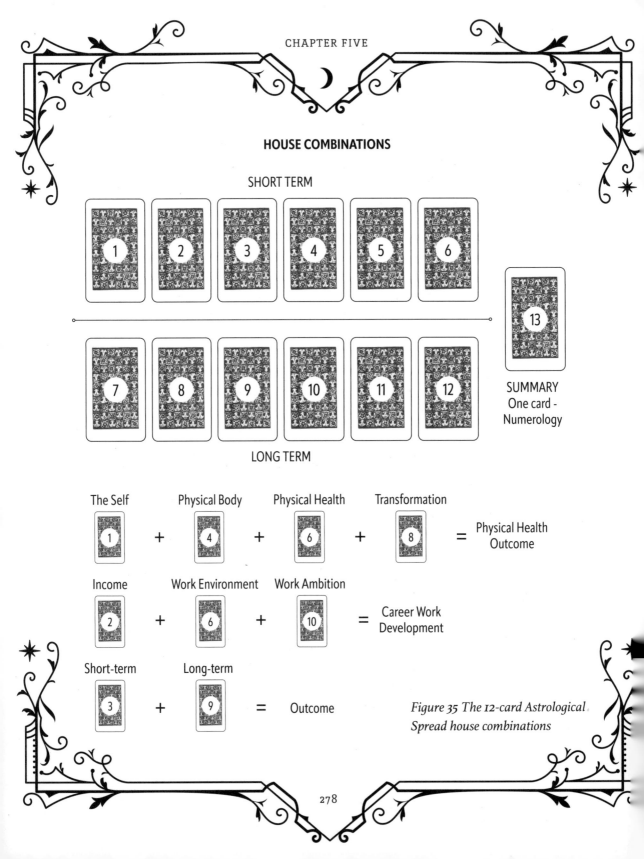

LONG TERM

SUMMARY
One card -
Numerology

The Self + Physical Body + Physical Health + Transformation = Physical Health Outcome

Income + Work Environment + Work Ambition = Career Work Development

Short-term + Long-term = Outcome

Figure 35 The 12-card Astrological Spread house combinations

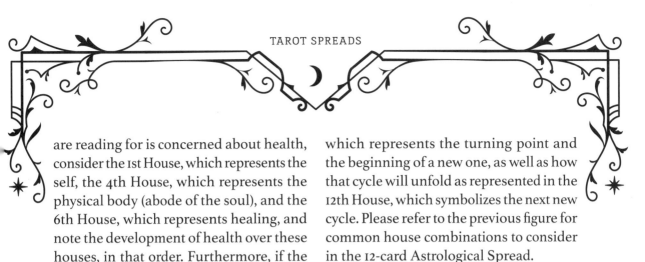

are reading for is concerned about health, consider the 1st House, which represents the self, the 4th House, which represents the physical body (abode of the soul), and the 6th House, which represents healing, and note the development of health over these houses, in that order. Furthermore, if the health situation is critical, look to the 8th House to discover how the transformation will play out.

Career development is another housing combination to check for: 2+6+10 represents the ability to earn money, the work atmosphere, and any promotions, in that order. When examining personal growth and transformation, examine 8+12,

which represents the turning point and the beginning of a new one, as well as how that cycle will unfold as represented in the 12th House, which symbolizes the next new cycle. Please refer to the previous figure for common house combinations to consider in the 12-card Astrological Spread.

Sample Reading: Maria is in her late fifties. She had an illustrious career, is retired now and remains single. Her eyesight started failing her recently in addition to other 'niggly' problems that doctors could not find a reason for. She spent nearly two years at home with family during lockdown, and is just beginning to emerge and resume her

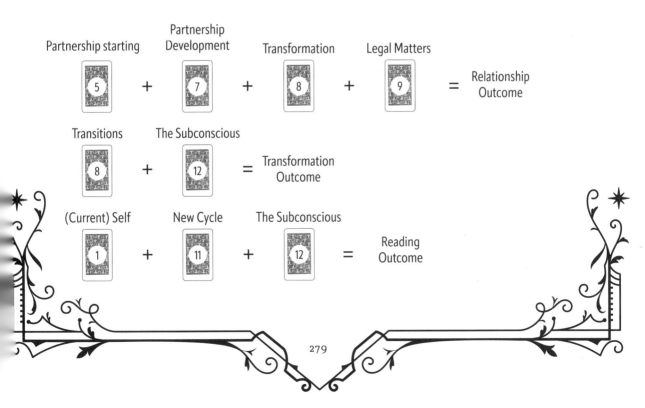

life. Maria is wondering what the future holds for her.

Question: *"What about important changes in Maria's life; what does she need to know?"*

First Impression Interpretation

Do not be alarmed by the number of cards in this spread. Let us take a look, step by step using the house combinations template in Figure 35.

Overview

Take a look at the Major cards first. Looking at the 12 cards, three 'spiritual cards' stand out: Strength, The High Priestess, and The Hermit. They imply that Maria is self-aware and may have a regular spiritual practice that nourishes her well-being (The Hermit in the 6th House). Strength in the 1st House and The Star in the final follow-up house reinforce this insight. Both cards signal that she has begun the healing process and that everything will be fine in the end. Furthermore, the 1st and 5th Houses, when considered as combined, indicate Maria's innate psychic or spiritual gifts or abilities. Perhaps a mentor (The Hermit) will come into her life and guide her to a higher level of consciousness, and further wisdom.

Tarot House Combinations

Because Maria's health is a concern, let's evaluate the physical health house combination: Strength, The Sun, and The Emperor reversed in Houses 1, 4, 6 and 8, respectively (for the meaning of Tarot combinations, please refer to Figure 32).

The first three cards are all positive, representing healing (rather than medical or surgical intervention). The Sun in the 4th House represents the physical condition of the body, which is wonderful! So far, the cards suggest that her minor issues are the result of a disrupted energy pattern, for which energy healing treatment would be appropriate (<u>never diagnose with the Tarot; always consult a medical practitioner to determine health status</u>).

The Emperor reversed in the 8th House, on the other hand, indicates that Maria's physical body is suffering as a result of her overburdening herself with chores that stress her and her body. Because The Emperor represents foundation, her issues could be with her legs or feet (the foundation of the body). Moreover, weight can also be an issue, though it is not explicitly stated; because the foundation is weak and there is too much pressure on the legs and feet, the physical weight of the body can be an added issue – too much for the legs to carry. However, The World card in the 9th House representing the long-term future is very favourable; it implies that Maria will regain her balance and recover with focused effort and discipline, much like The Emperor's!

Next, examine the transformation outcome combination of the 8th and 12th Houses. Interestingly, both Major cards, The Emperor and The Fool, are reversed. They indicate that Maria is rejecting the transformation that she needs to go through in order to evolve and advance in her life. She is also hesitant to share her true essence, creativity and talents with the external world. The Fool reversed refuses to express his gifts in public. The High Priestess in the 5th House, which represents hidden talents and creativity (in the short term), also means that Maria has hidden talents that she is not yet aware of! It's the equivalent of being pregnant with abilities and creative potential but refusing to give birth to them!

The 3rd and 9th Houses, which symbolize mental abilities, learning, communication, travel and long-term outcomes of higher education, are the next combination to consider. They indicate that if Maria applied herself to developing ideas consistently and regularly, perhaps even developing a skill she's inclined toward, or travelling a short distance to take a course, the world would benefit from her innate abilities and

gifts – particularly since she is no longer creating an outcome, as the Judgement card indicates.

Maria's demeanour and, as a result, her well-being must have suffered the consequences of her retirement from employment. She appeared to be retiring from life, reluctant to socialize or be motivated by friends (11th House), and inadvertently refusing to grow and show her skills and abilities. The reading outcome combination, Houses 1, 11 and 12, imply, however, that if she made an unbiased decision to begin doing so (Justice), the situation would improve. And, as The Star's follow-up card indicates, she would finally discover hope, inspiration and emotional recovery, and flourish at delivering her 'gift' to the world.

House 1: The Self

Major Card: Strength

Strength in the 1st House represents the female aspect of The Hermit, the wise feminine, which reflects Maria's nature. She is most likely someone who is trusted by those who seek her wisdom and advice. She appears to be a conduit for wisdom and a comfort to others. According to the following card, Judgement, Maria's life changed when she stopped working. As a

SHORT TERM

1 The Self	2 Income	3 Communication	4 Home Life

7 Partnership/ Development	8 Crisis/Transitions	9 Long term/Outlook	10 Work/Ambition

LONG TERM

5 Partnership/Creativity

6 Physical Health/
Daily Routine

THE HIGH PRIESTESS

THE HERMIT

Follow-up card 1

Follow-up card 2

THE HANGED MAN

THE STAR

THE FOOL

JUSTICE

11 Next Cycle

12 Subconscious/
Next Cycle

Figure 36 Maria's Major Arcana reading of the 12-Card Astrological Spread

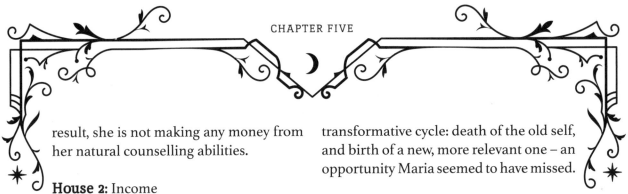

result, she is not making any money from her natural counselling abilities.

House 2: Income

Major Card: Judgement

Every action we take in life has long-term consequences. Judgement in the 2nd House indicates not only that Maria is no longer earning an income, but also that this was intended to happen in order to inspire her to reveal latent skills and abilities, improving her life and the lives of others around her. Although leaving work was a stressful experience (a sudden interruption) and may have appeared unfavourable at the time, it was, in effect, to encourage Maria to create her own income and financial independence.

She was called to recognize that she must now seek to express her own skills, that she has a purpose to fulfil. In a manner, life may have been rewarding her for past efforts in her job by offering her an opportunity to achieve what she yearned for most: financial independence.

Because Judgement is a card of self-awakening, and the death of the previous life, the end of her employment was a catalyst for her spiritual development, prompting her to create an income via her abilities and talents. Judgement is an unescapable transformative cycle: death of the old self, and birth of a new, more relevant one – an opportunity Maria seemed to have missed.

House 3: Intellect, Mental State, Communication, Self-expression, Short-distance Travel

Major Card: The Chariot

The Chariot is the most mystical card in the Tarot, implying that Maria has mental mastery. If she sets her mind to something, she will most certainly succeed, overcoming all hurdles in her path! She appears to have balanced mental abilities, both creative and intellectual. In addition, she appears to be a master at expressing communication, speaking or writing ideas and concepts on her mind. The 3rd House denotes a person's ability to express or convey their ideas and thoughts, as well as what is unique about their personality (their soul). Furthermore, she appears to have a naturally organized mind and thought process.

This is a person who has control over their thoughts or enjoys a positive mind-set as well as someone who values expanding their knowledge or intellect. Furthermore, it denotes a desire to travel and learn about other cultures.

House 4: Home

Major Card: The Sun
The Sun in the 4th House represents both the physical body and life at home, implying that Maria's life at home with her family is full of joy and happiness. Furthermore, it denotes a comfortable lifestyle, money, success and good health. However, it also implies that now is the time for Maria to explore her creativity and put any concepts that she wishes to expand in the future into action. She can begin by doing that from home (the 4th House). Now is the time for growth and success. She will feel fresh vigour and vitality if she chooses to do so. Remember that the meaning of the card strongly suggests that innocence and purity are necessary in the mystical path for unification with spiritual wisdom, and that efforts are rewarded with success and abundant creative energy (no room for resisting change!)

House 5: Partnerships/Creativity

Major Card: The High Priestess
The High Priestess in the 5th House represents both Maria's latent gifts and psychic abilities and an unexpected romantic relationship. Temperance in the 7th House represents a wonderful coming together of two partners. The absence of definite cards in the 8th House of legal problems, such as Justice or The Hierophant, means that neither marriage nor a business partnership are in the cards (yet) for Maria. However, it may be so after a time of waiting, as suggested by the 12th house and follow-up cards (Justice, The Hanged Man and The Star).

Furthermore, The Emperor reversed means that Maria is avoiding any form of partnership, either because she is afraid of being controlled by a man, or because of a dominant male at home (a brother), or a prior relationship that resulted in her losing her footing.

However, it appears that discovering her hidden qualities or creative potential is the key to unlocking the prospect of finding a loving companion. Furthermore, because of her intuitive nature, she could delve deeper into both issues by dealing with her dreams. Her subconscious appears to be aware and ready to provide her with insights if she will just listen! Nonetheless, The Hermit in the adjacent house foretells someone entering her life.

House 6: Daily Life

Major Card: The Hermit
Many interpretations of Maria's future are

suggested by The Hermit in the 6th House. Apart from expressing deeper spiritual development and being guided by a mentor, it also represents everyday routine or life. It implies that Maria has been a bit of a recluse recently, but that a knowledgeable and mature male figure is about to enter her (everyday) life. It can denote someone older, or more mature than his age, but it always denotes a knowledgeable, self-aware and enlightened man.

The potential companion does not show in the 5th House of relationships, indicating that this relationship is not yet known to Maria; it is not a current relationship but there is a possible affair in the near future. Also, she is unaware that someone is interested in her at the moment. However, the potential partner would be someone easy to get along with and get to know. Or, he would seem familiar, as The Hermit indicates a longer connection, as opposed to The Fool, who suggests someone utterly new and unknown to the seeker.

House 7: Partnership/Development

Major Card: Temperance
Given the next card, Temperance, when the two partners meet, they would feel a natural affinity or familiarity, as if they had met or known each other before. Coming together

with this partner would feel natural, and the relationship will unfold smoothly. Temperance denotes emotional healing and balance, a coming together of hearts and minds. Temperance also suggests that Maria requires a period of emotional healing and relaxing, perhaps travelling abroad or a short vacation (The Chariot and The World both indicate travelling) to regain her balance and re-charge her energy.

The triangle encircled by a square on Temperance's chest symbolizes that Maria can seek inspiration from her higher mind, or Spirit, through meditation or reflection to mend past relationships or emotions in order to manifest the future partnership. It also implies that Maria must exercise moderation in order not to deplete her physical energy while running errands or giving advice to others.

House 8: Transformation/Joint Finance

Major Card: The Emperor reversed
The interpretation of The Emperor in the 8th House has already been discussed in several combinations above. The 8th House, however, also represents joint finances. And, given that Maria is currently single and lives with her family, it appears that the family's joint finances have recently

experienced a setback. Furthermore, joint financial affairs are not as well managed or organized as they need to be (The Emperor upright would have signified a stable long-term financial foundation).

The Emperor reversed can refer to a male relative who is directly involved in family finances too, and who is not open to any advice or suggestions Maria may provide. Because the 8th House also represents the future of joint finances, this appears to be a critical matter that must be addressed, or else the family will be forced to live with financial constraints for an extended period of time. The Emperor reversed appears to reflect Maria's concerns about this matter, to the point that it is affecting her physical well-being and diminishing her body's vitality.

House 9: Long-Term Outlook

Major Card: The World
The World in the 9th House, which represents the long-term future and is directly below the 3rd House, which represents communication and self-expression as well as intellectual mastery, foretells the end of a cycle of total transformation and the beginning of a cycle of fulfilment, joy, achieving goals and transcending life's challenges. It also denotes that Maria's efforts with her friends and family will be recognized, as might her talents be, if she chooses to develop them. Regarding her talents, her impact would be recognized around the world, not just in her close circle.

Furthermore, following the 7th and 8th Houses, The World indicates a harmonious life with a partner, as well as possible long-distance travel or movement together in the future. If The Fool was upright in the 11th House, it would indicate that she would be moving to a new country with a partner, as her network of friends or acquaintances would be 'new', or she would be embarking on a new adventure. However, for the time being, The World represents frequent travel with a partner (we'll see what the Minor cards bring to this spread later).

However, life's cycles do not end there. The World heralds the start of a new cycle by revealing Maria's skills, which are ripe and ready to be born into the world. If this transpires, she will experience a new degree of fulfilment, growth and expansion, as well as increased self-mastery and transcendence. That appears to be an important challenge for Maria to conquer.

House 10: Work

Major Card: The Empress
Maria's commercial objectives are revealed

by the Empress in the 10th House of work, career and ambition, though the specifics may be unknown to her at the present (The High Priestess, in the house of creative talents and abilities). However, because both aspects of feminine energy, the intuitive and the businesswoman, are present, both cards indicate that Maria may be inspired with a business that nurtures womanhood in general in combination with the travel cards (The Chariot, The Hermit, and The World; this could very well be a resort or a retreat, for example, especially when Strength is present in the 1st House).

The Empress in the 10th House possesses qualities or attributes that go beyond the specifics of motherhood, highlighting the substance of its meaning as giving life to ideas, projects and enterprises that nourish through loving care and devotion. She also serves as a reminder that the time is right to start such a business, and that Maria will reap the advantages of her efforts and labour.

She encourages Maria to make the required efforts to materialize whatever ideas she may have, to grow them, and to reap the rewards of consistent efforts to sustain them. It's a positive card with a message of success and financial fulfilment. It represents luxurious living and taking care of one's physical health and body in order to accomplish one's life's objective. It undoubtedly denotes a profession related to beauty, or a business or service related to women.

House 11: Ambitions

Major Card: The Fool reversed
The 11th House represents social activities, external ambitions, and having suitable friends who are supportive of one's ambition, vision and goals. The Fool suggests that Maria may not have much support around her at the moment, and that she should reconsider connections that might discourage or distract her from achieving her goals. It also suggests that she currently lacks any realistic aspirations. Whatever her vision for her personal future is, it appears ambiguous, to say the least. It is an invitation to pay attention to her gut feelings and instincts, and to leave any 'connections' that are not beneficial or supportive. In a sense, The Fool reversed is nudging her to take a leap into the unknown, to move forward, even if the future is uncertain or unknown to her.

House 12: Next Cycle

Major Card: Justice
Despite the apparent abrupt ending

of Maria's career, and the financial predicament around her family at the moment, Justice in the 12th House brings a sense of fairness when evaluating Maria's past actions and decisions that contributed to her current situation. Justice depicts how opposing forces can result in decisive action! Whatever the following cycle brings, Maria's dispassionate decision must be taken to attain balance and harmony in her life once more. Her decision needs to be based on facts – after considering all the factors involved – rather than emotions. Would she continue as she is, even if it meant jeopardising her health? Or would she instead rise to meet her challenges? A follow-up is required.

Follow-up Card 1: The Hanged Man
The Hanged Man represents Maria's ability to discover solutions to her troubles if she surrenders and accepts the truth of her circumstance. She needs to take a fresh look at her life, and address the way she is living it and the toll it is taking on her health, especially since the emotional causes appear to be severely impacting her well-being. The 'incarceration' imposed by The Hanged Man is teaching her to willingly give up the way she's currently approaching her life, and to evolve a higher sense of self-awareness. A fresh cycle of growth brings a

new attitude as well as a purposeful desire to move forward. To know the outcome, another follow-up card is required.

Follow-up Card 2: The Star
The Hanged Man is followed by The Star, which seems appropriate because it signifies a new dawn following the dark tunnel of reflection imposed by The Hanged Man! The 'purification' Maria needed to undergo was a lack of a meaningful partnership and overburdening herself, helping her friends and family in order to make a conscious decision to change her attitude about her life and awaken her innate talents and abilities.

The Star declares that Maria is ready for this purification, which will allow her to receive her true wishes. The Star contributes further healing, rejuvenation and unification of 'heaven on Earth'. It is a 'wish' card that is about to come true whenever Maria decides! This is indeed a fabulous conclusion to her reading.

Now, let us take a look at the Minor cards that cover the Major cards in the 12-card Astrological Spread and see what additional details and insights they offer.

House 1: The Self

Minor Card: Five of Wands
Although Strength is a positive card to

have in the 1st House, the Five of Wands indicates that Maria is in the midst of a minor transformation cycle, where she is 'fighting' for her place at home and in the world; it is as though she is battling to get her voice heard at home, and her expression noticed.

Instead of a confrontational approach, she should adopt a flexible one. She struggles when she does not. The minor cycle of change she is experiencing is about to bring about new circumstances. The Five of Wands is all about changing or adapting one's behaviour, plans, thoughts and feelings. Moreover, she has the inner strength of the enchantress to accomplish this through calm negotiations.

Although Maria's life appears to be chaotic, lacking organisation at the present (she is overwhelmed with commitments to others, and her health is failing her), this lack of structure represents a lack of emphasis on her personal life and leads to uncertainty about the future and a sense of despondency. A shift in mind-set will help her get what she desires: an outlet for her abilities and ideas, as well as a loving, supportive relationship. This necessitates her overcoming obstacles in order to accomplish her life's mission.

House 2: Income

Minor Card: Eight of Wands reversed
This card signifies the need to get out of bed and get to work. It is the time for new starts and activity. It is, however, reversed, meaning that Maria is overdue in adopting this mentality, and because it is in the 2nd House of finance and income, it indicates the necessity for her to start earning her own money again, from her ideas! Her circumstances will improve if she changes her mind-set. It is worth noting that most of the Minor cards are either Wands or Swords, indicating that she is worried, overthinking and not taking enough initiative. A lively and exciting period awaits, signifying travel and possibly relocation, or that the business will be set up abroad.

House 3: Intellect, Mental State, Communication, Self-Expression, Short-Distance Travel

Minor Card: Ten of Cups
This card foretells a joyous event or celebration after a long period of hard labour. It's like a dream come true! It is also in the 3rd House, indicating a cheerful mental shift that will make Maria happier – perhaps news from abroad (The Chariot) that will cheer her up. It can also imply that she will be taking a short-distance journey soon, or that a welcome guest from abroad will be visiting her. Considering the two Minor cards preceding it, the Ten of Cups

suggests that Maria is capable of making a mental shift that will transform things for the better and make her happier.

House 4: Home

Minor card: Three of Wands
This card complements the Major card, The Sun, showing that much has already been accomplished in terms of success, material gain and joyful, luxurious living. However, it also means that there will be greater growth, expansion and material gain in the future. It's time to celebrate! Following the excellent news of the Ten of Cups preceding it, it might also signify a party at home to celebrate the forthcoming good news.

The overarching theme throughout Maria's reading thus far has been restoring balance to her life by focusing on herself and taking action. Keeping this in mind, the Three of Wands foretells the success and advancement of whatever plans she has in mind for her personal objectives. This could be accomplished through expanding a business by opening new branches or franchising a business globally.

House 5: Partnerships/Creativity

Minor Card: Knight of Pentacles

The image of The Knight of Pentacles is one of calm. The High Priestess is in the 5th House, which means that one of Maria's hidden skills is unlimited patience and tolerance; she will accomplish her work no matter how long it takes. She never fails to achieve her goals once she has decided, because she never gives up. Furthermore, she has a financial, analytical and methodical approach to her business goals.

Furthermore, it can represent someone she is about to meet or does not know yet, as it covers The High Priestess, who can be a dark-haired young man who is also meticulous, reliable and logical. This individual is sensible, systematic and stable in his approach, and she can rely on him. This person may be able to inspire her or support her in bringing her business ideas to fruition. In any event, he represents a joyful outcome of a scenario, particularly a business enterprise that has been delayed for long time.

House 6: Daily Life

Minor Card: Knight of Swords
The Knight of Swords, in comparison to the previous Knight of Pentacles, has an attractive, fascinating personality that quickly grabs the attention and affection

of others. He does, however, have a ruthless streak, and while he is not evil, he tends to pursue his own goals at the possible expense of hurting people close to him. This card signifies someone known to Maria, or someone who is about to enter her life (The Hermit indicates someone who either travels or is familiar).

Although pleasant, this individual is somewhat selfish and does not provide any emotional support to those around him. This is not how he works. He does, however, have a smart mind and good business sense. When dealing with this individual, Maria must exercise caution. She will listen to any helpful advice, but that is all. Any guarantee of continued support should be viewed with scepticism. If a professional relationship is formed, it is likely that it will burn out shortly, leaving chaos in its wake as he fades out of Maria's life.

House 7: Partnership Development

Minor Card: King of Wands
This is the third male Court Card in the spread so far, which is intriguing. Keep in mind that Court Cards can symbolize an aspect of the seeker or someone in their life. You can deduce how the card relates to the seeker by considering where it falls and the cards around it.

The Knight of Pentacles, for example, appears to reflect an aspect of the seeker – her hidden talents – while the Knight of Swords signifies someone who storms in and out of the seeker's life. And finally, the King of Wands, in the 7th House, symbolizes the character (and complexion) of the man Maria is about to meet. This man is quite accomplished; wands imply movement, which can portend a change of country or residency when Maria meets him (or frequent travel, as denoted earlier). Wands also represent the element of fire – charisma and sexual attraction, which might be appealing given his wit and charm. The King of Wands is attractive, with strawberry blonde or light brown hair and a freckled complexion.

He is kind and generous, with a great sense of humour and a strong desire to have a good time, breaking Maria's loneliness and languishing. As a successful entrepreneur, he could provide immense emotional support as well as sound business acumen when Maria requires it.

House 8: Transformation/Joint Finance

Minor Card: Knight of Wands
The Knight of Wands is the fourth Court Card that appears in the 8th House of shared finances (or relationship development). He

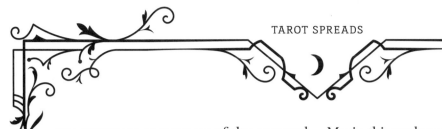

can represent one aspect of the reversed Emperor covered by this card, or a sibling who is likewise involved in the family's joint finances. A person who is younger than The Emperor represents stabilising impacts on the family's combined finances.

The reversed Emperor can also suggest a partner or business associate whose influence is having a detrimental impact on the family's finances; and the Knight of Wands represents the end of this negative influence. The business associate may be leaving. In either case, it's great news!

House 9: Long-Term Outlook

Minor Card: Seven of Wands

This card, like the cards in the preceding house, is about the family finances. Despite the fact that the family is facing a stifling struggle as a result of a competing business associate, the Seven of Wands indicates that the family has the fortitude and dedication needed to succeed in this matter. Perhaps Maria (Strength) is the one who keeps the family together by providing moral support (which is taking a toll on her body). Despite the fact that the competition has taken a toll on the family's finances, their perseverance and courage will triumph in the end.

Moreover, this card represents knowledge as well as talents. Considering Maria, this card covers The World, the long-term outcome of Maria taking initiative and conquering her personal challenges. It denotes Maria receiving excellent training or developing a platform for her communication skills or business ideas despite any existing competition.

House 10: Work

Minor Card: Six of Cups

The Six of Cups covers The Empress; both are joyful cards. It denotes a happy reunion with an old friend who shared wonderful memories with Maria. As it is in the 10th House of work, it can also signify this old friend helping Maria in establishing her business.

House 11: Ambitions

Minor Card: Eight of Swords

This card, which depicts a woman bound by her own thoughts, complements the reversed Fool in the 11th House. It reveals that Maria's impasse is of her own making, and that a mental shift in attitude is all that is required to unblock her aspirations and self-expression – the ultimate step in her evolution. The streaming water beneath the confined and blindfolded woman in this image represents that if Maria were to

open her eyes and listen to her true feelings, she would be able to liberate herself and transcend her obstacles.

House 12: Next Cycle

Minor Card: Queen of Cups
Toward the conclusion of the spread, two queens – the Queen of Cups and the Queen of Pentacles (covering The Star as the second follow-up card) – represent attributes of Maria.

This is intriguing because both emphasize that Maria has control over how she spends the rest of her life. The two queens represent her having dual aspects in harmony: the businesswoman and the intuitive. Furthermore, in the two previous Major cards we saw the dualistic aspects in harmony as well: Strength in the 1st House, and The High Priestess in the 5th House. Additionally, we later met The Empress in the 10th House. All of these cards related to Maria herself, her talents, her professional goals and her future self in the next cycle, if she chooses.

Essentially, Maria has the intellect, commercial acumen, intuitive insight and inner resources to create and materialize her dreams. The Queen of Cups is an invitation for Maria to contemplate and trust her true feelings and her intuition. The prize will be attaining what she genuinely desires: the big cup held by the Queen.

Follow-up Card 1: Five of Pentacles
The Five of Pentacles covers The Hanged Man, explaining the delay in activating her ambitions. Maybe it's fear of failure, or maybe it's because the family's funds are tight right now. However, it also provides Maria a route out that she is unaware of – just like the two figures on the card, who are overwhelmed by poverty but refuse to enter the church that can shelter them. In reality, her concerns are unjustified. All she has to do is make a choice. The next set of follow-up cards reflects her accomplishment.

Follow-up Card 2: Queen of Pentacles
This Queen covers The Star, one of the auspicious cards that represents success, transcendence and healing. The association of both cards in this house is significant. This healing will be brought about by the Queen of Pentacles: Maria, expressing her business acumen and talents through launching her own business. If you will, it is both an incentive and a challenge for her to complete her spiritual path of self-awakening. It underlines Maria's ability to conquer this challenge.

Reading Summary: Using The 12-house spread to answer Maria's concerns, we began by asking what the significant changes in her life will be. Take note of how framing the inquiry, or the intention of the reading, opened the door to getting a plethora of insights. The 12-card Astrological Spread lends itself to evaluating those insights on multiple levels. The spread contributed to a more complete picture of what was going on in Maria's life. It brought to light the underlying concerns that were causing her stress. Furthermore, it pointed to a significant underlying element, which is the family's financial situation and the competing business associate – despite the fact that Maria did not discuss any of it at the start of the reading.

THE FOOL

More importantly, it highlighted what Maria actually desires: the ideal relationship, and to realize her vision of helping women. The reading showed Maria how to overcome her difficulties by expressing her abilities and skills; it even offered a suggestion indirectly (the resort or retreat that can be franchised).

Retaining her financial independence after retirement was a critical factor. Building a vehicle for expressing her skills and innate talents will help her regain balance and feel fulfilled. Her personal development is the goal of all that she is going through. The results will be enormous, however, if she chooses to take a leap of faith into the unknown. Finally, it gave Maria her power back by ascertaining what her inner attributes were, which was all she needed to be herself: her intuition, her caring nature, and her business skills and entrepreneurial nature that was ignored after retirement.

As with The Fool's quest, obstacles are often what the seeker needs to conquer, overcoming their vulnerabilities or impurified dualistic essence such as worries or concerns, lack of trust in their abilities, or interest in expressing what they are truly gifted with. The ultimate reason, of course, is self-awareness by regaining one's self-will and self-empowerment as they discover how to create the finest life possible.

The Tarot began more than 10 centuries ago as a set of cards to play money tricks and entertain. It sparked the imaginations of the numerous cultures it passed through, as its popularity increasingly grew. So much so that each culture felt they needed to imprint their own input onto the cards until the deck became what we today know as the Tarot: a creative visual 'game' of symbols to inspire and empower, finding answers to life's journey.

We hope that *The Book of Tarot* has inspired you, too, to begin your Tarot adventure as courageously as The Fool did, to go through your life experiences seeking wisdom as boldly as he did, and that your readings will restore seekers' self-will and inspire them to take a leap into the unknown – where fulfilment lies.

The End

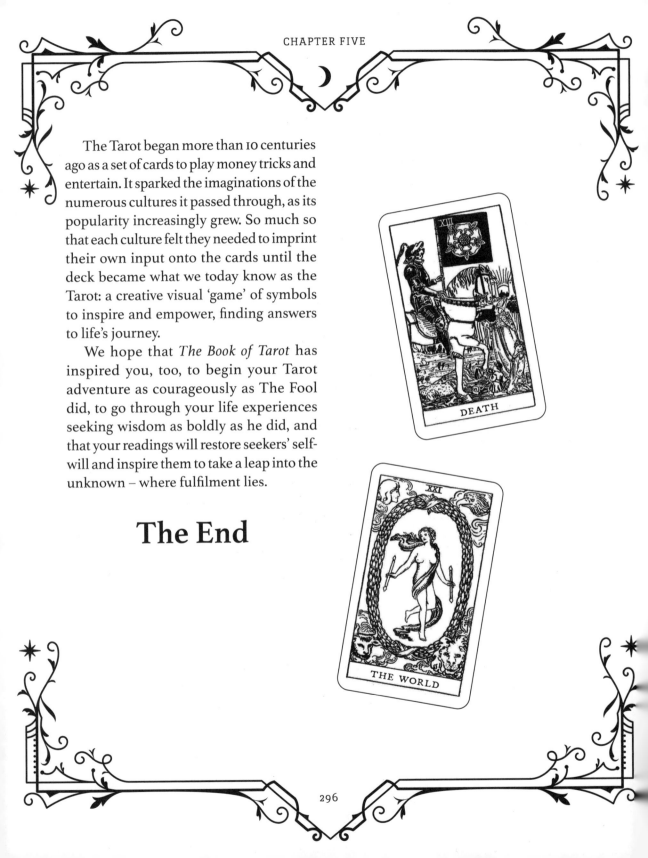

Index

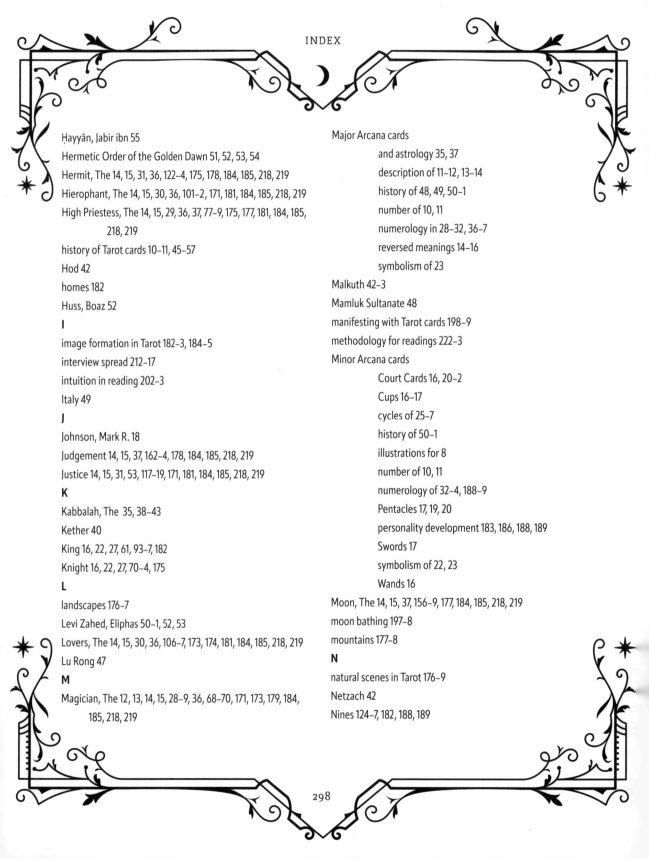

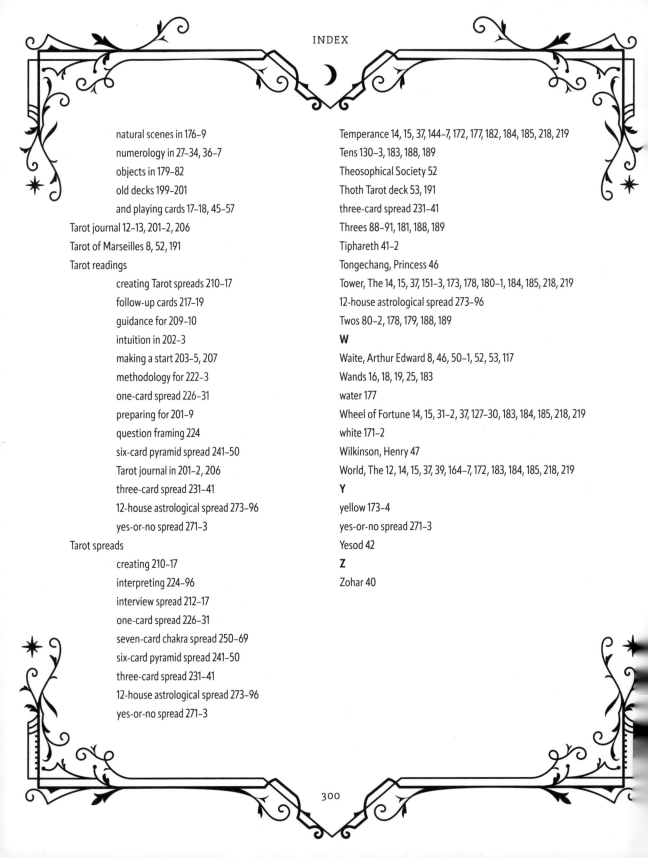

List of Figures